THE CRAFT OF
POETIC SPEECH IN
ANCIENT GREECE

A volume in the series

MYTH AND POETICS

edited by GREGORY NAGY

A list of titles appears at the end of the book.

THE CRAFT of POETIC SPEECH in ANCIENT GREECE

CLAUDE CALAME

Translated from the French by
Janice Orion

Preface by
Jean-Claude Coquet

CORNELL UNIVERSITY PRESS

ITHACA AND LONDON

First published as *Le récit en Grèce ancienne*, © Méridiens Klincksieck, 1986.

Translation copyright © 1995 by Cornell University

The publisher gratefully acknowledges the
assistance of the French Ministry of Culture
in defraying part of the cost of translation.

First published 1995 by Cornell University Press.

Printed in the United States of America

⊛ The paper in this book meets the minimum requirements of the
American National Standard for Information Sciences—Permanence
of Paper for Printed Library Materials, ANSI Z39.48-1984.

Library of Congress Cataloging-in-Publication Data
Calame, Claude.
    [Récit en Grèce ancienne. English]
    The craft of poetic speech in ancient Greece / Claude Calame ; translated from the French by Janice Orion; preface by Jean-Claude Coquet.
        p.   cm. — (Myth and poetics)
    Includes bibliographical references and index.
    ISBN 0-8014-2743-6. — ISBN 0-8014-8022-1 (pbk.)
        1. Greek literature—History and criticism. 2. Mythology, Greek, in literature. 3. Semiotics and literature. 4. First person narrative. 5. Narration (Rhetoric). 6. Rhetoric, Ancient. 7. Poetics. I. Orion, Janice. II. Title. III. Series.
PA3014.N37C3513 1995
881'.010923—dc20   94-24167

To the memory of Michel de Certeau,
in gratitude for his generous encouragement
of the publication of this book.

Contents

Foreword

GREGORY NAGY

The Craft of Poetic Speech in Ancient Greece, by Claude Calame, is a radical book. It challenges classicists to rethink the principles of myth-making in the poetry and the art of the ancient Greeks. Taking as his point of departure the linguistic studies of Emile Benveniste on the interactions of the first, second, and third persons in their spatial and temporal components, Calame applies the methodology of semiotics in formulating altogether new ways of looking at the poetics of Homer, Hesiod, lyric, tragedy, and even history. As we see Calame's arguments develop, we begin to reconfigure our own preconceived pictures of poet and audience, poet and Muse, poet and mask.

Calame's argumentation is often not easy, but it is precise, consistent, and always leading toward a point. The system of analysis that he brings to bear stems in part from a branch of semiotics and narratology perfected by Algirdas Julien Greimas. I say "perfected" because Greimas has actually worked out with his colleagues in Paris an interchangeable French-English vocabulary of academic discourse, assembled as a two-volume "dictionary" of semiotic terms in which each entry is clearly specified in both French and English.[1] In order to help the reader, the translator of Calame's book, Janice Orion, follows this remarkable reference work of Greimas, consistently checking against it as she renders Calame's French semiotic terms into their exact

[1] A. J. Greimas and J. Courtés, *Sémiotique: Dictionnaire raisonné de la théorie du langage*, 2 vols. (Paris, 1979/1986).

counterparts in English. Salient examples are *enunciation* (along with the adjectives *enuncive* and *enunciative*), *subject*, and *shifter*. The meaning of each such word is carefully explained at its first mention. The author himself has collaborated with the series editor and the translator in reviewing the use of each technical semiotic term.[2] In this regard, the reader is further aided by the inclusion, in this English-language version, of the original preface written by Jean-Claude Coquet for the French edition; it helps explain not only the distinctly French intellectual context in which Calame's book took shape but also, more specifically, the impact of the book on semiotic studies.

The effort required to read Calame's work is repaid by the insights that emerge with ever increasing frequency as reading proceeds. For classicists, these insights will extend to such timely questions as the relationship of authorship and authority, the role of the first person in choral lyric poetry, the dichotomy between lyric and epic genres, the literariness of history, the tragic mask as a projection of identity, and the "poetics" of the gaze in iconographic traditions. More generally, all who are interested in myth and ritual will be drawn to Calame's challenging new way of looking at the fundamental dichotomy between them. Many of the topics are singularly striking in and of themselves, as with Calame's comparative analysis of the Cyclops story in the *Odyssey*. There is a pervasive sense of newness throughout the book. Moreover, thanks to the author's extensive collaboration in the translation process, numerous changes and additions to the original French text render this English-language version a definitive new edition.

[2] The author and the series editor wish to acknowledge the able assistance of Derek Collins, Katherine Collins, and Fred Porta.

Acknowledgments

The present book is a collection of essays written at intervals over a period of a dozen years. It bears the mark of the different phases of my thinking concerning the enunciation and its utterance. Certain inconsistencies that may be found in it will be seen as my attempt to preserve a sense of groping inherent in research in progress. Nine more years have passed since its publication in French. I have therefore tried not only to update the bibliographical indications given in the footnotes but also to state more precisely for this English translation the concepts used in analyzing the texts. Even if they appear quite abstract to the reader, the essays remain in the field of applied semiotics, or "soft semiotics." I would like to express my gratitude to Gregory Nagy for his many suggestions and for having had the courage to propose that this translation be included in his series. The work of revising and updating the translation has been supported by a subsidy granted by the Fonds du 450e anniversaire of the University of Lausanne. I thank the members of the committee of the Fonds for their attention. Having presented these essays at various conferences and lectures, I have benefited from the advice of many friends, among whom I would like to mention G. Arrigoni, C. Bérard, D. Bertrand, P. Borgeaud, F. Fabbri, C. Grottanelli, F. Hartog, E. Landowski, D. Lanza, N. Loraux, E. Pellizer, H. Pernet, M. Pop, J. Rudhardt, J. Sherzer, and F. Zeitlin. A. Habib helped me with reading the proofs.

The text of Chapter 1 was previously published in *Semiotica* 43 (1983): 245–73. An abridged version was presented at the International

Congress "Oralità: Cultura, letteratura, discorso," Urbino, July 1980, and at the Colloquium "Pouvoir et dire," Albi, July 1982.

Chapter 2 is the definitive version of an essay published as a working paper in *Actes sémiotiques. Documents du Groupe de recherches sémiolinguistiques* (Paris) 4, no. 32 (1982).

An abridged version of Chapter 3 was given as an inaugural lecture to the Faculty of Arts of Lausanne in October 1985; it was published in *Etudes de lettres* 3 (1986): 27–52.

A first English translation of Chapter 4 appeared in *History of Religions* 26 (1986): 125–42.

The text of Chapter 5 was presented in an abridged form at a conference organized at Lausanne in February 1983 and published by C. Bérard, C. Bron, and A. Pomari in *Images et société en Grèce ancienne: L'iconographie comme méthode d'analyse* (Lausanne, 1987), 77–88.

The text of Chapter 6 was read at the conference on mythological analysis organized by the Centro internazionale di semiotica e di linguistica at Urbino in July 1975; it was published in *Etudes de lettres* 3, no. 10 (1977): 45–79.

Written for a colloquium on proper names organized by the Centro internazionale di semiotica e di linguistica at Urbino in July 1982 and read in Rome at the conference "Mondo classico: Percorsi possibili" (February 1984), the text of Chapter 7 appeared in a shorter form in the *Cahiers roumains d'études littéraires* 4 (1984): 4–11, and in Italian in *Mondo classico: Percorsi possibili* (Ravenna, 1985), 27–37.

Chapter 8 takes account of some of the results of a much larger study, subsidized in part by the Fonds national suisse de la recherche scientifique and published in 1990 (see the bibliography). It was given as a lecture in Geneva, Milan, Paris, and Trieste and was included as a prepublication in *Degrés* 35/36 (1983): 1–15.

C. C.

Preface

JEAN-CLAUDE COQUET

Claude Calame's book has, in my opinion, the special merit of making us reconsider the eternally absorbing problem of the "subject." We cannot, of course, impose our categories on those of other cultures. The subject in ancient Greece has little to do with our definition of the term today. "There is no reference to a 'self,' " as Jean-Pierre Vernant says when speaking of the Greek gods; "none speaks of an ego with an individual will, emotions, destiny."[1] The texts and the objects examined with such virtuosity by Calame (whether a passage by Herodotus or a vase painting) direct us elsewhere, however, onto the terrain of the narrative, away from history and philosophy. As good philologists, we can (and should) rely on the forms of language. Grammar is used here, however, less to analyze discourse (a combinatory principle) than to register the conditions under which it is formulated or, more important, altered and, finally, to discover who takes responsibility for it. The complexity of the process is obvious. It is not the least of the strengths of this book that its readers are induced to adopt three points of view. By applying them successively, we arrive at a better understanding of how the "subject" is constituted. I shall call them the points of view of subordination, of self-reference, and of recognition.

To start with, I should like to refer to a remark of Emile Benveniste, our best guide to the semiotics of discourse. When he considers the

[1] J.-P. Vernant, *Mythe et pensée chez les Grecs* (Paris, 1974), 2:86.

semantic transformation of the Greek verb *hēgeisthai*, as implied in its transcription from "to be a leader" to "to be a guide (in opinion)"—in other words, its transition on the modal level from the dimension of power (*pouvoir*) to that of knowledge (*savoir*)—Benveniste comments: "There is the suggestion here of the judgment of an authority," and more precisely, "the authority of the individual's judgment, not the authority of power." I should like to reconsider the opposition set up here. I seem to discern three modal stages in this transformation, described as "direct" by Benveniste. The verb *hēgeisthai* does indeed mean "to precede the others in an action" and therefore to "be the leader" (the modality of power). The same modality of power is then presupposed and the modality of knowing suggested when *hēgeisthai* takes on the meaning, as in Herodotus, of "to have the authority (in opinion) to. . . ." It is on a relationship of this sort that the category of performance verbs is based. But we need a third alteration of the term *hēgeisthai* to arrive at the meaning of "to think by assuming full responsibility for one's own judgment." And if you acknowledge that the act of judgment in the third sense arises from the modality of the will (*vouloir*)—in every willing there is a "nucleus of approbation," writes Paul Ricoeur—the successive transformations of *hēgeisthai* would be a good illustration of the links between the modalities. It would be possible to extend the discussion using the Latin *judicare* and show how it passes in the same way from a position of authority (the modality of power), "to judge as a sovereign judge," to an individual's position, "to express a judgment [of thought]" (modality of the will).[2]

It would be pointless to object that usage determines acceptance and that there is thus no reason to be surprised by this polysemia. We have to establish an order here: power (*pouvoir*) is the modality being taken into account; it gradually changes and becomes will (*vouloir*). This is the "tunnel effect" I want to show.

Judging is the activity by which the subject is recognized (inversely, the nonsubject shows no such activity); it is clearly not connected either with the notion of reflexive transparency, a secondary sense effect sometimes used in psychology and philosophy, or with the notion of syntax function, which would take us into the realm of linguistics, or even with the presence of this or that pronominal form. Continuing to cull our examples from Benveniste, we find that whether we adopt the

[2] E. Benveniste, *Le vocabulaire des institutions indo-européennes* (Paris, 1969), 1:153.

form *I*—"I command that . . ." (performative)—or the form *he/she*—
"he/she commands that . . ." (asserting a fact)—the subject is implied
by the semantics of the verb "to command."

"To think and assume full responsibility for one's judgment" is no
small affair. Calame shows the steps by revealing the relationships
between the personal pronouns, the *I*, the *you*, the *we*, the *he/she*. . . . It
is a problem of judging distances or, more precisely, of interpreting the
reciprocal variations of the actantial positions.

Creating distance has two opposite effects. On the one hand, it
validates one actant to the detriment of the other: for example, the
human *I* is subordinate to the divine *you*. On the other hand, it tends to
lend an objective solidity to the *I* (*I* becomes *he/she*). It is clear that in
the *Iliad* the Muses occupy a position hierarchically superior to that of
the narrator who is represented by an *I* or a *we*. The Muses are
goddesses invoked by the poet in the second person plural; "present
everywhere," they know everything; and we, who only hear their
sound, know nothing. This use of the modality of knowing (to know
everything, to know nothing) leaves no doubt as to the subordinate
status of the person who says *I* in epic poetry. He does not need to be
named; his role—I quote Calame—"can be assumed by any bard who
acquires and recites the poem in question." But Calame's study lets us
watch a reversal of proportion in Hesiod. It is true that "without the
help of the Muse speaking through its mouth, the *I* is powerless," but a
public has been formed. It is this other, collective actor who, recognizing a "poet-artisan" in the one who says *I*, authorizes him, as it were,
to avail himself of a proper name. This reciprocal recognition (recognition of the other, of the *you*, and recognition of the *I*) constitutes, to
my way of thinking, one of the operations that must be carried out by
the actors so that we can rightfully speak, syntagmatically or, more
precisely, transformationally, of a "subject." Calame puts it very well:
"The poet reveals in the text his involvement in a situation in which he
communicates with the exterior by expressing the identity conferred
on him by his name; he is the poet who transmits to a public, as yet
unnamed, his own poem. In the utterance of the enunciation, the song
of the Muse henceforth appears subordinate to the *I*, which communicates the song by taking it over completely." In addition to the proper
name, however uncertain the meanings that can be attributed to it (this
subject is dealt with most interestingly in Chapter 7), the signature
(*sphragis*) offers the actor another occasion to name himself; by creat-

ing a distance, "he gives himself a precise identity." By passing from the *I* to the *he/she*, the subject is placed among the objects of this world and doubtless hopes to benefit from their stability.

In this way the subject is formed. By being associated with these signs, the subject shows the position he occupies: *I, you, we, one, he/she.* . . . In Chapter 3, Calame rightly points out that "at the very moment . . . when the narrower confines of the city were expanding into the Athenian 'empire,' it is likely that history was made in the enunciative transition from the *I/you/we* to the *they*, in the passage from the limited collective, focused on the source of the enunciation, to the quasi universal." The "work of making heroes" that seems so natural in a "commemorative perspective" can be cited, and we can take into account a sort of logic of history that cancels chronology. Nevertheless, it is clear that in the last analysis it is up to the "subject-*I*" to decide. It is an ancient custom. In litigation (Benveniste takes this rule from the *Śatapatha Brāhmaṇa*) it is the one who has seen that must be believed and not the one who has heard.[3] What is 'true is thus in keeping with the absence of distance. It is up to anyone, "whoever he may be," says Herodotus, to decide if he should approve or not of what he, the logograph of Halicarnassus, reports concerning what he heard from the Egyptians. In short, as is sensible, it is up to the logos to decide how far to go. "As for me," proclaims Herodotus, "I owe it to myself to report what is said, but I am not bound to believe it; let this rule apply to the whole of my story." In this way the modality of judgment (the will) is revealed by often circuitous routes.

I have perhaps not done sufficient justice to the richness of Calame's book by focusing on the formation of the subject. Tractent fabrilia fabri! I should like at least to have dwelt on the quality of an analysis in which the study of relationships, or rather clusters of relationships, always prevails, as it should, over case studies. The semiotics of the discursive has here a reference work. And Claude Calame is to be thanked for it.

[3] Ibid., 2:173.

ENUNCIATIONS

The Enunciation, Its
Utterance, and Its Subjects
in Ancient Greece

The philosophical implications of the structural method appeared still quite recently to be on the verge of tolling the death knell of the *subject*, whose autonomy was already diluted in economic infrastructures or in a universally shared unconscious. The productions of the subject, particularly literary productions, were expected to reflect this interlacing of social and psychological parameters. A literary analysis could emphasize either the influence of social conditions or the presence of the structures of the unconscious, according to whether the approach was Marxist or psychological. Yet it was also in this same structural context that the linguistic concept of immanence, formulated by Louis Hjelmslev using principles set forth by Ferdinand de Saussure, was applied to the productions of meaning in semiotics. The construction and articulation of signification, the object of investigation in the field of semiotics, thus became an internal process that takes shape mainly in discourse. Within this tangle of relationships, which are in effect structural, the subject seemed to be no longer the victim of dilution, but of exclusion.

In the 1970s, however, voices were being heard with an increasing regularity affirming and reaffirming the central place held by the subject in all productions of meaning. Jean-Claude Coquet, for example, responding to the problems raised by Lacanian psychoanalysis, says: "The 'I' [*moi*] of the (individual) subject is not the same as the 'I' [*je*] of its discourse." Jean-Blaise Grize, responding to the necessity of removing the marks of natural logic governing the discourse of a purely formal system, asserts in a similar vein: "The key phenome-

3

non, the one that fundamentally distinguishes natural languages from any formal system, is the presence of an enunciating subject."[1]

So it is within the framework of *enunciation*, the process whereby all forms of discourse are produced, that the problem of the subject is posed for semioticians, to the exclusion of all philosophical and substantialist ideas. Though Emile Benveniste limited these forms to linguistic discourse, we are still indebted to him for the notion that discourse is structured by enunciation, and for focusing attention on the signs of enunciation to be found in it.

1. The Uttered Enunciation and the Communication Situation

A well-known analysis of pronouns shows that, in addition to the linguistic elements which surround and sustain the narrated story in any text, there are others that have to do with what Benveniste calls "les instances de discours," or *instances of discourse*; they correspond to the acts performed by an individual speaker whereby language becomes speech. Speech or *utterance* is the result of a pragmatic process, and it often reveals traces of the act of its enunciation. These traces can be divided into three categories: (1) variation in the verb tenses (imperfect/aorist, on the one hand, present/future, on the other); (2) the elements of deixis (*there* as opposed to *here*); and (3) pronouns created by the opposition between the nonperson represented by the *he/she*, actant/actor of the utterance, and the duo *I/you*, actants/actors of the uttered enunciation. It is from these three categories of marks or indicators that the plane of discourse is constructed, parallel to the narrated story (or description) with its own space-time structure, and without the speaker's intervention. It is on the plane of discourse that those elements which produce the story—the subject, with its own time and place—are formed.[2]

[1] J.-C. Coquet, *Sémiotique littéraire: Contribution à l'analyse sémantique du discours* (Paris, 1973), 15f.; J.-B. Grize, "Logique et discours pratique," *Communications* 20 (1973): 95. On the philosophical implications of the semiological resurgence of the subject, I cite P. Ricoeur's article, "La position du sujet: Le défi de la sémiologie," *Social Research* 34 (1967): 1–30, reprinted in *Le conflit des interprétations: Essais d'herméneutique* (Paris, 1969), 233–62.

[2] Benveniste 1966, 251ff. and 258ff., and 1974, 68f. and 72f.; see also Adam and Goldenstein 1976, 296ff., and Ricoeur, 1984, 92ff. Cf. K. Bühler, *Sprachtheorie: Die Darstellungsfunktion der Sprache* (Jena, 1934), 102ff. As will be seen in Chapter 1, §8, the pronouns do not correspond to syntactical positions alone; that is why I use the mixed

The question then arises as to how story and discourse are articulated in speech. Starting out with the concept of the *shifter* (*embrayeur*) introduced by Roman Jakobson, I have tried to define the procedure used to install the signs of the enunciation in speech as a "shifting-in" (one can also speak of "anchoring"); shifting in contrasts to the inverse procedure of "shifting out," in which these elements are withdrawn from the utterance to make the latter coincide with the story. The shifting-in, or anchoring, procedure is thus always coupled with a shifting-out procedure. When the actors of the enunciation (represented by *I/you*) are installed in the utterance, there is a corresponding expulsion of the actors (personified by the *he/she*'s) of the utterance; in this case we speak of *enunciative* shifting in/out, or *enunciative* anchoring. The other side of the coin is the disappearance of the actors of the enunciation, who in turn give way to the *he* of the utterance: we then have a shifting-in/out of the *enuncive* type.[3]

This analysis leaves something to be desired, however, as regards the terminology and its underlying concepts. In the ideas formulated by Benveniste of how language is realized in words, and of the presence of the enunciation in speech, an *instance of discourse* implies the idea of an action. If it is true that the utterance of the enunciation is linked to the act of producing speech, we must distinguish carefully between the "real," *referential* communication situation, with its particular social and psychological parameters, and the enunciation situation as it is glimpsed in the utterance through the use of language. To simplify, the communication situation corresponds to the actual act that produces the utterance: if we resort to the terminology introduced by Algirdas Julien Greimas, an *enunciator* (Jakobson uses the term *sender* or *transmitter*) addresses his utterance to an *enunciatee* (*sendee* or *receiver*, according to Jakobson). The uttered or spoken enunciation, in contrast, is the linguistic record of the communication (or referential) situation as it is expressed in the utterance: its actors/actants are called *narrator* and *narratee* (Benveniste employs the terms *locuteur* and *allocuté* or *allocutaire*).[4]

---

term of *actants-actors* of the narration. For the difference between actant and actor, see Greimas and Courtés 1979, 3ff. and 7ff., and Greimas 1983, 49f.

[3] On this subject, see Jakobson 1963, 178ff., and Greimas and Courtés 1979, 79ff. and 119ff. The history of the successive contributions of Benveniste to the theory of enunciation, often wrongly attributed to Jakobson, has been recorded by C. Normand, "Le sujet dans la langue," *Langages* 77 (1985): 7–19.

[4] See Greimas and Courtés 1979, 94 and 125f., for a systematic organization of Benveniste's thoughts (1966, 252f., and 1974, 81f.); see also T. Todorov, "Problèmes de l'énonciation," *Langages* 17 (1970): 4, and the recent details contributed by Adam 1985,

At this point, I should stress that the distinction Benveniste draws concerning the instances of discourse separates the utterance of the enunciation from the story being told. Abandoning the criterion of the past tenses, one could enlarge the concept of the story being told to the more general one of the *assertion*: a distinction would be drawn between the utterances modalized by the *I* or the *you*, the *here and now*, and so on, and the neutral utterances of the story, of the description, and the like. Keeping in mind the distinction proposed by Benveniste, however, in what follows I will use the terms *speaker* and *allocutee* as well as *narrator* and *narratee*: the archaic Greek poet is mainly, but not only, a storyteller.

It would have been possible to choose here the concepts of *fiktiver Autor* and *fiktiver Leser*, as elaborated in German reception theory, or the Italian formula of the *lettore modello*. But in taking over the terms "author" and "reader," these concepts derived from written texts induce possible confusions with the extradiscursive and biographical figures that correspond to them. They are also only partially based on precise textual indications. To that extent they are often confused with the more vague concepts of "implicit author/reader" or "abstract author/reader."[5]

178ff., who, in addition to the utterance and to the uttered enunciation, distinguishes two different levels in the enunciation (/communication): the level of the enunciation as "discourse," in which a real author addresses himself to a real reader, and the level of the enunciation as an "act," with the instances of the "enunciator" (abstract author) and the "receivers" (abstract readers) constructed by the discourse and looking at the act of discourse (see also below, n. 5). Borel, Grize, and Miéville 1983, 34ff. and 59ff., revise Benveniste's theses and reverse the meaning of the terms referring to the actants of the enunciation: the "locutor" takes part in communication, while the "enunciator" is the reference to it in the utterance. Ducrot 1984, 192ff. and 203ff., uses the term "locutor" for narrator and "producer" (or "empirical author") for enunciator in order to keep the term "enunciator" to designate the "character" that the locutor sometimes places in the utterance to represent himself.

As regards the utterance of the enunciation, it is possible, by means of a form such as dialogue, to introduce in the utterance a purely fictitious communication situation; the actants of this interactive structure are then called "interlocutor" and "interlocutee"; see Greimas and Courtés 1979, 80 and 191. As far as archaic Greek poetry is concerned, the complex relations between narrator and protagonists of the dialogues inserted in the narration have been explored by M. Steinrück, *Rede und Kontext: Zum Verhältnis von Person und Erzähler in frühgriechischen Texten* (Bonn, 1992).

[5] See, for instance, H. Link, *Rezeptionsforschung: Eine Einführung in Methoden und Probleme* (Stuttgart, 1976), 23ff., W. Iser, *Der implizite Leser* (Munich, 1972), 88ff., and *Der Akt des Lesens: Theorie ästhetischer Wirkung* (Munich, 1984), 50ff., and U. Eco, *Lector in fabula: La cooperazione interpretativa nei testi narrativi* (Milan, 1979), 53ff. J.-M. Adam, *Langue et littérature: Analyses pragmatiques et textuelles* (Paris, 1991), 27ff., proposes introducing between the " 'real' author/reader" and the "narrator/narratee" (as inscribed in the text) the figures of the "virtual author/reader" (see above, n. 4).

Between the utterance of the enunciation and its referential counterpart there can be a greater or smaller distance, so that the enunciation when uttered does not by any means faithfully represent the relationship of communication (i.e., the act of discourse, put more simply). So, for example, the *narrator*, installed in the discourse by the indications referred to above, is not necessarily the linguistic equivalent of the *enunciator*, nor is the *narratee* that of the *enunciatee*.[6] This distance means that the uttered enunciation is to a certain extent independent of the actual production of discourse; it also explains the creative and fictional potentialities of the spoken text. This helps make us particularly aware that the works of Antiquity "speak" to us still, even though the modern reader has practically no point of connection with the audience/enunciatee for whom the original enunciator intended them.

It must be stressed that already in the ancient world, critics had become aware of the essential difference between enunciator and narrator. More precisely, one must remember that Plato, looking for a place and a status for poetic discourse in the ideal city of the *Republic*, draws a clear distinction between *diegesis*, that is, simple narrative, and "mimetic" narrative. He also notes the existence of a third form that mixes these two narrative modes. The first type, simple narrative, is assumed by the poet himself (we would speak of the narrator), and the second, "mimetic" narrative, through a process of dialogical imitation, puts the story in the mouth of the protagonists of the narrated action. Homer was the master of mixing precisely these two modes: the direct narrative and the mimetic and dramatized narrative. Taking over in the *Poetics* the distinction made by Plato and seeing these three narrative modes as three kinds of mimetic representation, Aristotle seems moreover to be sensitive to the eventual presence of the narrator in the story told. Later literary critics, like the author of the treatise *On the Sublime*, have noticed quite clearly that, for instance, the passage from the third to the second person would enable the narrator—the voice supporting the diegesis—to have a narratee and to call out through him/her to an enunciatee, with a certain psychagogical effect.[7]

The relative autonomy of the utterance does not mean, however,

---

[6] See Genette 1972, 225ff. and 259ff., and Ducrot 1984, 206ff.; for the Homeric epic, see Nagy 1979, 5ff., and de Jong 1987, 31ff.

[7] See Plato, *Republic* 3, 392c ff. as well as Aristotle, *Poetics* 3, 1448a 19ff., and 24, 1460a 5ff., with the commentary on those difficult texts offered by D. W. Lucas, *Aristotle: Poetics* (Oxford, 1968), 66f. and 266f. Pseudo-Longinus, *Sublime* 26, 1ff.

that there is no overlap between the enunciative, or discursive, world it creates and the empirical world in which it is produced and operates. There is a positive aspect to the enunciative approach in that it exposes the trap of the principle of immanence, the trap of assuming that the text of the utterance is structurally closed.

2. The Semantic Composition of the Subject

"The 'ego' is the one who *says* 'ego,'" Benveniste affirms; and Coquet adds, "*ego* is the one who says *ego* and who says himself or herself to be *ego*."[8] Not only is the subject formed "in and by language," but every act of enunciation expresses a predicative relationship between the *I* and what the *I* says about itself through the act of enunciation. If it is true that the subject exists for certain only when it is enunciated, if it is true that "the basis of subjectivity is in the exercise of language" (Benveniste), then the subject, through its linguistic activity, affects the world that surrounds it and on which its very existence depends. When first defined, such activity might seem philosophically solipsistic or analytically autistic, but it is turned toward the exterior on two counts, because the subject, in order to acquire a distinctive character, is immediately faced with a *you*, and because its physical existence, its "corporeality," is of the world, a world it perceives through its senses and endeavors to represent and reconstruct by putting it into words.

So we are twice brought back to the enunciation situation. Having accepted the *I* as subject of the enunciation, and as a narrator who names himself, we are obliged to postulate the existence of an *I* (*ego*) that I shall call for the moment extralinguistic or, more precisely, extradiscursive. The *I* is therefore not a purely linguistic construct; its reality is not uniquely self-referential, but its self-referentiality has as well an external component, an extradiscursive aspect. The *I* is specific only insofar as it is situated and determined in relation to a *you*; and this *you*, like the *I*, refers to a *referent* that is external to language. Caught in a net of intersubjective relationships that have only a linguistic existence, the *I* bears the mark of the sociological and psychological conditioning to which, particularly when the *you* intervenes, its *exteriority* is exposed. Just as the *I*'s construction must bow to the rules of

---

[8] Benveniste 1966, 259f.; Coquet 1989, 14ff.

language on the linguistic level, its enunciative nature depends on its psychological reality and on its cultural and social relevance; it thus undergoes the constraints of both the intersubjective world and the natural world in which it is embedded.[9] The terms used here should not be deceptive: if I have had to use the word *exteriority* to define the elements implied by the marks that install the subject in language, the linguistic and discursive expressions of the *I*, and the *referent* of the predicative act by which the *ego* calls itself *I*, are only, to borrow an image from Saussure with all its metaphoric implications, the two sides of one sheet of paper.

To pose the problem of discourse and of enunciation is more than just posing the philosophical problem of the subject; it is to inaugurate a semantics or a semiotics of the *ego*, especially in its relation to the *you* that allows it to take on the role of *I*, and also in its connection with the exterior world. Such an open semiotics breaks with the theory and principle of immanence; it allows for the integration of all the elements belonging to what might be called, when the *ego* under consideration is from another culture, the "ethnographic context." But we must not forget that its openness will always start with the traces of the enunciation in the discourse, thus avoiding saddling it with predefined "production conditions."[10] It is indispensable, as regards the literary and iconographic productions of ancient Greece, to make the connection between the narrator or speaker and his or her manner of enunciating the self, along with what we know about the act of enunciation.

But if this seems to open discourse to an "exterior" world, we must avoid an overly simplistic and reductive separation of interior discourse and exterior world. Returning to the image of the two sides of one sheet of paper, we must not forget that we already perceive the exterior or natural world as a series of significant images, and that it is the object of meaningful operations which, in turn, give it sociological shape. The speaking subject is thus a point of articulation between a

[9] For a discussion, see the communication schema as reformulated by Kerbrat-Orecchioni 1980, 17ff., by F. Rastier, *Sens et textualité* (Paris, 1989), 47ff., and by J.-B. Grize, *Logique et langage* (Paris, 1990), 27ff.

[10] A criticism of this principle concerning the problem of the inference and of the reference is formulated, for instance, by J.-M. Adam, *Eléments de linguistique textuelle: Théorie et pratique de l'analyse textuelle* (Liège, 1990), 11ff., and by J.-C. Coquet, "Réalité et principe d'immanence," *Langages* 103 (1991): 23–35. Moreover, for an open "immanentism," see Kerbrat-Orecchioni 1980, 220f., as well as the reflections on "intersemioticity" in Greimas and Courtés 1986, 119, 185, and 187, in spite of their reaffirmation of the principle of immanence.

semiotics which looks at the meanings of the world and one which the subject itself produces in discourse when faced with the *you*. Still remaining within the semiotic framework, we can affirm that the utterance and the utterance of the enunciation are reformulations of an already meaningful exteriority.[11] Studying enunciative marks and whence they come leads to a much more general problem of how discourse is created, of the world of significations assumed by discourse; it also leads to the question of the impact of discourse on the world itself and on those who experience it. We have, therefore, not only an exchange between the signifying context in which discourse is produced and the discourse itself but also the mutual structuring of one by the other and of one within the other, with the speaking and uttering subject as go-between.

Discourse is formed by the subject on the basis of the latter's psychological and social makeup and his or her own vision of the natural world; in the same way, the subject's discourse tends to modify, by constantly restructuring it, the "reality" in which enunciation operates. This back and forth movement is particularly noticeable when the *I* exists only in its exchange with a singular or plural *you*; the *I* constantly repositions itself in relation to the *you* and in relation to the world that it transforms by its discourse. Enunciation is therefore not just a construction, it is also an action; it can always be seen in material signs and in the effects it brings about. Since the uttered enunciation exists only in the material aspect of the linguistic sign, whatever its substance may be, it reinforces the fundamentally materialist and realist position of semiotics, in spite of accusations of idealism leveled against it.

3. Enunciation as Action

Even before the development of pragmatism, Benveniste realized that the enunciative character of language is just as visible in the functions of supposition, interrogation, injunction, and the like, as it is in the signs that anchor the enunciation and its space-time structure in the utterance.[12] These operations make real actions of the utterance

[11] See A. J. Greimas and E. Landowski, "Pragmatique et sémiotique," *Actes sémiotiques: Documents* 5, no. 50 (1983), Landowski 1989, 190ff., and Calame 1990, 38ff.
[12] See Benveniste 1966, 264ff. (this study on "subjectivity in language" dates from 1958), and 1974, 79ff.

containing them, and the speaker can then intervene in the situation surrounding the discourse. The fuzzy line separating the illocutionary from the perlocutionary act is not a subject for discussion here; but Oswald Ducrot attempted to distinguish between the self-referential acts of language that utilize the rules of discourse and those which introduce the causality of the "exterior" world. The illocutionary act, such as "promise," creates an obligation that is valid only "in the world depicted by the enunciation" at the very moment the utterance is being enacted; the perlocutionary act, in contrast, such as offering consolation, has a direct effect on the situation outside the discourse.[13] This distinction is particularly pertinent for early Greek poetry in which the act of enunciation manifests itself in the utterance by way of performance verbs such as *to sing, to praise, to invoke*; it leads us again to those complex relationships which link the linguistic domain marked out by the utterance of the enunciation to the empirical domain corresponding to the enunciation/communication situation and its psychosocial protagonists.

These same relationships are central to Antoine Culioli's reflections on enunciation; his main idea is that any utterance, by taking over the predicative relationship, implies an enunciating subject and a situation that triggers the "enunciation."[14] In relation to the enunciation situation, the "marks" represented by the elements that anchor the protagonists and the space-time structure in the utterance are then only the visible tip of an enormous enunciative iceberg; this idea of a generalized enunciation, implied by an expansion of linguistic activity, in the end comes up against the all-pervasive problem of *référenciation*, that is, of the extradiscursive reference.[15]

In fact, it is arguable, if we follow Hermann Parret, whether the enunciation, if indeed it underlies the act of discourse, should not be thought of as an "utterance effect" not necessarily visible in the utterance in the tangible form of marks and signs. The enunciation would then be the precondition for an utterance and thus a "translation" of

---

[13]O. Ducrot, "Illocutoire et performatif," *Linguistique et sémiologie* 4 (1977): 17–53, reprinted in *Dire et ne pas dire: Principes de sémantique linguistique* (Paris, 1980), 279–305.

[14]A. Culioli, C. Fuchs, and M. Pêcheux, *Considérations théoriques à propos du traitement formel du langage* (Paris, 1970), 32ff.; A. Culioli, "Rapport sur un rapport," in *La psychomécanique et les théories de l'énonciation*, ed. A. Joly (Lille, 1980), 37–47, and "En guise d'introduction," in *La langue au ras du texte*, ed. A. Grésillon and J.-L. Lebrave (Lille, 1984), 9–12.

[15]On the subject of *référenciation*, see D. Bertrand, *L'espace et le sens: Germinal d'Emile Zola* (Paris, 1985), 30ff.

that utterance. It would be seen far away at the base of the iceberg, forming the transcendental level of the "enunciative community." Only by going down to this deep level would the contradiction between an uttered enunciation having the character of a stage production and the communal values underlying it be surmounted.[16]

Whatever the case may be, the enunciative perspective inevitably expands to include the problem of the production of discourse, involving the effect on the utterance of its procedures of actorialization, temporalization, and spatialization, to say nothing of how the more abstract semantic structures are translated into "figures."[17] It is from this angle that we must approach the thorny problem of the relationship between the world constructed in discourse and the world of nature or society as well as the complex question of the pragmatic influence of the one on the other. Why then limit ourselves to the tip of the iceberg? Why not try to track down all the traces left in the utterance by the innumerable marking procedures of a referential situation? While we are about it, why not analyze all the pragmatic implications of the language act that any discourse represents? Why not turn to philosophy and try to understand the transcendental element beyond the utterance underlying all the operations that produce discourse?

4. The Communication Situation in Antiquity

If we hesitate to cross the threshold of such an all-inclusive vision of discourse production, it is mainly because our understanding of Antiquity—and this is a truism—is gained primarily through texts. We can know the implications of these written utterances, and the community that wrote them down, only through these same utterances. In the absence of an observable enunciation situation, Hellenists interested in the processes by which literary meaning is produced must deal only with "finished products"; from an enunciative point of view, they risk being reduced to the illocutionary act, in the self-referential concept developed by Ducrot. Threatened by tautology or anachronistic projection, the Hellenist's best bet, therefore, is to start with the most

[16]H. Parret, "L'énonciation en tant que déictisation et modalisation," *Langages* 70 (1983): 83–97.

[17]See D. Bertrand, "Narrativité et discursivité," *Actes sémiotiques: Documents* 6, no. 59 (1984), 30ff.

obvious enunciative indicators and conform to the fundamentally materialist conception of enunciation and semiotics articulated above.

The different interpretations, over the last hundred years or so, of the renowned *Hymn to Aphrodite*, which opened the Alexandrian edition of Sappho's poems, prove the value of this approach. Addressing the divinity by evoking her qualities, recalling her past kindnesses, making a new request on the basis of previous assistance, all these are the enunciative marks of the relationship between the *I* and the *you* contained in Sappho's verses and make this a cletic hymn, a hymn of invocation. Philologists are unanimous on this point. When we pass from the illocutionary elements of the poem to the analysis of its perlocutionary effect, however, the dissonance is as jarring as the previous harmony was perfect. Between a reference to an objective situation, on the one hand, in which Sappho asks Aphrodite to bring back into her circle a young deserter and, on the other hand, the autonomy of literary fiction, the specter of interpretations engenders an almost infinite number of possibilities.[18] The prologue of Hesiod's *Theogony*, with the importance assumed there by the Muses' vision as evoked by the narrator/speaker, confronts us—as we shall see—with a similar problem.

However difficult this departure, based on the marks of enunciation, toward the nonlinguistic and nondiscursive may be, it is nevertheless necessary. In much the same way that we do, the Greeks obtained information from their texts, to which they were a great deal closer than we are, and they have passed down to us a fragmentary knowledge of the conditions under which the earliest Greek poetry was communicated. It must be said that, with the exception of Homeric poetry, ancient Greek poems are rich in enunciative "shiftings-in" of all sorts and that a burgeoning literary criticism, beginning with Plato and continuing among Aristotle's students, was aware of these interventions in the text of the circumstances of enunciation. But the biographies of the ancient poets, starting with Hermippus or Aristoxenus of Tarentum, are there to show that the Ancients were not able to avoid the circular reasoning that reconstructing the conditions of communication on the basis of the work itself inevitably leads to.[19]

---

[18] Sappho, fr. 1 Voigt; see the commentary by A. P. Burnett, *Three Archaic Poets: Archilochus, Alcaeus, Sappho* (London, 1983), 243ff., and the forty-odd interpretations listed by H. Saake, *Zur Kunst Sapphos: Motivanalytische und kompositions-technische Interpretationen* (Munich, 1971), 54ff. and 67ff.

[19] See M. R. Lefkowitz, *The Lives of the Greek Poets* (Baltimore, 1981), 25ff.

It is true, however, that Greek poetry of the earliest period is, in essence, a poetry of occasion; each composition is ordered for a particular festival and composed for a specific public. And the poetic utterance bears many marks of this process, which at times goes so far as to reach the point where the poem is itself the description of the ritual and of the public performance that is its occasion, with the result that the poem serves as its own context, in a process of external self-referentiality.[20] With this in mind, the enunciative perspective is useful for comprehending a literature that, at least until Herodotus and although poetry gradually gave way to prose, was profoundly dependent on the practices surrounding its production. I shall now examine the *I* in its role as the source and focal point of enunciation and utterance. But we have just said that the ancient Greek enunciator, at least in sociological terms, is defined in relation to the enunciatee to whom he addresses himself and who in effect provides him with his material means of support. Thus as we analyze the *I* of the self-enunciating narrator, our attention will inevitably focus on the *you* who appears vis-à-vis the narrator and on the organization of space and time in which these two actants/actors of the uttered enunciation evolve. The interaction between the two is present in different forms on the sociological level as well as in the utterance of the enunciation.

5. The *I* as Simulacrum

If it is difficult to estimate the effect of the relation between the uttered enunciation and the real circumstances of communication in early and classical Greece owing to a lack of precise data on the subject,[21] the finished character of the literary works makes it all the more necessary to understand their sociological context. But let us not be tempted to "sociologize"! Nor should we forget that during the referencing process, the utterance of the enunciation does not in the least give a direct reflection of the communication situation or its circumstances. We must realize that the functioning of the uttered enunciation has a certain autonomy—this has already been stated, and I will give

---

[20] Lastly, see Gentili 1988, 153ff., for the specific character of archaic Greek poetry.

[21] An exception might be the remarks of Aristotle on the effects of tragic dramas on the passions; Aristotle, *Poetics* 1449b 24ff.; for fear and pity aroused by tragedy and their *katharsis*, see Dupont-Roc and Lallot 1980, 188ff., with the contributions now reprinted in *Die Aristotelische Katharsis*, ed. H. Luserke (Hildesheim, 1991).

concrete examples later. Semiotically speaking, the utterance of the enunciation creates its own world, just as the story creates its own fiction. Without reducing them to pure "facsimiles," the protagonists of the uttered enunciation are creatures of the written text in the same way, for example, that characters in novels are. What distinguishes them from the latter is the act of producing utterances; they may be facsimiles, but they are facsimiles situated in the time of the enunciation. "*Ego* is the one who says *ego* and who says himself or herself to be *ego*" in the present, at the very moment of speaking. And an *I* that creates itself as it creates its product is enough to break the bonds of linguistic immanence.[22]

As it enunciates itself, the subject can play hide-and-seek with its psychosociological "reality"; it is capable of constructing itself in the text in any way it wishes. But it cannot hide the fact that its capacity to attribute to itself the predicates that suit it has the same origin as the affirmation of its existence in the enunciation, in the word. As I said earlier, it is in the subject that psychological "reality" and language production intersect.

6. Narrativization of the Enunciation

The Actantial Structure

With the intersection of psychological "reality" and language production in mind, it is interesting to note that the discursive subject is constructed as if it were the protagonist of a narrative. In early Greek poetry especially, we see it occupy various positions in the actantial structure defining the logic of any story. In what follows, I highlight with initial capital letters the various actants of the Greimassian narrative grammar. In the oldest poetic texts, the *I* is projected on a *you* that takes over the position of the Sender by assuming the figure of the Muse; the *I*, narrator and Subject of the uttered enunciation, is then in the position of Receiver, represented by the linguistic form of the

[22]On the simulated *I*, see Landowski 1989, 77ff., with added remarks by Greimas and Courtés 1986, 193 and 206. Only within the framework of the assertion of the *I* and its space-time character in the utterance of the enunciation is it possible to resolve the differences between the philologists who see in the lyrical Greek *I* a biographical reflection and those who recognize in it only a poetic personage with no social reality; this problem is articulated by W. Rösler: see Chapter 3, n. 29; see also the references cited in n. 35 below.

dative and by an effect of actantial syncretism. From the viewpoint of the Predicate that is attributed to it in this micronarrative, the *I* becomes both the Subject and the Receiver of the action of singing entrusted to it by the Sender.[23] The constant change in this type of poetry from the singular form *I* to the plural *we* causes the *I* to install, at times, a second *you*, an Antisubject, with which it is only very partially at odds: narrator/speaker and narratee/allocutee are thus brought together in the same linguistic form. I note in passing that the narrator and the narratee seem to be defined in this narrative framework not so much as actantial positions but as actors assuming a specific semantic role. We shall see how, as time passes, the *I* tends gradually to oust the Muse from the Sender's position and itself takes over; the second *you* is then called on to give up its Antisubject status and to take on that of the Receiver. As the history of early Greek literature proceeds, while one genre replaces another on a synchronic line, we see the enunciation situation being narrativized in the utterance and, more important, a displacement of the actors occupying the actantial positions in the uttered enunciation. That displacement can be diagrammed as shown in Figure 1.

Situation A:

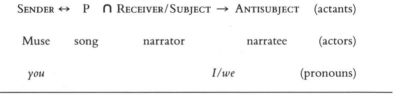

Sender ↔	P	∩ Receiver/Subject →	Antisubject	(actants)
Muse	song	narrator	narratee	(actors)
you			*I/we*	(pronouns)

Situation B:

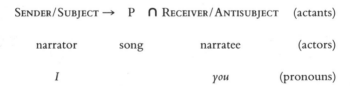

Sender/Subject →	P	∩ Receiver/Antisubject	(actants)
narrator	song	narratee	(actors)
I		*you*	(pronouns)

Figure 1. Actantial structure of the utterance of the enunciation

[23] As mentioned, the capitalization used here is to distinguish the actants of the narration that have positions only in the syntax from the actors who can assume positions and invest them with the semantic values attached to them. Also within the actantial structure, the idea of the Object has been replaced by the Predicate,

With the transfer of the *you* from the actantial position of Sender to that of Receiver, we leave the uttered enunciation and must ask ourselves what the disappearance of inspiration, as represented by the Muse, means in sociological terms. The question brings us to the enunciation/communication situation; here, as the poem is recited, and independently of the actantial positions assumed by the *you*, the enunciatees receive from the enunciator useful knowledge that will reformulate for them semiotically the data of the natural and social world.

Toward a Modal Analysis of the Actors of the Enunciation

The transmission of knowledge represented by the poem serves as the point of intersection between the uttered enunciation and its converse, the circumstances of enunciation. By way of its intermediary, the communication situation can also be understood in terms of a narrativization; by investigating the use of the modalities that animate the actors engaged in the process of narrativization, we can see how the circumstances of enunciation intersect with the uttered enunciation during this process.

The starting point for our analysis as it moves in this new direction is the enunciation's focal point, namely, the subject that enunciates and that also enunciates itself. Subordinate in its actantial status to a Sender it projects outside itself, the *I* occupying the actantial position of the Subject places power (*pouvoir*) over it rather than duty (*devoir*); it then fits itself into the modal sequence "will, power-knowledge" (*vouloir, pouvoir-savoir*); like the Muses who are supposed to inspire him, and because of them as well, the poet knows everything.[24] In this way, the will of the poet, by being projected onto a Sender with divine qualities, is transformed into power-knowledge. Before the Subject-

corresponding to the remarks in my "La formulation de quelques structures sémio-narratives, ou comment segmenter un texte," in *Exigences et perspectives de la sémiotique: Recueil d'hommages pour A. J. Greimas*, ed. H. Parret and H.-G. Ruprecht (Amsterdam, 1985), 135–47; for the "canonic schema" of narration and for the new formulation of the actantial structure implied by it, see Adam 1985, 24 and 76ff., and *Les textes: Types et prototypes: Récit, description, argumentation, explication et dialogue* (Paris, 1992), 45ff.; see also Calame 1990, 55ff.

[24] Concerning this modal definition of the subject of the narration, see Coquet 1989, 27ff.; Coquet's ideas are here used toward a definition of the subject of the uttered enunciation, allowing the circle of the immanence of the text to be broken (see also n. 10 above).

narrator's sphere of competence can be considered complete and find expression in performance, the modality of duty must be present. It will not be found on the level of the uttered enunciation; it is on the related plane of communication that duty is included in the Subject's competence. The sponsor of the poem and of the poetic performance becomes the Sender of the Subject because of the material means he puts at the disposal of the author; the sponsor manipulates the power the poet possesses and in this way defines the poet's duty. The Sender/actant is thus doubled: on the plane of the uttered enunciation the Sender is embodied in the figure of the Muses who confer power, while in the communication process that position is taken over by the sponsor, a Homeric prince or member of an aristocratic family who formulates for the poet, in a financial contract, the poet's compositional duty.

In the first situation, the competence of the Subject is defined both in the utterance of the enunciation and in the communication situation: the power-knowledge that the Muses transmit, the simulacrum, and the power-knowledge possessed by the poet finally come together in the effect produced on the enunciatee, with the help of the duty imposed by the sponsor. The illocutionary strength of the poetic utterance, appearing in the uttered enunciation as the power-knowledge conferred by the Muses on the narrator, is transformed into a perlocutionary act; and it makes a definitive appearance in the communication situation as the power-knowledge which the sponsor wants to put into effect and which the poet/enunciator effectively exercises over his public.[25] The unique source of this illocutionary, or perlocutionary, effect is the enunciating *I*, which—as we shall see—causes the Muse to intervene in the uttered enunciation so as to disguise the social manipulation to which it is subject.

And when inspiration represented by the Muses becomes merely a literary convention, it is the *I* of the narrator that inherits the power-knowledge previously bestowed by the Muses. From an actantial point of view, the Subject stops being the Receiver of the Muses and becomes the Sender for a Receiver *you* that then appears frequently on the level of the uttered enunciation; similarly, the communication of the utterance, the song as Predicate-Object taken up by the Subject, will also be seen on this level. It is thus possible to construct a chart

[25] Concerning the power of the ancient Greek poet vis-à-vis his public, see Gentili 1988, 203ff.

illustrating the historical and generic change that the poet's position, both enunciative and social, underwent (see Figure 2).

Situation A:

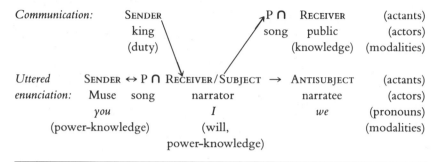

Situation B:

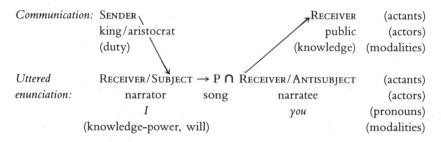

Figure 2. Communication, uttered enunciation, and modalities

When the cases of pronouns are reversed, the double shift that the *I*-narrator undergoes in situation A is simplified in situation B by being "linearized"; but as the focal point of the diffusion of knowledge, the *I* remains at the point of articulation between uttered enunciation and communication. The process of narrativization which involves the subject guarantees that these two levels will be closely coordinated.

We also see in Coquet's modal classification of subjects that the change from situation A to situation B shifts the Subject-narrator from the modal sequence "will, power-knowledge" to the sequence "knowledge-power, will."[26] The narrator/speaker no longer projects

---

[26] Concerning the subjects "w–pk" (will, power–knowledge) and "kp–w (knowledge–power, will), see Coquet 1989, 38ff. and 65ff.

his power-knowledge onto the Sender (simulacrum) represented by the Muses; he becomes a subject conscious of his (partial) identity as poet. He is not entirely possessed by the Muses; he is also the owner of a *tekhnē* and a *sophia*, a technical competence and knowledge that allow him to compose and sing.

The interest in a modal analysis of the enunciating subject thus resides in the fact that the combination of modes characterizing him is situated at the point where the uttered enunciation and the social communication intersect. If will (*vouloir*) seems to refer to the subject's psychological reality, duty (*devoir*) necessarily refers to the action of an exterior Sender of a social nature. So, in the end, it is his psychosocial identity and actions that the subject of the enunciation reveals, in a series of transpositions, through his manner of constituting himself modally in what he says. By projecting power-knowledge (*pouvoir-savoir*) outside himself in order to double the duty defined by an exterior Sender, and by the will to dominate thanks to power-knowledge, or conversely, by collaborating with knowledge-power (*savoir-pouvoir*), the enunciating subject asserts and assumes his function and position.

7. The Enunciative Games of the Narrator: Alcman

In conclusion, I will give a single example of the complex enunciative interplay discussed in the previous section, partial and incomplete though the poetic crumbs may be from which to cull such an example. The player is an *I* that transposes its sociological identity in order to dissemble it, for the purpose of settling itself more firmly in its poetic reality.

In one of the fragments of the Spartan poet Alcman, a feminine *I* describes in the present tense the moment when she will be awakened by the Muses to take part—as the continuation of the fragment shows—in a ritual during which she will sing the very poem she has already started to perform.[27] This strange projection into the near future of a moment already gone by in relation to the time of the uttered enunciation (the description of the ritual is in the present tense) makes the Muses' intervention coincide with the tense of the enunciation. The Muses assume the role of the Sender, since it is they who "lead" the *I*

[27] See Alcman, fr. 3, 1ff. Page = 26, 1ff. Calame, with the commentary that I present in *Alcman: Introduction, texte critique, témoignages, traduction et commentaire* (Rome, 1983), 396ff.

(by intoning the strains of the song?) toward the place where the poem is performed. The power that these daughters of Zeus have over the *I* strengthens the will of the *I*-narrator. Its effect is immediate, making the *I* the Subject of the action described: the *I* thus becomes the protagonist of the ritual which it evokes; it is the *I* that performs the poem which brings the *I* into being. The complexity of the utterance of the enunciation becomes visible during performance.

The power of the Muses in the realm of song and music is often reaffirmed in Alcman's poetry, particularly in certain fragments where the daughters of Zeus, invoked in the second person, paradoxically occupy the position of narratee. Though this position seems to coincide with that of the Receiver in the narration, we need not find it unusual; the Muses' position is simply subordinate to the supplication that the *I*—here implicitly present in the form of the imperative—addresses to them. The narrator/speaker sets up an opposing *you* in order to request that it start to sing the song, promising the speaker's musical and choreographic accompaniment. The Muses are the narratee because of the linguistic forms used, but in fact they take over the position of Sender in relation to the narrator—a Sender who serves to establish the choral competence of the Subject of the speech act. The apparent inversion of the actantial roles implied by the use of the pronouns *I* and *you* merely indicates the projection of the narrator/speaker onto the divine authority invoked to exercise its power over the *I*; I shall have occasion to return to this projection. Another sign of the power conferred on the Muses is the effacement of the *I* behind a third person plural that immediately reveals the narrator's social identity, thus sending us back to the communication situation:

> "O Muse, Muse with the melodious voice,
> Muse of the eternal song,
> sing for the maidens
> a new tune!"

The movement from singular to plural should not disturb us; it is normal in early choral poetry for the performer to be described as an individual as often as a group.[28] But this projection onto a divine

---

[28] See Alcman, fr. 14(a) Page = 4 Calame (see on this subject Chap. 1, § 7) and 27 Page = 84 Calame, with the commentary of Calame [n. 27], 349ff., and of Gianotti 1975, 43ff. On the alternation *I/we* in the expression of the subject in choral lyric poetry, see Calame 1977, 1:436ff. and 2:45f.

authority of modal values that establishes the competence of the Sub-
ject/enunciator by no means prevents the *I* from appearing in other
fragments as the subject of its song; in the presence of the Muse, the *I*
thus takes a first step toward affirming the autonomy of its poetic
competence.[29] The poet—psychosocial and biographical author of the
verses recited—is not excluded from this power game between an *I*
narrator and Subject of the poem's enunciation, on the one hand, and,
on the other, a Muse both narratee and Sender of the song being
performed; the poet hides behind a third person situated by the aorist
of the story in the tense of the utterance:

> "Alcman has found the words
> and the melody . . .
> listening to the voices of the
> partridges."[30]

It is time to compare the two sides of the situation. On one side we
find a Subject, a feminine plural narrator, projecting as its counterpart,
in the position of narratee, its own Sender; this Sender possesses the
modal competence necessary for the production of the song, although
that does not prevent the *I* from taking it over on other occasions;
lastly, we note the presence in the utterance of the "composer" of the
poem, as distinct from the narrator, removed from the level of the
utterance of the enunciation in order to appear under his own name in
the third person, in the tense of the story. On the other side, thanks to a
great deal of outside evidence, we note the presence of a poet active in
Sparta in the seventh century B.C. during the most productive period
of cultural expansion the city ever knew; not only did this poet produce verses of which we have a few fragments, he also directed the
young women who sang them in chorus. Their poetic performance
had its context in various Spartan civic cults. These cults were often
part of the ritual practices that reintegrated young initiates into the
city; they consisted mainly of public rituals and performances of poetry. It was therefore the political authorities of the city that acted as
the sponsors of the poet Alcman, who was most probably supported
in Sparta by the State.[31]

---

[29] Alcman, fr. 29 Page = 89 Calame and 28 Page = 85 Calame; see also fr. 1, 39
Page = 3, 39 Calame.
[30] Alcman, fr. 39 Page = 91 Calame; see also fr. 95(b) Page = 92 Calame and 17, 6
Page = 9, 6 Calame.
[31] On this subject, see Calame 1977, 1:393ff.

In light of what we can gather regarding the utterance of the enunciation in Alcman's poetry, the schema I have outlined takes on the form shown in Figure 3.

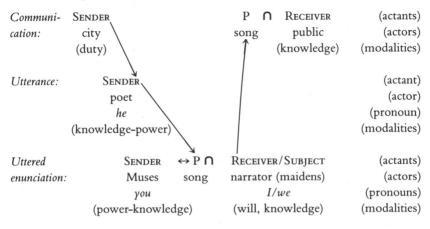

Figure 3. Communication and uttered enunciation in Alcman

The enunciative shifting-out, along with the enuncive shifting-in, or anchoring, the object of which is the figure of the poet, is significant for the role played by the poet with respect to the poetic performance. The city delegates to this custodian of knowledge-power (*savoir-pouvoir*) the function of preparing for the poetic performance those who will say *I*, but the poet does not intervene in the choral execution itself; hence the custodian appears in the poem only at the level of the utterance, as if he were an actor from the outside. Following Ducrot's polyphonic analysis of the enunciation, one could say that in Alcman's poems the author, instead of establishing himself as narrator, puts himself in the position of one of those "enunciators" who are there to take over positions at a distance from that of the narrator/speaker.[32] Possessing, however, like the Muses, the modality of power, he communicates it only partially to the *I*-narrator, who can be considered as much the Subject of the poetic performance as its Receiver: by singing the poems composed by Alcman, the young women become initiated and acquire knowledge, as does the public that is present at the choral performance. In this way, the realization of the supreme power-knowledge attributed by projection to the Muses combined with knowledge-power of the individualized Subject pos-

[32]Ducrot 1984, 203ff.

sessed by the poet creates in Alcman's poetry a unique enunciative situation motivated by the subordinate social status of the performer or performers of the poem. This situation is translated, narratively speaking, by a modal impoverishment of the speaking Subject and by an inversion in the complementary actantial role that the Subject assumes in the uttered and narrativized enunciation: from being the Sender, the Subject becomes the Receiver.[33]

8. Questioning Distinctions in the Classical Genres

Thus we find that in a situation where the narrators tend to project their power onto a higher authority, the *I* can take on various actantial positions covering a wide range of enunciative possibilities. These possibilities are closely connected with the particular circumstances in which the poems examined are performed, even if they sometimes reverse the terms of such a connection. This will not surprise those who have realized that in ancient Greece consistency in the poetic genres stems from their being defined relative to the different rituals at which they were regularly performed. It has, of course, already been said, and we shall see again, that the different positions assumed by the self-enunciating *I* in its own discourse seem to be arranged in a linear series: from the epic poems to the victory odes of Pindar, the *I* appears to occupy an ever more objective and conscious position, a position in which the modality of will appears in ever higher relief. But this seemingly linear historical development is partly due to our own tradition, which makes lyric poetry come chronologically later than epic texts (I use the term *lyric* without intending any reference to "lyric individualism" and with the understanding that it includes iambic and elegiac forms); in fact, the epic and lyric, along with their individual spoken forms of enunciation, had long existed concurrently: the distinctions between them, rather than being historical, are a function of the various genres known in archaic Greek poetry. We shall see how the work of a Herodotus, who also introduces historical discourse, interrupts this apparent line of development and takes on, in certain respects, epic intentions.

The foregoing statements will at any rate prevent us from confusing the different forms assumed successively or concurrently by the utterance of the enunciation in the genres of ancient Greek poetry with a

---

[33] Note that the unique enunciative situation represented by Alcman's poetry produces a far more complex schema than that projected by Kerbrat-Orecchioni 1980, 18ff.

linear transition from the oral to the written. It is true that within choral lyric poetry the effacement of the narrator behind a *he*, such as we have observed in Alcman's poetry, gives way a century later in Pindar to a strong affirmation of the narrator as *I*; and this despite an enunciated context similar to the one we find in Alcman: like the poet from Sparta, Pindar delegates to a chorus or to its *khorēgos* the power to perform his own song.[34] It cannot be stressed enough that the position of the narrator/speaker corresponding in archaic Greek poetry to the use of the pronoun *I* is only a simulation; it refers only quite indirectly to the biographical, intradiscursive person of the author.[35] True, the processes of the *sphragis*, or "signature," a subject to be investigated at a later point, sometimes give to this *I* the identity conferred by a proper name; but the proper name itself belongs in its own right to the domain of the extradiscursive; it does not necessarily refer to an *empirical author*. It is only within a complex interplay of discursive constructs and enunciative masks that it is possible to grasp the fictional character of ancient Greek literary works.

At the time of Alcman, we see how the *I* that makes its appearance in Sappho's poems probably refers back to the author, while the elements that characterize the space-time context of the utterance of their enunciation not only refer to the here and now of the moment of their performance but define an idealized context, repeatedly evoked, that closely resembles a mythic setting; the *I* and the *you* which is its corollary are invited to be part of this, often with memory as an intermediary, so that their sensibilities may take on a predictable, divinely guaranteed existence.[36] And it is in this sense that we should

[34] For the circumstances of enunciation in Pindar's *Epinicia* in relation to the uttered *I*, see T. K. Hubbard, *The Pindaric Mind: A Study of Logical Structure in Early Greek Poetry* (Leiden, 1985), 145ff., Nagy 1990, 337ff., and the collection of studies published by M. R. Lefkowitz, *First Person Fictions: Pindar's Poetic 'I'* (Oxford, 1991); the unilateral position defended by this scholar, who prefers to refer the Pindaric *I* to the author rather than to the chorus performing and singing the poem, has triggered a long polemic. See its latest development in *Class. Philol.* 86 (1991): 173–91 and 192–200, and 88 (1993): 1–15.

[35] See on the question of the *I* for epic poetry, n. 6 above, and for lyric poetry, W. Rösler, "Persona reale o persona poetica? L'interpretazione dell'io nella lirica greca arcaica," *Quad. Urb. Cult. Class.* 19 (1985): 131–44, B. Gentili, "Die pragmatischen Aspekte der archaischen griechischen Dichtung," *Ant. u. Abendl.* 36 (1990): 1–17, and the three contributions edited by S. R. Slings in *The Poet's 'I' in Archaic Greek Lyric* (Amsterdam, 1990); unfortunately these three studies deal essentially with so-called monodic poetry. See now also the various contributions published in *La componente autobiografica nella poesia greca e latina fra realtà e artificio letterario*, ed. G. Arrighetti and F. Montanari (Pisa, 1993).

[36] Burnett's interpretations [n. 18], 229ff., move in this direction, though Burnett sometimes forgets to mention that the fiction constructed in the poem is based on a real

understand the appeal in the *Hymn to Aphrodite*. The goddess is certainly invited to intervene in the here and now of the recitation of the cletic poem, but the repetition of some of the elements that indicate both space and time in the poem's enunciation places the request of the *I* in a reality outside time, a divine reality; the speech act represented by the pact the narrator/speaker proposes to the goddess at the end of the poem will now assure that the justice of Love, guaranteed by Aphrodite herself, will prevail.

An enunciative approach to archaic and classical Greek literature, while permitting us to define the author's situation as speaker and narrator in his own discourse, leads to a redefinition of the classical literary forms. In undertaking this redefinition, we make a break with linear developments and with genres that have overly precise, predetermined contours. We redefine the way these genres relate to their contexts of enunciation. Indeed, we redefine the very status of the narration/description that is contained in and assumed by the different modalities of the utterance of the enunciation. In a perspective that aims to bring to the fore the complementarity and mutual imbrication of the levels of the uttered enunciation and of the communication circumstances, the focal role played by the *I* cannot be emphasized enough. Even if the *I* loses one of these modal values and becomes simply the performer of verses composed by another, as it does in Alcman's poetry, it nevertheless assures, through the various actantial positions it occupies, that the two different layers meet. The utterance of the enunciation always refers to the social aspects of a transmission of knowledge, knowledge constructed, through assertion and narration, in a work of literary creation. Let us not forget that the literary work in question was composed outside a tradition that sees historic evolution moving inexorably toward a Western culture believed to be the only possible end.

---

experience and that it generally has a precise role to play during the occasion on which the poem is performed. Also in this regard, see the article by J. Latacz, "Realität und Imagination: Eine neue Lyrik-Theorie und Sapphos *phainetai moi kenos*-Lied," *Mus. Helv.* 42 (1985): 67–94; this article was written in reaction to the ideas defended by Rösler (1980, 200f., and the article cited in Chap. 2, n. 35), who associates early melic poetry, supposedly depending on an oral tradition in a linear way, with a concrete and referential deixis (*Demonstratio ad oculos* as opposed to a *Deixis am Phantasma*, which would be appropriate to written literature); the discovery of "fictionality" would then be reserved for the literature of the classical period insofar as it is supposed to use writing more extensively. See the response of W. Rösler in "Realitätsbezug und Imagination in Sapphos *Gedicht phaínetaí moi kēnos*," in *Der Übergang von der Mündlichkeit zur Literatur bei den Griechen*, ed. W. Kullmann and M. Reichel (Tübingen, 1990), 271–87.

CHAPTER I

Epic and Lyric Poetry: The Projection of the *I* and Its Oral Discourse onto the Divine Authority

1. The Levels of Enunciation

The appearance of the subject of the narration in the text is sometimes quoted as evidence when attempts are made to isolate the characteristics of written literature as opposed to oral literature.[1] As we shall see, merely reading the transcription of an oral text is enough to show that the appearance of the *I* is not a distinctive trait of written literature. A study of the more global problem of enunciation can lead, however, to conclusions of definite interest, particularly in the early period in Greece, when the oral tradition gives way little by little, starting in the eighth century, to the written word.

We saw in the Introduction how the linguistic and semiotic definition of the enunciation process has been greatly expanded and deepened since the landmark studies of Emile Benveniste. Within this wider definition, the expression of "subjectivity" in the form of the pronoun *I* and in the actantial position of the Subject/narrator seems to serve as a pivot between the level of uttered enunciation and that of communication. But the problem of the impact of an oral tradition on literary works does not emerge only at this point of articulation, since

---

[1] See, e.g., A. J. Greimas, "Conclusions générales," in *Strutture e generi delle letterature etniche* (*Atti del simposio internazionale,* Palermo, 5–10 April 1970) (Palermo, 1978), 339f.; see also, for Homeric poetry, Russo 1968, 483ff.

in early Greek poetry the expression of the *I* occupies a privileged place. Hence the dual interest of the enunciative perspective opened up by Benveniste's research. To examine either of the modes of production and enunciation in Greek poetry, we must inevitably begin with an analysis of the traces that they leave in the poetic utterance.

The problem of the expression of the *I* in early Greek literature will be examined within the framework of the procedures for producing discourse and its linguistic signs. The very manner in which we pose the problem of the utterance of the enunciation in its relation to the communication situation implies, for a literature that is just passing from the oral to the written, an examination of this basic change in the mode of production and transmission of the literary artifact. We can then give a preliminary idea of the degree to which the first Greek literary productions that have come down to us still depend on an oral tradition. But in order to avoid imposing on the text external "conditions of production," it is necessary to start with the utterance of the enunciation in order to understand the variation it undergoes during the three centuries of the early period. This will allow for an a posteriori evaluation of the impact of the transition to writing on the utterance of the enunciation in various kinds of literary texts, and it will also prompt us to modify the often too narrowly applied relationship between the form of these various literary productions and the transition from oral to written.

2. The Oral and Written in Archaic Greece

I am not going to spend much time on the question of the oral and the written, a problem which has been the object of many studies during the last few decades and which, along with a series of new theories, has led to a number of difficulties. It is well known that the earliest inscriptions that have survived allow us to date the adoption and the gradual diffusion of the Phoenician alphabet in Greece from about the middle of the eighth century.[2] But it was some time later that a particularly gifted *aoidos* (or two of them), perhaps called Homer, had

---

[2] See L. H. Jeffery, *The Local Scripts of Archaic Greece* (Oxford, 1961), 12ff.; on the same subject, see also the articles published in *Das Alphabet: Entstehung und Entwicklung der griechischen Schrift*, ed. G. Pfohl (Darmstadt, 1968), and the historical perspective presented by Heubeck 1979, 73ff., and by B. B. Powell, *Homer and the Origin of the Greek Alphabet* (Cambridge, 1991), 5ff.

the idea of reworking and transcribing, by means of the newly introduced system of writing, some of the epic poems he was in the habit of
performing, probably with the purpose of ritually consecrating those
texts (for instance, in a temple) rather than "publishing" them. The
poems were subsequently conserved under the names *Iliad* and *Odyssey*.[3] Two facts are certain: first, we see the transition from the oral to
the written tradition in Greece in the first written literary text, and the
distance in time separating us from that period prevents us from
understanding the state of the tradition before the adoption of the
Phoenician alphabetical system. Second, even if the use of the sylla-
bary called Linear B probably ended with the extinction of the Mycenaean civilization during the twelfth century, it is still true that one
part of the historical reality underlying the *Iliad* and the *Odyssey* is
rooted in this civilization of the written word through the numerous
mediations set up by the narrative system of the epic story.[4] Linear B's
use was probably limited to the writing of administrative documents
of the Mycenaean palaces, and the existence of literary works transcribed in Linear B is more than doubtful. In this connection, at least
one explicit reference to the use of writing (*Iliad* 6.169ff.) can be found
in the Homeric poems; this allusion concerns the utilitarian production
of a message, however, and not the use of writing in the literary
domain. These facts are all too often passed over in silence in articles
based on theories asserting that the manner of communication lends a
particular flavor to the contents of the message communicated.[5]

[3] On Homer as a person, see, in particular, J. A. Davison, "The Transmission of the
Text" and "The Homeric Question," in *A Companion to Homer*, ed. A. J. B. Wace and
F. H. Stubbings (London, 1962), 215–33 and 234–65, Lesky 1968, 687ff., and G. S.
Kirk, *Homer and the Oral Tradition* (Cambridge, 1976), 201ff.

[4] Concerning the historicity of the "reality" described in the Homeric poems, see
D. L. Page, *History and the Homeric Iliad* (Berkeley, 1959), 218ff., and Kirk 1962, 3ff.,
with the summary given in *The Iliad: A Commentary, Volume II: Books 5–8* (Cambridge,
1990), 36ff., but also M. I. Finley, *The World of Odysseus* (New York, 1977), 49ff. and
185ff., A. Heubeck, "Geschichte bei Homer," *Stud. Mic. Egeo-anatol.* 20 (1979): 227–
50, I. Morris, "The Use and Abuse of Homer," *Class. Ant.* 5 (1986): 81–138, S. Scully,
Homer and the Sacred City (Ithaca, N.Y., 1989), 81ff., and various contributions in
Zweihundert Jahre Homer-Forschung: Rückblick und Ausblick, ed. J. Latacz (Stuttgart,
1991).
  For a modern example of maintaining an oral tradition in a civilization that writes,
see B. Gentili, "Lo statuto dell'oralità e il discorso poetico del biasimo e della lode,"
Xenia 1 (1981): 13–24.

[5] See, for example, J. Goody, *The Domestication of the Savage Mind* (Cambridge,
1977), 36ff. and 74ff.; for Antiquity, see Havelock 1978, 336f., B. Gentili, "Lirica greca
arcaica e tardo arcaica," in *Introduzione allo studio della cultura classica* (Milan, 1972), 63f.,

Until now I have been careful to consider only the "transcription" of oral epic poems using the Phoenician alphabet adopted and adapted by the Greeks during the eighth century. There are actually various possible ways of considering this process. As regards the distinction made between the processes of composing and transmitting the literary product, some scholars have claimed that the *Iliad* and the *Odyssey* were orally composed poems, improvised at each performance and subsequently copied down, even perhaps transcribed from dictation.[6] Others think these poems are the result of a very long oral tradition in which they remained more or less unchanged for several decades before finally being copied out.[7] Whatever the truth may be, these views are too simplistic. As soon as the use of writing spreads, and in spite of the definitely oral character of the diction of the Homeric poems (formulas, typical scenes, etc.), it is not possible to exclude the use of writing from the process of composing epic poems, at least in the state in which they have come down to us. As regards their transmission, we have to distinguish clearly between the moment of communication to the public, when the poem is recited by an *aoidos* (the moment of the "public-ation," of the performance), and the tradition which uses this technical means as soon as it appears, at the same time that the singer continues to use his memory to recite the epic poems.[8]

To summarize, the first Greek literary product for us consists of

---

and R. Thomas, *Oral Tradition and Written Records in Classical Athens* (Cambridge, 1989), 15ff. On the mention of the use of writing in the Homeric poems themselves, see also Heubeck 1979, 126ff., and A. Ford, *Homer: The Poetry of the Past* (Ithaca, N.Y., 1992), 131ff.

[6] See Notopoulos 1964, 50ff., as well as A. B. Lord, "Homer's Originality: Oral Dictated Texts," *Trans. Am. Philol. Assoc.* 84 (1953): 124–34 (reprinted in *Epic Singers and Oral Tradition* [Ithaca, N.Y., 1991], 38–47), and "Homer as an Oral Poet," *Harv. Stud. Class. Philol.* 72 (1967): 1–46 (see also "Homer as an Oral-Traditional Poet," *Epic Singers*, 72–103), with the study of M. L. West, "Archaische Heldendichtung: Singen und Schreiben," in Kullmann and Reichel [Introd., n. 36], 33–50. The "oral dictated text" theory has been reshaped by M. Skafte Jensen, *The Homeric Question and Oral-Formulaic Theory* (Copenhagen, 1980), 96ff., who situates the dictation of our *Iliad* and *Odyssey* in sixth-century Athens, in the time of Peisistratos; see now G. Nagy, "Homeric Questions," *Trans. Am. Philol. Assoc.* 112 (1992): 17–60.

[7] See, for example, Kirk 1962, 98ff., or Powell [n. 2], 187ff.; for an overview of the various hypotheses, see W. Rösler, "Alte und neue Mündlichkeit: Über kulturellen Wandel im antiken Griechenland und heute," *Altsprachl. Unterricht* 28 (1985): 4–26.

[8] See Finnegan 1977, 16ff.; I prefer to use the term *tradition* for the third moment because it is more precise than the term *transmission* used by Finnegan. For the problem of tradition in Greek poetry, see Notopoulos 1964, 18ff., Lesky 1968, 704, and Lord 1960, 124ff.

epic poems that display numerous traits generally considered characteristic of oral poetry; but it is impossible to discount the intervention
of writing in the process of composition, at least in the state in which
these poems have been passed on to us. Moreover, they are in part the
product of a society that had knowledge of a system of writing,
although it does not seem to have made use of it for literary purposes.
Lastly, we can assert that the epic poems were communicated orally,
given the descriptions of performances contained in them, but that
after the Phoenician alphabet was adopted, their tradition was confined to the written word, probably more as a means of consecration
than of real "publication."

3. Texts Chosen for Analysis

The problem of the appearance of the subject of the enunciation in
Greek literary texts can therefore be determined only at that moment
when the culture that produces those texts adopts writing. We then
find ourselves faced with a complex situation in which the transition
from the oral to the written is already in progress; it is impossible,
from a historical viewpoint, to reconstruct a priori the "pure" oral
stage. Only comparative ethnography can complete our knowledge of
the beginnings of Greek "literature."

Given the importance traditionally attributed to inspiration and
memory in the production of any oral literature, the criterion I use for
selecting the texts is based not only on the presence of an *I* in the
utterance but also on the mention of the act of singing, which corresponds in epic poetry to the performance of the enunciation itself. This
act is present either in the verbs *humneō* (to celebrate in song), *aeidō* (to
sing), or *mimnēiskomai* (to remember, recall) used in the first person or
else in an invocation to the Muses or to one of the Muses. Consequently, I exclude from analysis all the utterances in which the *I* is tied
to a predicate, the semantic content of which has no relation to the
poetic performance, in other words, to the enunciation process. Similarly, I leave aside the rhetorical questions using a form of the third
person, as in "what man could tell forth from his heart the names of
the other Achaeans?" (*Iliad* 17.260f.); in such situations the narra-
tor/speaker appears only in an implicit manner. It goes without saying
that all the situations of mimetic communication represented by the
many dialogues punctuating the utterance of some of the poems stud-

ied are also not considered. It is the *I*-narrator/speaker, actant of the uttered enunciation, and not the *I*-interlocutor that will be the subject of the following reflections.

Given the period covered by my investigation, modifications in the uttered enunciation caused by the transition from oral to written imply the introduction of a diachronic perspective. This study will therefore consider not only those passages in the *Iliad* and *Odyssey* to which the criteria described above apply but also passages in the works of Hesiod (from the end of the eighth or beginning of the seventh century B.C.), in the *Homeric Hymns* (dating mostly from the seventh and sixth centuries B.C.), and in the fragments of lyric poetry (from the seventh and sixth centuries B.C.), excluding Pindar and Bacchylides. Still, we must be aware that the various poetic genres represented by the works under consideration here are not to be inscribed on a continuous line of historical succession: they developed, in general, simultaneously, and their apparent succession is only the result of blanks in the tradition as it has survived. The exclusion of Pindar and Bacchylides is due to the complexity of the appearance of the enunciation at the level of the spoken text. A study of this complexity would require special treatment that would not be appropriate here; however, I shall refer to it in my conclusion. The literary production under consideration therefore extends from the middle of the eighth century to the end of the sixth; it includes the epic and lyric poetry of this period, with the exception of verses attributed to the pre-Socratic philosophers.

4. The Context of Enunciation

As has already been suggested, the system of enunciative indicators in the enunciation (of which the most important is the narrator/narratee connection) entails a complex relationship with the communication process of the utterance (the enunciator/enunciatee connection). Owing to the distance in time separating us, the ethnographic context of ancient Greece can be understood only through texts, texts, moreover, that correspond in large part to the very ones chosen here for the analysis of the enunciation. Thus the extradiscursive phenomenon that I am attempting to pin down and the textual manifestation of the enunciation process I wish to compare it with risk being treated on the same semiotic level. The tautology can nevertheless be avoided to a certain degree: indirect evidence (Plato, Aristotle), on the one hand,

and contemporary iconographic representations of the texts being analyzed, on the other, can furnish external confirmation of the "reality" found in the literary texts, thus avoiding a total referential illusion.

These different levels of testimony allow me to formulate three different communication situations in ancient Greek literature. All three of them are present in scenes described in the Homeric poems; this proves that they must not be assigned, as all too often happens, to a fixed order of historical sequence.

On the first level, a singer (enunciator), probably also the composer of his song, recites in front of an audience (enunciatee) poems he knows by heart, the content of which is by nature epic, such as the *Iliad* or the *Odyssey*; he accompanies his recitation with music played on the lyre. This singer-composer is called *aoidos* or *rhapsōidos*, two terms which some think correspond to two different functions but which in fact are synonymous or at least overlap in a relation of inclusion.[9] Sometimes the *aoidos* is accompanied by dancers, in which case his poem is no longer a simple rhythmic performance but a real song. The compositions performed to accompany dancers are shorter—the heroic songs composed by Stesichorus come to mind. This kind of delivery, called *kitharōidia*, is often described in Homeric epos; the singer in such cases is called *kitharōidos* to distinguish him from the *rhapsōidos*. The enunciatee in this context is generally represented by the public gathered together for the performance of the song in a palace worthy of Homeric epic.[10]

On the second level, the poet is generally accompanied by a pipe or a lyre and sings a relatively short poem he himself has composed with the help of writing. Plato used the term *monody* to refer to the work corresponding to this type of performance. The forms and themes of monodic compositions are highly varied: they range from the polemics and personal attacks of Archilochus's iambics to the amorous and pedagogical musings of Sappho's strophic songs or the politically engaged elegiac verses of Theognis. The enunciatee of this type of

[9] See C. O. Pavese, *Studi sulla tradizione epica rapsodica* (Rome, 1974), 15ff., and A. Ford, "The Classical Definition of *Rhapsōidia*," *Class. Philol.* 89 (1988): 300–307. On the content of the poems sung by the rhapsodes, see Pavese 1972, 215ff., and Nagy 1990, 21ff.

[10] See, in particular, *Iliad* 18.567ff., and *Odyssey* 8.261ff. and 23.130ff.; see the bibliographic references in Calame 1977, 1:104 n. 126; in addition, see Kirk 1962, 274ff., Notopoulos 1964, 13ff., and C. P. Segal, "Bard and Audience in Homer," in *Homer's Ancient Readers*, ed. R. Lamberton and J. J. Keaney (Princeton, 1992), 3–29.

poetry generally corresponds to a circle of intimate friends of the enunciator: such a group may have an institutional character, as did Sappho's circle in Lesbos, or be brought together on the occasion of a banquet or symposium, as in the case of the iambic performance.[11] An early form of this type of song, sung by an individual without the accompaniment of a chorus, can perhaps be found in the song that Achilles addresses to Patroclus in the *Iliad* or in the song described in the *Odyssey* intoned by Calypso or Circe as she weaves.[12] The descriptions of these songs contain of course no reference to writing, and the poems, fragments of which are probably to be found in the anonymous *Carmina Popularia*, are in the oral tradition by virtue of both their composition and their mode of communication.

Lastly, on the third level of enunciation situations from the earliest Greek poetry, the poet-composer is no longer the one who sings his own song; its execution is entrusted to a chorus singing in unison and dancing. By providing an instrumental accompaniment, the poet himself can lead the chorus, but it is more often directed by one of its own participants, in which case he or she assumes the function of *khorēgos*, or chorus-leader. This kind of production is traditionally called choral poetry. This category often includes ritual songs sung at a religious festival; among the best known are Alcman's *Partheneia* and Pindar's *Epinicia*. The enunciatee in this category of songs is represented by the audience present at the ritual. As in the case of monody, we also find descriptions of this type of choral performance in the Homeric poems. The most famous concerns the singing of the lamentations at the funeral of Hector; the lament of the singers, probably professional, is punctuated by the refrain taken up by the women present at the ritual; no composer, or author of the song, is mentioned.[13]

This brief attempt at a morphological classification of poetic performance in archaic Greece leads to two considerations. On the one hand, the person who has composed the song does not necessarily perform it; the person occupying the actantial position of the transmitter in the communication process is therefore split in two; it is necessary to distinguish between the author, who has composed the poem, and the

[11]Plato, *Laws* 764de; cf. Bowra 1961, 4ff., Pavese 1972, 219ff., B. Gentili, "Storicità della lirica greca," in *Storia e Civiltà dei Greci* I.2, ed. R. Bianchi Bandinelli (Milan, 1978), 382–461, and Nagy 1990, 84ff.; performance of the "monodic" type crosses the boundaries of genres: see M. Davies, "Monody, Choral Lyric, and the Tyranny of the Hand-Book," *Class. Quart.* 38 (1988): 52–64.

[12]Homer, *Iliad* 9.185ff., *Odyssey* 5.61 and 10.221. On this subject, cf. M. Wegner, *Musik und Tanz* (*Arch. Hom.* III, U) (Göttingen, 1968), 29ff.

[13]Homer, *Iliad* 24.720ff. (see also 18.37ff.); see Calame 1977, I:51ff. and I:143ff.

enunciator, an individual or choral group, who sings it in the presence of the enunciatee.[14] But the highly occasional character of this poetry implies that its communication process has nothing of the spatial and temporal distance separating the enunciatee and the enunciator in modern literature.[15] The oral recitation or even the oral repetition of one of the poems mentioned above on a different occasion from that for which it was composed is rare in the archaic period.

On the other hand, we must recognize that in the three situations described, the song may not have been composed by a specific author and the performance may consist of a traditional song sung by an individual singer or a group of chorus members; along with the *Carmina Popularia*, previously mentioned, some of the *Homeric Hymns* probably belong to this class of songs; they are objects of regular *reenactment*—to apply the idea developed by Gregory Nagy. Historically speaking, this reenacting type of performance, which most likely belongs to a period when writing was not used either in composing a song or in communicating it, endures after the adoption of the Phoenician alphabet, subsisting alongside the type of performance based on songs by named and known authors. At the Spartan Feast of Gymnopaidia, for example, an anonymous popular song was performed, a fragment of which is extant, along with compositions of well-known poets like Thaletas of Gortyn or Alcman.[16]

5. The Uttered Enunciation in Homer and in the *Hymns*

Among the texts I have chosen for this analysis, the most complete and, in spite of its historical heterogeneity, the most homogeneous corpus is the collection of thirty-three *Homeric Hymns*. Almost all of

---

[14] A similar distinction between author and enunciator has been given by Ubersfeld 1977, 254f., in the area of drama. In the process of dramatic communication, the instance of the enunciator is also doubled, and we must differentiate the author (the writer) from the "character" who acts on the stage. This doubling is also present for the enunciatee (doubling between the public and the "character," the interlocutor on the stage), but here it is valid only for dramatic representation; the comparison loses some of its relevance as regards the performance mode of ancient Greek poetry, where the recitation is not necessarily a stage production. For the enunciative consequences of this doubling, see the thoughts of Ducrot 1984, 205ff.

[15] Regarding the question of the distance between enunciator and enunciatee, see, for example, Dubois 1978, 118f.

[16] *Carmina popularia* fr. 870 Page, Sosibius, *FGrHist.* 595 F 5, and Pseudo-Plutarch, *Music 9.*

these compositions, anonymous and used to introduce the performance of longer poems, begin by installing in the statements elements indicative of the enunciation. A perusal of the beginning of each of these poems reveals, in the enunciative shifting-in/anchoring corresponding in this process of installation, three different ways of proceeding and consequently defines a typology.

Typology

a. In the first and commonest case (eighteen occurrences; see Appendix, Texts A), an *I* is introduced as the subject of a verb meaning "to sing" (usually *aeidō*). This verb is usually in the future and dependent on the form *arkhomai* "I begin"; the object of the verb is represented by the god who is the subject of the narrative development of the poem. No sooner has the *I* of the altered enunciation been installed in the utterance than we move on, by means of a relative pronoun whose grammatical antecedent is the god, object of the verb "to sing," to an utterance in the third person, in other words, to the appearance of the not-*I*. The relative clause thus introduced corresponds to an enunciative shift; it marks the start of the recitation, in the third person, of the qualities and exploits of the god sung by the *I*. The function of the initial enunciative shifting-in is therefore only to engage the description and/or the story itself.[17]

We shall see later that among the *Homeric Hymns* in the category just defined, the majority of the compositions end in an invocation addressed directly to the god evoked in the poem. This second introduction into the utterance of elements indicative of the enunciation can be

[17] See the first verses of *Homeric Hymns to Demeter, Apollo, Aphrodite* and 7, 10, 11, 12, 13, 15, 16, 18, 22, 23, 25, 27, 28, 30, to which must be added Homer, *Iliad* 2.493, *Ilias parva* fr. 28 Bernabé, Hesiod, *Theogony* 1 and 36, *Works and Days* 10, Alcman, fr. 29 Page = 89 Calame, fr. mel. adesp. 936 Page, Theognis, 943, and Hesiod, dub. fr. 357 Merkelbach-West. For fr. mel. adesp. 938(e) Page, see n. 34 below. See the particular case presented by Homer, *Iliad* 12.176.

Not considered here are the incomplete fragments in which the enunciation situation is the object of one or more conjectures: see, for example, Alcman, frr. 3.1, 5.2 (column 1), 23f. and 8.9ff. Page = frr. 26.1, 81 and 21 Calame, or Corinna fr. 655.2(b), 2ff. Page.

In some rare cases, the narrator seems to be hidden behind a generalizing "they say" (*phasi*): see Homer, *Iliad* 2.183 and 17.164, and *Odyssey* 6.42, with the commentary of de Jong 1987, 48f. and 237f.

The hymnic predication through a relative clause has been described by E. Norden, *Agnostos Theos: Untersuchungen zur Formengeschichte religiöser Rede* (Leipzig, 1913), 168ff. Note that Race (1992, 20ff.) distinguishes only two kinds of enunciative shifting-in.

seen in the appearance of both an *I* and a *you*; introducing a *you* in opposition to the *I* creates a dialogical relationship. These two pronouns are often the actants of a verb signifying "to remember" (*mnêsomai*): the *I* is its grammatical subject, the *you* its object. If the analysis of this *you* is central to the development that follows, it can immediately be seen that a double enunciative shifting-in frames, as it were, the story in the third person.

b. The second case, of which there are eight occurrences in the *Hymns*, also includes the beginning of Homer's *Iliad* (see Appendix, Texts B) and of Hesiod's *Works and Days*. Similarly in this case, the enunciative shifting-in opens the poem; but instead of installing into the utterance an *I* signaling the enunciation, this type of shift introduces an actant *you*, the grammatical subject of a verb meaning "to sing" (*humneō, aeidō*). This *you* does not refer to the god or to the person who represents the theme of the poem but to the Muse invoked in the singular or in the plural. As in the first case, the *he/she*, the grammatical subject of the utterances that constitute the essence of the story and the center of the poem, is introduced by a relative clause which is the object of the verb "to sing"; thus this clause assumes the role of an enuncive shifting-in.[18]

I must point out that when the verb of which the *you* and *he/she* mentioned occupy the actantial positions is in the imperative, the presence of an *I* that speaks the injunction contained in the imperative form is presupposed; there is therefore an implicit dialogic relationship. In spite of this presupposition, however, the *you* is still the subject of the verb "to sing"; this implies that it is the narratee/allocutee and not the narrator/speaker who is thought to offer the utterances which make up the song. This situation becomes even more complex, at least as regards the *Homeric Hymns*, in that the poem ends with the same formula described in the first case outlined above (a). Thus, in this new enunciative shift, the narratee addressed by the *I* (explicit this time) is not the Muse invoked at the beginning of the poem but the divinity who is the *he/she*, the "nonperson" subject of the narrative utterances at the heart of the poem. At the end of the poem we find not only the explicit appearance of the *I* that was merely presupposed in the enunci-

[18] This type of shifting-in is seen at the beginning of *Homeric Hymns to Hermes* and 9, 14, 17, 20, 31, 32, 33; in Homer, *Iliad* 1.1; in Hesiod, *Works and Days* 1, and even *Thebais* fr. 1 Bernabé; in Hesiod, fr. 1, 1 Merkelbach-West; in Alcman, fr. 27 Page = 84 Calame; and in Stesichorus, fr. 278 Page and Pig. fr. West; see also probably Sappho, frr. 124, 127, and 128 Voigt, and Theognis 15ff.

ative shifting-in at the beginning but a substitution of the actor occupying the actantial position of the narratee.

Establishing this fact invites us to go further into the analysis of the
narratee. Not only is the latter provided with a mobile syntactical
(subject or predicate) and semantic (actorial variations) status, but
he in no way corresponds to the group that occupies the position of
the enunciatee in the communication situation described above. One
might naively suppose that the *you* of the narratee/allocutee refers to
the enunciatee, the recipient of the production and transmission of the
poem, in other words, to the audience. But this is not the case: from a
semantic point of view, the actant narratee of the uttered enunciation
corresponds to a divinity, a Muse or god, who may also occupy the
actantial position of the narrator when the enunciatee, as has been
pointed out, is the audience; extended or not, the latter is always
present in Greece at the poetic performance. I shall return to this point
later.

c. In the third case, the least common of the three (two occurrences;
see Appendix, Texts C), the *I* and the *you* appear together.[19] The
actantial position of the narratee is occupied, as in the preceding case,
by the Muse or Muses invoked in the vocative case; the verb of which
the Muses are the grammatical subject is again a verb meaning "to
sing" or "to recite" (*aeidō* or *ennepō*). The *I* appears as a pronoun in the
dative case depending on the verb mentioned; the impact of this very
special syntactical appearance of the *I* (implicit in the verb in the
imperative; explicit in the dative) is still to be defined. The object of
the verb "to sing" is generally represented by the god or the principal
hero central to the piece. The sequence of third-person statements that
make up the narration is also engaged by a relative pronoun the
antecedent of which is the divinity, itself the object of the verb "to
sing" or "to say." The narrator/speaker asks the narratee/allocutee,
the Muse, to recite on his behalf the utterances that make up the story
immediately following his or her request; thus the Muse is again put in
the position of narrator.

This form of introduction to a poem or to a new section in the poem
occurs four times in the *Iliad*;[20] it is also to be found at the beginning of

[19] See the first verses of *Homeric Hymns to Aphrodite* and 19; see also Homer, *Iliad*
2.484 and 761; 11.218; 14.508; 16.112, *Odyssey* 1.1; *Ilias parva* fr. 1 Bernabé, Hesiod,
Theogony 114, Hipponax, fr. 126 Degani, and Semonides, fr. 17 West and fr. lyr. adesp.
935, 1ff. Page.
[20] Note that in the citation of Aristoxenus, the Aristotelian musicologist (fr. 19a
Wehrli), the first book of the *Iliad* also opened with the same type of enunciative

the *Odyssey* and is the effective beginning of Hesiod's *Theogony* (verses 114f.), the prologue of which forms the object of a special section (§ 6).

It is remarkable that the only two poems in the *Homeric Hymns* beginning with this type of enunciative engagement end, as do most of the poems in the collection, with an invocation to the god described above. So here too we have a substitution in the semantic investment of the narratee, represented at first by the Muse who sings for the *I*, then by the god who was the grammatical subject of the third-person utterances of the story.

Uttered Enunciation and Communication

The gap between the actors of archaic Greek literature who occupy the actantial positions of the linguistic enunciation and those who play roles in the referential communication situation is now clear (see Figure 4). The absence of homogeneity between the two levels that are represented here prompts two remarks.

	Narrator/Speaker	*Narratee/Allocutee*
Uttered enunciation	*I* (speaker)	*you* ⟨ Muse / divinity (*he/she* of the descriptive and narrative statements)
	Enunciator	*Enunciatee*
Communication	*aoidos* ———— poet-author ————— poet-author/chorus ⌐	audience

Figure 4. The uttered enunciation and the communication situation

First, concerning the *I*, there are some occurrences in which its grammatical form is not singular but plural; a *we* is substituted for the *I*. An immediate explanation presents itself: the *we* of the narrator

---

shifting-in and not with an engagement of the second type as the canonical tradition would have it. This potential for variation shows the formulaic character of the verses invoking the Muse.

corresponds in the communication context to a choral group, the plural enunciator of the poem. The popular song fragments 851(b) and 885 Page seem to confirm this hypothesis. However, the same form in the plural is also to be found in the opening verses of Hesiod's *Theogony*, and it is well known that this type of dactylic poem was recited by a single enunciator.[21] Fragment 29 Page (= 89 Calame) of Alcman, by contrast—which, with its indication of a feminine person (*aeisomai arkhomena*), was sung by a chorus of young women and not by its author—is a case in which the *I* of the uttered enunciation (narrator/speaker) is singular while the enunciator is plural. Several studies of the *I* in choral poetry show that the alternation of *I* and *we* in the utterance of the enunciation does not necessarily correspond to a distinction between singular and plural. The *we* is more likely polyphonic in nature and refers to both the enunciator and the enunciatee on the referential level.[22]

Such a hypothesis, and this is the second of my two remarks, may be confirmed by the fact that the enunciatee in these poems, represented by the audience, is never expressed linguistically in the uttered enunciation. The *you* refers to the person invoked in the poem, the Muse or god: it is a purely linguistic formula without a referent; the dialogue suggested by the forms *I* and *you* is therefore internal to the text. Moreover, when the Muse, if she is invoked, appears at the beginning of the poem as the one who has been invited to sing, she occupies, in spite of the use of *you* for her, the actantial position of the narrator rather than that of the narratee. By virtue of the syntactical play of different cases (*you* in the vocative, then in the nominative; *I* in the dative) and of the object status of the *you* ("to sing") as go-between, the Muse comes to occupy the position of the narrator, a position normally taken by the *I*. Brought into existence as the Muse, this *you* is really a simple double or projection of the *I*. In the poly-

---

[21] The verse shaped in exactly the same way in the opening of *Homeric Hymn* 26 has, in contrast, a verb in the singular! We also find a variation between the singular and the plural in the grammatical expression of the *I* contained in the enunciative engagement that introduces the Catalogue of Ships (*Iliad* 2.486, to be compared with verse 488) and the one opening the *Odyssey* (1.10, to be compared with verse 1); see also *Hymn to Apollo* 174ff. and the beginning of the *Epigonoi* (fr. 1 Bernabé), where the form *arkhōmetha* is combined with an address to the Muses.

[22] See the references in Calame 1977, 1:436ff., as well as above, Introduction, § 7. For a linguistic analysis of *we*, see Benveniste, 1966, 233, R. Lafont and F. Gardès-Madray, *Introduction à l'analyse textuelle* (Paris, 1976), 94f., and Kerbrat-Orecchioni 1980, 42ff.

phonic conception of the enunciation developed by Ducrot, the Muse would correspond to one of the "enunciators" introduced into the utterance by the "locutor" (for us, the narrator) to represent himself/herself or to lend to the self a point of view different from the self's own.[23]

In the poems examined, there is almost no correspondence between the planes of the uttered enunciation and the communication structure.

The Hic and the Nunc

As Benveniste, followed by Greimas and Courtés, have shown,[24] the shifting-in affecting the actants is generally accompanied by both a temporal and a spatial engagement. When this procedure has to do with the installation in the utterance of the indicators of the enunciation, the temporal shifting-in takes the form of a *now* and the spatial shifting-in, of a *here*.

The linguistic forms corresponding to this double procedure have been present in the texts we have been considering. But, significantly enough, they do not appear in the texts of the first category that I defined. In this case the tense of the verb (present or voluntative future) of which *I* is the subject and the presence of this *I* are sufficient to define the space-time structure of the *hic et nunc* of the enunciation.[25] Conversely, in the other two cases, the imperative of the verb "to sing" is not always considered explicit enough to define the *here* and the *now*; that is perhaps why the enunciative expression opening the *Works* of Hesiod includes in its syntactical form the adverb *deute* 'here',

[23] See Ducrot 1984, 203ff.; for the term *enunciator* as Ducrot uses it, see the Introduction, n. 4. This type of discourse with a single enunciator but implying in the utterance of the enunciation, if not a dialogue, at least a communication with a fictional instance who moves dialogue onto the plane of diaphony or polyphony would need precise analytical categories; the mono- /dialogal, the mono- /dialogue, and the dia- /polyphony redefined by E. Roulet et al., *L'articulation du discours en français contemporain* (Bern, 1985), 69ff., are not sufficient.

[24] See Benveniste 1966, 253ff. and 262f., as well as Greimas and Courtés 1979, 81f. and 127.

[25] Analyzing the utterance of the enunciation in inscriptions, J. Svenbro, *Phrasikleia: Anthropologie de la lecture en Grèce ancienne* (Paris, 1988), 47ff., has shown, after others, that as pronoun of the "here," *I* can replace the pronouns of the *deixis* (*tode*) to designate the present space. For the modal and not only temporal value of the future tense in Greek, see E. Schwyzer and A. Debrunner, *Griechische Grammatik*, vol. 2 (Munich, 1950), 290ff.

whereas the formula found four times in the *Iliad* contains the adverb *nun* 'now'.[26] In most of the cases discussed so far, however, the tense and mode of the verb are enough to define the space-time structure of the enunciation. As regards the uttered enunciation, the spatial and temporal shiftings-in in the texts under consideration play only a subordinate and marginal role in relation to the actantial engagement.

Some Variations

Degree Zero

I must first mention that in the *Homeric Hymns*, certain poems, unexamined as yet, represent a sort of degree zero in relation to the three cases of uttered enunciation I have defined. In some of these compositions the central figure of the divinity is evoked directly by the *I*, without the intervention of the Muse. These poems also begin with an actantial shifting-in of the *I* (sometimes presumed) and *you* forms, but the predicate is not the song; the song is only mentioned in the final formula of the poems in question, where it appears, as it does in the other poems of the collection, as the means of communication between the *I* and a given divinity. In their direct address to the divinity, these poems take over the form (and the function) of prayers, with a typically triadic structure: *invocatio/pars epica/preces*.[27]

This type of shifting-in, typical of Greek prayer, is significant to the degree that the relation established between the *I*-narrator and the *you*-narratee represented by the divinity becomes the center of the poem: the *you* is generally transformed into a *he/she*, the subject of the story at the core of the composition (*pars epica*). When the invocation is addressed to the Muse, by contrast, the prayer affects the instances of discourse and the poetic competence of the *I*; it also introduces a

---

[26] See also Ibycus, fr. 282, 10 Page and fr. lyr. adesp. 935, 1ff. Page, and the fragmentary invocations found in Stesichorus, fr. 240 Page, and Sappho, frr. 127 and 128 Voigt.

[27] See the first verses of *Homeric Hymns* 8, 21, 24, and 29 (the *Homeric Hymn to Dionysos* is incomplete); see also Sappho, fr. 1, 1ff. Voigt, Theognis 1ff. and 11ff., etc. The recent studies of J. M. Bremer, "Greek Hymns," in *Faith, Hope, and Worship: Aspects of Religious Mentality in the Ancient World*, ed. H. S. Versnel (Leiden, 1981), 193–215, and of A. M. Miller, *From Delos to Delphi: A Literary Study of the Homeric Hymn to Apollo* (Leiden, 1986), 1ff., are based on earlier attempts to compare the structure of the *Homeric Hymns* with that of cultic prayers; see my study "Variations énonciatives, relations avec les dieux et fonctions poétiques dans les *Hymnes homériques*," *Mus. Helv.* 51 (1994).

narrative in the third person of which a divinity can be the subject, but this story is subordinate to its circumstances of production. Thus the enunciative shifting-in that modifies the song takes on the role of mediator for the story and functions as a focal point for the instance of discourse, while the shifting-in that brings a divinity onto the scene is an end in itself. Hence the complexity of the poetic relations of the pious Greek with his gods: it is possible to invoke them directly or to offer their interventions to the assembled community by means of poetry itself.

Combinatory Principle

From Homer on, we find utterances of the enunciation in which the formula corresponding to the first case described above is combined with the formula corresponding to the second and third cases.

Such a combination occurs in the prologue of the Catalogue of Ships in the second book of the *Iliad* (verses 484ff.). The opening begins, as in all passages of the same type in the *Iliad*, with a shifting-in, by virtue of a verb "to say" in the imperative, of a *you* represented by the Muses and of an *I* in the dative. After these four lines of introduction, however, lines that contain the usual enunciative shifting-out/enuncive shifting-in by means of the relative pronoun, there is a new enunciative engagement whereby only the *I* is installed in the utterance. If the predicate attributed to this *I* is first the object of a preterite (the exact enumeration of all the warriors fighting under the walls of Troy is left up to the Muses), the *I* is then affirmed as the unique instance of discourse in a shifting-in of the first type (*arkhous neōn ereō* . . . 'I will tell of the lords of the ships . . .', verse 493).[28]

As in the prologue of Hesiod's *Works and Days*, the shifting-in of a *you* behind which lurk the Muses is immediately followed by the introduction, using the relative-pronoun procedure, of the first theme of the work, namely, Zeus, who appears as the subject of acts in the third person. But in verse 10, after a brief introduction addressed to this same god (who is introduced by means of *you* as the actant of two verbs in the imperative), the *I* appears as the grammatical subject of a verb "to say"; we therefore have an enunciative shifting-in of the first type (a). The text also presents a new element: the second actant of the

[28] See, on verse 2.493 of the *Iliad*, the commentary of de Jong 1987, 48 (with bibliographic references). In Ibycus, fr. 282, 23ff. Page, there is a preterite construction of the same type but in which the *I* is only implicitly present.

verb "to say" is represented by a narratee who, instead of appearing in the pronominal form as a *you*, is named in the third person. The name quoted in this actantial position, Perses, can probably be related to the enunciatee of the communication situation: even if this figure can have a generic value, in terms of the name's meaning, it corresponds to Hesiod's brother to whom the Boeotian poet addresses his work.[29]

6. The Invocation to the Muses in the *Theogony*

These variations on the way in which the indices of the enunciation are incorporated into the utterance are minor when we consider the complexity of the enunciation in the long prologue that opens Hesiod's *Theogony* (see Appendix, Texts D).

The introduction begins, as I have indicated, with a shifting-in of the first type: the *I*, in the linguistic form of *we*, is installed as the subject of the verbal phrase "to begin to sing." The object predicate of this act is not the divinity usually celebrated in a poem's prologue, however, but the Muses themselves. The Muses are thus the antecedent of the relative pronoun that provokes the enunciative shifting-out/enuncive shifting-in described above: they take the place of the third-person grammatical subject of the narrative statements in the verses that follow. It is thus in the guise of a grammatical subject in the third person that the Muses appear in verse 11 as the actant of a verb "to sing"; the complement of this verb is represented by a series of gods, evoked later. As a result, this evocation of the divinity, usually the object of the act of singing initiated by the person of the narrator, is instead conveyed in the song of the Muses, itself an act described in the third person; thus the evocation of the gods is engaged by a second enuncive shifting-in that depends syntactically on the one I have just mentioned. Everything happens as if the *I* were handing over to the Muses the act of broadcasting the contents of the poem.

The sequence of utterances in the third person, with the Muses as

[29]For the real existence of Perses in the communication situation, see West 1978, 33ff. The point on the authenticity of this proem to the *Works and Days* has been made by A. Lattes, "Sull'autenticità del proemio degli 'Erga' di Esiodo," *Riv. Stud. Class.* 1 (1954): 166–72. I have attempted to define the function of this prelude in its particular form in "Le proème des *Travaux* d'Hésiode: Prélude à une poésie d'action," to be published in *Hésiode* (Lille, 1994); see also P. Pucci, "Auteur et destinataire dans les *Erga* d'Hésiode," to be published in the same collection.

their subject, continues up to verse 22, where the divinities are said to have "taught [*edidaxan*; see *Odyssey* 8.481] Hesiod a fine song one day." This utterance is a sort of "narrativization" of the uttered enunciation defined in our third category (c); its two actants show up as *he*, and the tense of the verb, the simple past, refers back to the tense of the narrative. The transformation of the *I* into a proper name, by contrast, implies a reference to the communication situation, for, once named, the narrator possesses an identity on the *referential* level. The equation between the level of the spoken enunciation and the communication situation is far from being complete, however, since the actor called Hesiod, who of course fills the actantial role of enunciator on the extradiscursive level, turns up in the utterance in the accusative. This linguistic form confers on him, in the narrativization of the uttered enunciation at issue here, the position of the narratee and not that of the narrator, a position occupied by the Muses. This enuncive shifting-in, which objectifies the situation of the uttered enunciation but without making it coincide word for word with the communication situation, represents the outline of a procedure to be developed in other types of poetry and which is called *sphragis*.[30]

Beginning with verse 24, we come upon another enunciative shifting-in. This one remains incomplete; if the *I* appears as receiver of the Muses' song (narratee) because of its syntactical form, the Muses continue to be shown in the grammatical form of the third person. In addition, the tense of the statement is not shifted-out in the same way as in previous verses; it continues in the past and we remain on the plane of the narration. The objectified expression of the spoken enunciation situation is thus immediately followed by a partial shifting-in projected onto the *I*: this maneuver is obviously used to connect the *I* of the narrator/narratee with *Hesiod*. Only from those verses on is it possible to give to the figure of the speaker the identity conferred by the proper name Hesiod.

In the verses that follow, the introduction of a summary of the remarks which the Muses address to the *I* in direct discourse initiates a brief dialogue (verses 26–28). After that dialogue, the utterance continues its course between the uttered enunciation (*I*) and the narration

[30]Cf. West 1966, 161, W. Kranz, "SPHRAGIS," *Rhein. Mus.* 104 (1961): 3–46 and 97–124, as well as G. B. Walsh, *The Varieties of Enchantment: Early Greek Views on the Nature and Function of Poetry* (Chapel Hill, N.C., 1984), 31f., and n. 36 below. Notice that, contrary to what Benveniste 1966, 256, says, the *he/she* can echo the "instance de discours."

(*he*, verbs in the past). These verses are essential because they tell how the Muses confer on the *I* the power of the song, in other words, narrative and poetic competence. From the enunciative point of view, the realization of this competence is contained in two subordinate clauses in which the *I* becomes the subject of a verb meaning "to celebrate" (verses 32 and 33); note that the object of this praise is the Muses themselves (verse 34)! The remarks addressed to the *I* by the Muses are the beginning of the discourse of the *I*, a discourse, to come full circle, whose object is the Muses.

That is why, in verse 36, the *I* reappears, relying on the competence transmitted by the divinities, as the subject of the verbal expression "begin (to sing)," in a complete enunciative shifting-in. We find that the verb in question here becomes subjunctive and that by means of it, the *I* addresses an injunction to itself; this doubling of the *I* is also found in the form *tunē*, a second-person pronoun in the vocative, that opens this utterance. As at the beginning of the poem, the object of the verb "to sing" is represented by the Muses, and through the relative pronoun, of which they are the antecedent, they become the grammatical subject of a sequence of utterances in the third person. The statement relating to the enunciation is thus immediately disengaged and followed by an enuncive shifting-in involving a story that continues through verse 75. In this narration, the semantic content of the act whose subject is the Muses corresponds, as before, to the song, a song that at first has as its theme a sort of summary of the entire *Theogony* (verses 43–52).[31] From the point of view of the enunciation, this procedure is similar to the one used in the first part of the prologue: there, it was the Muses who finally praised Zeus through the voice of the *I*; here, too, the *I* delegates to these divinities the task of evoking the probable content of the work that follows. Here again, we have the insertion of two enuncive shiftings-in involving, respectively, an utterance with the Muses as grammatical subject and a sequence of utterances one step removed with the gods as subject.

One might think that in verse 53, where *tas* 'they (feminine) who' probably recalls the *tai* in verse 36 which engages the story of the Muses' actions, there is a return to an immediate utterance. This seems all the more likely in that the statements which follow tell the story of the Muses themselves. In verse 75, however, the phrase "the Muses

---

[31] Cf. Friedländer [Chap. 2, n. 9], 289 ff., and West 1966, 171f., with the complementary remarks of Race 1992, 22f., and the useful commentary of Leclerc 1993, 236ff.

sang this" suggests that the recital of their own story also forms a sequence of statements one step removed and that these divinities are the grammatical subject of it. Whatever the case may be, the list of their names in verses 76ff. begins a chain of narrative statements of the first order. This return to a series of actions of which the Muses are certainly the subject in the third person provides a new occasion for the (implicit) *I* to describe the authority conferred on the poet by the Muses (verses 94ff.).

Then in verse 104 the narrative undergoes a shifting-out procedure and the indicators of the enunciation are reintroduced by the *I* addressing the Muses, at first implicitly and then explicitly (verse 114). In a procedure that is characteristic of the conclusion formulas of the *Homeric Hymns* (as will be seen in Chap. 2), this address takes the form of a series of verbs in the second person plural imperative. This new invocation is thus structured according to the second type of enunciative shifting-in defined above (b) at the beginning and according to the third (c) at its close. Most of these imperatives involve verbs meaning "to say"; in conformance with the already familiar procedure, the first of them (verse 105) is followed by an object ("the race of the gods"), the antecedent of a relative pronoun that introduces a series of statements in the third person. This series represents a new summary of the contents of the poem introduced in the prologue; it is subsumed by the discourse addressed to the *I* by the *you*. And the enunciative structure of verses 104–15 is parallel to that of the beginning of the *Odyssey* (verses 1–10).

Then in verse 116, introduced by an enuncive shifting-in, the recital proper of the *Theogony* begins. This recital is also indirectly subordinate to the discourse that the Muses are asked to address to the *I* in verses 114 and 115; the form *prōtista* in verse 116 takes up the *prōton* of verse 115.

The prologue of the *Theogony* thus offers two important novelties. Deserving first mention is the assumption, on two occasions, of the song of the Muses and its contents by the *I*. The subordination of the musical activity of the Muses to the act of the *I* (verses 1ff.; verses 35ff.) represents a reversal of the third type of enunciative shifting-in: no longer does the *I* ask the Muses (*you*) to sing for it; rather, it evokes by itself the Muses in the act of singing (in the third person). The Muses are no longer in the narratee position, a projection of the narrator; they are now the theme of the narration uttered by the *I*.

Moreover, the distance set up between the *I* and the role played by the Muses is also visible in the sketch made in the *sphragis* in verse 22 and the following verses. In this case, however, it is not only the Muses who are objectified as actant of the narrative utterance but also the *I*, named in the third person and thus doubled. In the Homeric poems this process does not exist.

I mention here in passing that the complete communication situation underlying the utterance of the enunciation as illustrated in the prologue of the *Theogony* is expressed in a famous passage of the *Works and Days* (verses 646ff.). This will be discussed in the next chapter.

7. Diachrony: Lyric Poetry

As complex as the prologue to the *Theogony* may be from the perspective of the spoken enunciation, it nevertheless has its roots in what we are accustomed to call Homeric poetry. What becomes of the instance of discourse in the lyric poetry that, in our tradition at least, seems to follow it? It is possible to compare a series of enunciative shiftings-in in this poetry, alas, always very fragmentary, with the three types defined above on the basis of the collection of *Homeric Hymns* and the passages quoted in notes 10–12, but we will also find some variations on the theme.

First, we find a very clear affirmation of the *I*. "I am the servant of the Muses," says Archilochus at the beginning of one of his poems (fr. 1.1 West);[32] Solon makes a similar assertion: "I come as a herald" (fr. 1.1 West = 2.1 Gentili-Prato); and Theognis echoes the others: "I cannot sing like the nightingale" (verses 939ff.). It is true that the *I* stands alone in the first type of enunciative shifting-in defined above (a). In lyric poetry, however, the Muses, when referred to, play a rather subordinate role in relation to the *I*. Though the Muse is invoked in the second person in fragment 210 Page of Stesichorus and is asked to sing with the *I* (*met'emou* 'with me'), in Solon's poem 13 West = 1 Gentili-Prato, the Muses are called on as any other divinity would be, with no direct reference to singing.[33]

[32] See Hesiod, *Theogony* 100, which expresses the same thing but in the third person; by contrast, see below, Chapter 2, n. 3.

[33] The expression *met'emou* will also be found in fr. mel. adesp. 935, 1ff. Page, which features an enunciative engagement of the third type but in which the verb *aeidō* 'to sing' has the prefix *sun-* 'with'.

Frr. 729 and 796 Page, attributed to Timocreon and Timotheus respectively, are not

In the very short fragment 28 Page = 85 Calame (*Mōsa, . . . aeisomai* 'Muse, . . . I shall sing'), by contrast, we find a sort of summary of the procedure described in connection with the prologue to the *Iliad's* Catalogue of Ships and the prologue of Hesiod's *Works and Days*; this fragment combines the formula of the second type (b), which introduces, in the vocative case, a *you* represented by the Muses, and the formula of the first type (a), which installs an *I*-subject in the statement. Thus the invocation of the Muse, instead of installing this divinity as subject of the verb "to sing," is immediately followed by the introduction of the *I* substituting for the *you* in the actantial role. An enunciative shifting-in of the same type, introducing a *we* instead of an *I*, is found in the anonymous lyric fragment 1016 Page.[34]

But the most arresting example of the displacement of the role played by the Muses is surely afforded by Alcaeus's fragment 308.2(b) Voigt. Here it is the *thumos*, the heart of the *I*, presented in the dative, that becomes the grammatical subject of the verb "to sing", while the *you*-narratee, receiver of the song, is a god, Hermes.[35] This replacement of the figure of the Muses with an element of the poet's very person in the enunciative doubling of the *I* is also at work in the *sphragis*, the "signature" probably suggested in Hesiod's *Theogony*, of which Theognis gives us a very fine example (verses 19ff.; see Appendix, Text F); by appearing in the third person, the *I* is doubled in both cases on the enuncive level.[36] But the *sphragis* procedure implies more than a simple doubling of the *I*. The *I* is called on by this "signature" to name itself; it is thereby given a precise identity, whereas the projection of the *I* onto the divine authority represented by the Muses was a

---

examined here since these authors are not within the time frame established in the introduction to this chapter.

[34] Fr. mel. adesp. 938(e) Page suggests a similar form, but its lack of coherence in the syntax shows it to be composed from a combination of the formulas of the third and first types; see the reading I proposed of that inscription in "Apprendre à boire, apprendre à chanter: L'inférence énonciative dans une image grecque," *La part de l'oeil* 5 (1989): 45–53.

[35] A similar formula in fr. 697 Page attributed to Terpander is unfortunately corrupted. Another impersonal formula can be found in Ibycus, fr. 82, 10ff. Page.

[36] See Adrados 1976, 132ff.; according to G. Cerri, "Il significato di 'sphregis' in Teognide e la salvaguardia dell'autenticità testuale nel mondo antico," *Quad. Storia* 33 (1991): 21–40, this seal could represent the mark guaranteeing the authenticity of the work deposited in a temple. Alcman also speaks of himself in the third person, using his own name: see frr. 17, 39, and 95(b) Page = 9, 91, and 92 Calame (cf. above, Introd., § 7). See also fr. mel. adesp. 953 Page, a quite possibly late fragment in which an implicit *I* asks the Muse, *you*, to recite a song performed by Anacreon: the role of the Muse is therefore subordinate here to a *he* expressly named. See Sappho, frr. 1, 20, and 94, 5 Voigt.

negation of this identity. It is surely not by mere chance that this type of enunciation, which involves the level of the referent and that of the communication process, is found in the third person and not in the first; when it is made an object, the *I* naturally chooses the grammatical form of exteriority.

With regard to the involvement of the referential communication situation in the spoken enunciation, we see that in the introduction to Theognis's *sphragis* a *you* replies to the *I* and that this *you* refers to a person with a proper name, Kyrnos. So an enunciatee corresponds to the narratee/allocutee, just as the narrator/speaker is linked to the enunciator; this was not the case in Hesiod's *Theogony*, and a situation only partially comparable is present in the *Works and Days* (the reference to Perses), as we shall see in the next chapter. In the works of Theognis, the dialogue structure within the text implies a corresponding "dialogic" relationship on the communication level, whatever the referential status of Perses or Kyrnos may be: generic and textual, if not fictional, or biographical and real.

Two very different allusions to the concrete communication situation can be found in Alcman's fragment 14(a) Page = 4 Calame and also in Theognis (verse 1055ff.; see Appendix, Text G). The Alcman fragment, quoted in the Introduction, takes the following form: "O Muse, . . . sing for the maidens a new tune!" Thus this poem begins with an enunciative shifting-in of the third type (c), but the dative is occupied by the term "the maidens" (*parsenois*) instead of by the *I*. This is another allusion, in the third person, to the communication situation; we know that the chorus singing the poem was made up of adolescents. There is also an allusion in Theognis to the communication situation; the verses quoted mention a pipe player, accompanist to the enunciator of the poem. But in the utterance of the enunciation, this pipe player takes the place of the *you*, the narratee,[37] and is then joined with the *I* in a *we*. This *we* is placed in the actantial position as grammatical subject of the verb "to bring to mind" (*mnēsometha*), of which the Muses are the predicate, and subsequently in the position of the receiver (in the dative) of the Muses' gift, which confers musical competence on the *we*. This procedure recalls that of the prologue in

[37] Narratee and performer of the song correspond also in fr. mel. adesp. 934 Page. On other means proper to lyric poetry to designate the circumstances of enunciation, see J. Danielewicz, "*Deixis* in Greek Choral Lyric," *Quad. Urb. Cult. Class.* 63 (1990): 7–17.

the *Theogony*, where the *I* is made to describe still more precisely the enunciation conditions of its discourse. The *I* even mentions the public to whom the musical competence received from the Muses is addressed.

This tendency to vary the three types of uttered enunciation valid for Homeric poetry and to introduce syntactical positions and new semantic formations for the *I* and the *you* is naturally continued in the poetry of Bacchylides and Pindar. The variations in the enunciative shiftings-in at the beginning of the utterances of the compositions of these two poets are such that, as I have already said, they would need a special study. I shall limit myself to the following observations:

—Although Bacchylides offers two examples of enunciative shiftings-in of the second type (3.1ff. and 5.176ff.), there is no example in a "pure" state to be found in Pindar.

—Regarding the semantic formation of the *you*, the narratee's place in these two authors can be taken by one of the Muses (e.g., Pindar, *Pythian* 4.1ff., *Nemean* 3.1ff.; Bacchylides 15.47); or by the Graces (Pindar, *Nemean* 10.1ff.; Bacchylides 9.1ff.); or by the musical instrument accompanying the poet (Pindar, *Pythian* 1.1ff.; Bacchylides, fr. 20C.1ff. Snell-Maehler); or by the performer of the poem (Pindar, *Nemean* 2.24, *Isthmian* 8.1ff.); or by its receiver (Pindar, *Olympian* 11.11ff., *Pythian* 5.5, *Isthmian* 4.1ff.; Bacchylides fr. 28C.1ff. Snell Maehler); or by the city of the receiver (Pindar, *Pythian* 2.4 and 121ff., *Nemean* 1.5, *Isthmian* 7.1ff.); or even by the song itself (Pindar, *Olympian* 2.1ff., *Nemean* 5.1ff.). But the poem can also open with an invocation to a divinity other than the Muse, without alluding to the action of singing (Pindar, *Olympian* 4.1ff. [Zeus], *Olympian* 12.1ff. [Tyche], *Pythian* 8.1ff. [Hesychia], *Nemean* 7.1ff. [Eileithyia], etc.; Bacchylides 2.1ff. [Pheme]).

—The *I* no longer takes a single actantial position as the subject of a verb "to say" or "to sing"; it is also to be found as the subject of "to want (to celebrate)" (Pindar, *Pythian* 9.1), of "to know" (Pindar, *Olympian* 13.3), or of a predicate expressing the function of prophet guaranteed by the *I* (fr. 52f, 6 Snell-Maehler). As also in Pindar (fr. 150 Snell-Maehler), the *I* retains the role of prophet while reserving for the Muse, who appears in the second person, the function of divination.

—The *I* insists on a variety of ways of singing its subject (Pindar, *Isthmian* 4.1ff.; Bacchylides 19.1ff.).

—The Muse continues to play a subordinate role, as a mere assistant to the *I*; she is generally linked with the composition of the poem (Pindar, *Olympian* 3.1ff., *Pythian* 4.1ff., *Nemean* 4.1ff., *Isthmian* 6.1ff., etc.; *Bacchylides* 2.1ff.). This secondary position is often found in a third-person utterance. The same situation is often to be found as well in Hellenistic epic poetry, in particular in Apollonius of Rhodes; the indirect evocation of Apollo at the beginning of the *Argonautica*, with a variation on a formulation taken over from the *Homeric Hymns* and from Alcman (fr. 29 Page = 89 Calame), leads to a strong affirmation of the *I* (*mnēsomai* 'I will bring to mind', verse 2).[38]

8. Practice and Theory

The conclusions to be drawn from these different statements made about the utterance of the enunciation in archaic Greek poetry have as much to do with the question asked at the beginning of the study as with the instrument of analysis used in the attempt to respond.

The Marks of Writing

At least one conclusion is possible: in Greece, as elsewhere, the appearance of the *I* in discourse cannot be considered a characteristic of the written text as distinct from oral poetry. The first category of uttered enunciations offers, in the very first transcribed oral texts, a well-established *I*. And if our distance in time from ancient Greece does not allow us a glimpse of the moment of pure orality, insofar as it ever existed, anthropological comparison encourages us to confirm the irrelevance of the appearance of the *I* as a distinctive trait of the transition from the oral to the written.[39] A diachronic examination reveals, by contrast, that probably in conjunction with the adoption and spread of the use of alphabetic writing both in the transmission

---

[38] See also Pindar, *Isthmian* 2.1ff., with the commentary of L. Woodbury, "Pindar and the Mercenary Muse: *Isthm.* 2, 1–13," *Trans. Am. Philol. Assoc.* 99 (1968): 527–42, and of Svenbro 1976, 173ff.; the different passages quoted here are commented on by Gianotti, 1975, 52ff.; on the nature of the Pindaric *I*, see the Introduction to this volume, n. 34.

On the utterances of the enunciation in the *Argonautica*, see C. S. Byre, "The Narrator's Addresses to the Narratee in Apollonius Rhodius' *Argonautica*," *Trans. Am. Philol. Assoc.* 121 (1991): 215–27, and Goldhill 1991, 286ff.

[39] See the many texts cited, for example, by C. M. Bowra, *Primitive Song* (London, 1962), 34ff., and by Finnegan 1977, 181ff.; for Greece, see Rösler 1980, 15 n. 12.

For the relationship between the *I* and a partially fictive identification, see P. Smith, "Des genres et des hommes," *Poétique* 19 (1974): 297ff.

and in the composition of Greek poetry, the utterance of the enunciation underwent various modifications.

It has been possible, in particular, to recognize two different procedures for doubling the *I*. In the first, corresponding to the third case in my typology of uttered enunciations (c), the Muse occupies the position of the *you*; she thus takes on the role of the narratee, a narratee that in no way corresponds to the enunciatee of the communication situation. A purely fictitious being, the Muse represents a sort of double of the *I*, "a nonsubjective projection of the subjective person," to use Benveniste's terms. But because there is a substitution taking place in the syntactical positions, this "instance," which holds a position superior in the hierarchy to the *I* on account of the semantic qualities invested in it, becomes the subject of the verb "to sing": it assumes the actantial role of the narrator/speaker, therefore of the *I*. Thus, in the first place, the *I* projects itself through the form *you* onto a figure superior to itself (divine power) that takes over its actantial position. Given the religious values invested in the actor "Muse," this projection demonstrates the sacred status of the words spoken by the *I* in archaic Greek poetry; this does not prevent the narrator, in the same poem, from himself assuming other parts of his discourse, a discourse that is also the object of an apprenticeship.[40] While we are on this subject, let me draw attention to the fact that by taking the position of the *you*, the Muse blocks the appearance in the spoken enunciation of the enunciatee belonging to the communication situation. That is probably why the *I* in its plural form (*we*) includes both the enunciator and the enunciatee, referentially speaking. This enunciatee could as well be present in the few passages of the *Iliad* where a *you* intervenes in the narrative as grammatical subject of a verb of knowledge in the

[40] On the magic-religious status of the poetic utterance in archaic Greece, see Detienne 1967, 15ff., as well as D. Bouvier, "L'aède et l'aventure de mémoire," in *La mémoire des religions*, ed. P. Borgeaud (Geneva, 1981), 63–78. De Jong 1987, 45ff. and 227ff., sees in this manner of projecting the *I* onto a divine instance an example of the "double motivation," human and divine, which is at the origin of the heroic action in Greek epic poetry in general; cf. Russo and Simon 1968, 483ff. It is thus not possible to state simply, as does Lenz 1980, 27, after others, that the divinity sings the poem through the mouth of the poet. On the epic poem being the object of an apprenticeship, see, for instance, Homer, *Odyssey* 8.481 and 488, and Hesiod, *Theogony* 22 and 31. The religious status of the poetic word is not of course the prerogative of ancient Greece; see, in particular, examples cited by C. M. Bowra, *Heroic Poetry* (London, 1952), 15 (Kirghiz bard), and by Finnegan 1977, 204 (Apache song).

For the definition of *you* as "nonsubjective" opposite the "subjective" *I*, see Benveniste 1966, 232.

optative mood: "you couldn't tell on which side Tydeus's son is fighting" (5.85f.). Though the use of the second person and of the potential mood implies the presence of the narrator, this address is a rhetorical one; the *you* here has a general value and probably does not refer to a precise audience.[41]

In the second doubling I have analyzed, by contrast, a doubling that corresponds to the figure of the *sphragis*, the *I* is projected by way of an enunciative shifting-out/enuncive shifting-in onto a *he*. The latter receives, in its semantic form, a name corresponding to that of the author in the sociological circumstances of communication. Parallel to this, a process develops in which the hierarchical relationship that subordinates the *I* to the Muse reverses itself, as, for instance, in the prologue to Hesiod's *Theogony*. Independently of the genres, this transition from an *I* projected onto a divine being to an objectified *I* being some relation to the real identity of the author obviously has some connection with what was probably a growing awareness of the poet-creator's autonomy and with the secularization of his function in Greek society, a society taking on little by little the shape of the polis.

Similarly, in the communication process of choral poetry on the level of the spoken enunciation, we see a clear distinction being made between the composer-author of the song and its performer (choral group). The latter sometimes even takes over the actantial position of the narratee.

Finally, it is significant that the enunciatee appears on the level of the uttered enunciation, in the position of the narratee, as is its right, only in the era of Pindar and Bacchylides, with the suggestion of such an appearance in Hesiod's *Works and Days* and a definite attestation to it as early as Theognis.[42] This is only possible as the Muse takes the place of the *you*-narratee less and less frequently.

Now, since neither the emergence of the *I* in the utterance nor the expression of its autonomy can be considered distinctive characteristics of the written poem in relation to the oral song,[43] the presence in

---

[41] See also *Iliad* 4.223ff. and 429ff., 15.697ff., or 17.366f.; see de Jong 1987, 53ff., and, on those enunciative strategies to which one could add the addresses of the narrator to the heroes of his narrative, F. Frontisi-Ducroux, *La cithare d'Achille: Essai sur la poétique de l'Iliade* (Rome, 1986). On the question of the *we*, see above, Introduction, § 7, this chapter, § 6, and below, Chapter 2, § 3.

[42] See above, § 5 and § 7.

[43] Cf. Finnegan 1977, 201f.

the utterance of the communication situation outside discourse could possibly be connected with the spread of writing; doubtless writing helped objectify the communication process and express it in the discourse, to the detriment of the symbolic and purely discursive relationship of the *I* with the Muse, who is relegated to the rank of assistant. If the communication situation is objectified, perhaps in connection with the use of writing, and if it is present on the level of the utterance, it is always objectified in relation to the *I*, which occupies a central position in lyric poetry at the end of the archaic period. It does not exclude the introduction of this situation into an ideal world, as in Sappho, where it is given divine approbation. Far from distancing the narrative voice, as Walter J. Ong suggests, the use of writing in ancient Greece points up the central role played by the subject on the level of the uttered enunciation in lyric as opposed to epic poetry.[44] The *I*, instead of being defined by its relation to the Muse, is determined by its relation to the communication situation.

Therefore the gradual disappearance of the divine guarantee, as represented by the presence of the Muse, is less dependent on the adoption of writing than on the rules of the genres and on the process of profound social change taking place in the Greek city in the archaic period. Analysis of the elements affecting this process shows that writing helped the change along, but it should not be seen as the prime mover in the radical transformation that took place. The expansion of the word, which is at the root of the development of the assembly of citizens, center of the civic life of the classical polis, is an oral process; writing plays a secondary role, and we must stop seeing this technical advance—not the only one occurring at the time, the introduction of coinage being another—as the key to the evolution of archaic Greek society and its literary productions.[45]

The Theory of the Enunciation

When Benveniste shows that the pronouns *I*, *you*, and *he/she* are different from the other pronouns in that they introduce the instances of discourse, he presumes, without putting into words, the double nature of these linguistic forms.[46] The first two, besides having a

---

[44] See Ong 1982, 147ff.
[45] For this, see also Musti 1981, 70ff.
[46] Benveniste 1966, 125f.

linguistic function of a syntactical nature, also define narrative positions in the utterance of the enunciation; using Gérard Genette's terminology, Greimas and Courtés, as was mentioned previously, confer on these positions the narrative status of *actant* and call them *narrator* and *narratee*.[47] It has not generally been realized that this terminology implies a precise direction in the relationship between the *I* and the *you*. This direction is present on the narrative level and is also expressed on the linguistic or discursive level: it is determined by the syntactical positions of the pronouns *I* and *you*, positions defined by the nominative, dative, or accusative form in an inflected language like ancient Greek. Since the *I* does not necessarily occupy the grammatical position of the subject (nominative), corresponding to the narrator in the enunciation relationship, nor the *you* the position of the indirect object (dative), corresponding to the narratee, the *I-you* relationship is not directly homologous to the actantial relationship between narrator and narratee. In addition, the *you*, in contrast to the *I*, often has no referential analogue, but represents, from a semantic point of view, a simple projection of the *I*. And even when the *you* corresponds to one of the actors of the communication process, that actor can just as well be represented by the enunciatee, receiver of the song, as by its performer, a performer that could be defined as a sort of referential double of the *I*.

If, therefore, we continue to allow the terms *narrator* and *narratee* to designate actantial positions, in other words, to keep their quality as elements of the narrative syntax, we have to admit that the *I* and the *you* behave like actors capable of taking on one or another of these positions according to the context. We are forced to recognize that the *I* and the *you* are less the products of narrative syntax, as the terms *narrator/narratee* (or *allocutor/allocutee*, according to Benveniste) might lead us to believe, than of factors semantic in nature. This aspect of the personal pronouns has been noted, where the French language is concerned, by Benveniste.[48] He qualifies the form *moi*, "antonym" of *je*, as the "proper name of the speaker," thus recognizing, besides its "pronominal" function, a function he calls "onomastic."

[47] See Genette 1972, 225ff. and 265 ff., and also Greimas and Courtés 1979, 80 and 242.
[48] E. Benveniste, "L'antonyme et le pronom en français moderne," *Bull. Soc. Ling.* 60 (1965): 71–87. See also Kerbrat-Orecchioni 1980, 37 and 43f., who argues that the "semanticized" personal pronouns refer to extralinguistic objects. See also Apollonius Dyscolus, *Syntax* 3, 149ff., with the article of F. Lambert, "Aspects de l'énonciation chez Apollon Dyscole," *Hist. Epistém. Lang.* 8 (1986): 39–51.

Furthermore, analysis of the utterance of the enunciation implies the introduction of a third actantial position in addition to those of narrator and narratee: the position of the "object," of the predicate. This position, the semantic analogue of which is the content of the song in the texts studied, is syntactically expressed in the accusative form. It is thus necessary to distinguish carefully between the semio-narrative level, with its actantial syntax, and the discursive level, where the actantial positions of the semionarrative level take on different linguistic forms according to the morphology of the language used (by way of cases in ancient Greek). In this context the pronouns *I* and *you* play a doubly mediating role. Their status itself is double: while they are units more of narrative semantics than of narrative syntax, the *I* and the *you* nevertheless play a role in discursive structures by determining the form of the predicate. Besides being the point of contact between utterance and enunciation, the pronouns *I* and *you*, because of their ambiguous status, are one of the pivots between the surface semionarrative level and the discursive level.

So analysis of the enunciation not only points to the contact between the (discursive) linguistic level and the (semio)narrative level but forces us onto the level of the *referent* and of the semiotics of the natural world. In fact, it was the semantic element contained in the marks of the enunciation that led me to reflect on the transition from oral to written and to see how relative the influence attributed to writing is in the development of the enunciation process in Greek poetry and in the development of the culture from which it derives. The distrust expressed by Plato with regard to this technical instrument should be taken as a proof of the relativity of its impact.[49]

[49] See Plato, *Phaedrus* 274b ff., with the commentary of M. Vegetti, "Dans l'ombre de Toth: Dynamiques de l'écriture chez Platon," in *Les savoirs de l'écriture: En Grèce ancienne*, ed. M. Detienne (Lille, 1988), 387–419, and that of G. Cerri, *Platone sociologo della comunicazione* (Milan, 1991), 77ff.

CHAPTER 2

Hesiod: Mastery over Poetic Narration and the Inspiration of the Muses

1. Hesiod's Encounter with the Muses: An Authentic Vision?

The prologue that introduces Hesiod's *Theogony* is more than a hundred verses long, and—as noted in the preceding chapter—it is entirely dedicated to the Muses and to a description of their many attributes (see Appendix, Texts D). In this long invocation the poet tells of his encounter with the divine chorus on Mount Helicon. Since Antiquity scholars have questioned the authenticity of this vision as the narrator described it. The Ancients generally thought of the scene as a dream, but modern interpreters see either the sincerity of a real visionary experience or the fiction of a literary convention.[1] Research

---

[1] For the authenticity of the vision, see, in particular, K. Latte, "Hesiods Dichterweihe," *Ant. u. Abendl.* 2 (1946): 152–63 (reprinted in *Kleine Schriften* [Munich, 1966], 60–75), E. R. Dodds, *The Greeks and the Irrational* (Berkeley, 1978), 88 and 119f., A. Kambylis, *Die Dichterweihe und ihre Symbolik* (Heidelberg, 1965), 59ff., B. Deforge, "Hésiode: Initiation et nom," in *L'initiation*, Vol. I. *L'acquisition d'un savoir ou d'un pouvoir: Le dieu initiatique: Parodies et perspectives*, ed. A. Moreau (Montpellier, 1992), 79–85, and C. Grottanelli, "La parola rivelata," in *Lo spazio letterario della Grecia antica* I, Vol. 1, *La polis*, ed. G. Cambiano, L. Canfora, and D. Lanza (Rome, 1992), 219–64. For the contrary position, see, among others, F. Dornseiff, "Hesiods Werke und Tage und das alte Morgenland," *Philologus* 89 (1934): 397–415, esp. p. 400 (reprinted in *Antike und alter Orient* [Leipzig, ²1959], 76), who holds that the vision corresponds to a literary convention. F. Bertolini, "Dall'aedo omerico al vate Esiodo," *Quad. Storia* 12 (1980): 127–42, is uncertain.

For the interpretation of the Ancients, see Marcus Aurelius, *Letters to Fronto* 1, 4, 6 (p. 8 Van der Hout), with the commentary of Kambylis [n. 1], 55ff., and of West 1966, 158f.

by Kurt Latte and E. R. Dodds has shown that not until the end of the sixth century B.C. were a few intellectuals able to cast agnostic doubt on the reality of divine intervention in dreams and visions.[2] In order to prove the vision as lived experience, the author of a commentary on the *Theogony* compares a list of its features with other comparable visions in ancient Greek texts or in books of the *Old Testament*;[3] among the more important common features are the following:

> Instructions to the subject of the vision are given by a god.
>
> The encounter with the divine being takes place on a mountain.
>
> The protagonist in the encounter is a shepherd.
>
> The god speaks to him in supercilious tones using the formal, plural *you*, which includes other people.
>
> The protagonist of the encounter is suddenly endowed with great eloquence.

The recurrence of these elements suggests that the vision we find in the *Theogony* is a literary device, but during the archaic period in Greece, the conventional character of narrative and figurative elements does not necessarily mean that they were not authentically experienced. The parallels drawn from the books of the prophets in the Hebrew Bible are enlightening in this regard. But there is legitimate reason to be less certain about the Greek parallels taken for the most part from texts much older than Hesiod, texts that are the headwaters of a literary tradition (in the modern sense of the word). The texts said to attest to the authenticity of Hesiod's vision are thus not all to be trusted, a point I shall return to.

If the comparative method seems to lead to difficulties, the authenticity of the vision at the beginning of Hesiod's *Theogony* can still be approached on the linguistic level. In several works already quoted, Benveniste has shown how humans establish and shape themselves as subjects "in and by language."[4] In the act of enunciation, the subject turns language into discourse; it is here that the "subject" makes his or

---

[2] See note 1 and Gentili 1988, 110f. and 237.

[3] See West 1966, 159f., as well as the parallel experience of Archilochus according to the *Mnesiepes Inscription* (Archilochus, test. 4, E₁, 2, 22ff. Tarditi): cf. C. Miralles and J. Pòrtulas, *Archilochus and Iambic Poetry* (Rome, 1983), 61ff., and C. Brillante, "Archiloco e le Muse," *Quad. Urb. Cult. Class.* 64 (1990): 7–20. For ethnographic parallels, see S. R. Slings, "Poet's Call and Poet's Status in Archaic Greece and Other Oral Cultures," *Listy Filologické* 112 (1989): 72–80.

[4] Benveniste 1966, 259.

her appearance as *I*. But we have seen that the act of enunciation in discourse is not a factor solely of the presence of the *I*; that act is equally dependent on the presence of a second actant, *you*, in relation to which the *I* defines itself, and on the creation of a space-time structure determined by the tense of the verbs and the deictics (this structure differs, of course, from that of the narration). More recent studies have tended to make a very clear distinction between the enunciation as it is expressed in the utterance, by way of the indices mentioned above (I refer to the narrator/narratee relationship), and the social enunciation or communication situation of the text (I refer to the enunciator/enunciatee relationship).[5]

In narrating a vision in which the protagonist is the enunciator (author) of the text, there is naturally an overlap between the subject of the narrative statements who describes the visionary experience and the subject of the enunciation of those utterances. When the vision is given literary expression, the problem of its authenticity is then located in the relationships linking the enunciator of the text, protagonist of the visionary experience; the narrator/speaker, a linguistic expression of the enunciator (by way of the *I* form); and the subject (*he*) of the narrative utterances that recount the experience. The fictional or real character of an experience narrated by the *I* is therefore acted out in the connections between the narrative, the utterance of the enunciation, and the communication situation.

2. The Prologue of the *Theogony* as Oral and Traditional Poetry

Before I return briefly to the utterance of the enunciation in the prologue of the *Theogony* and in the narration/description of Hesiod's vision, I must emphasize two points: On the one hand, we have been told that the utterance of the enunciation is an indissoluble part of the extradiscursive (dialogic) communication process of the text. And in this connection we must remember that the *Theogony* was probably composed shortly after the Greeks borrowed the Phoenician alphabetical system of writing and adapted it to their own use. It has frequently been pointed out that Hesiod's language depends on the Homeric tradition or, more precisely, on a continental epic tradition

[5] See above, Introduction, § 1.

parallel to the one from which the Homeric poems derive.[6] The formulaic character of many of the terms used by Hesiod has been cited to situate his texts in the tradition of Homeric diction. And even if the value of this criterion is questionable, Milman Parry has related the formulaic aspect of epic language to the oral character of poetic transmission during the time of Homer and also of Hesiod.[7] Though Hesiod's poems were surely composed for an oral performance, it has nonetheless been argued that writing was used in their composition.[8] Thus it is generally assumed that Hesiod, at the end of the eighth or the beginning of the seventh century B.C., was composing at a time when writing was perhaps used in literary production but was not used to communicate the poem; during this period the tradition of the singers was still to perform from memory, but reliance on a written text may begin to appear.

On the other hand, numerous analogies have been drawn between the structure of the *Theogony*'s prologue and that of the *prooimia*, or preludes, represented by the songs in the collection of the *Homeric Hymns*. The comparison has been extended to the point where the main part of the present text of the *Theogony* (verses 1–964) is seen as a hymn to the Muses in the style of the *Homeric Hymns*, introducing a catalogue of heroes of which there is an extract in verses 965–1020.[9]

[6] See, among others, Pavese 1972, 111ff., and "La lingua esiodea come lingua della tradizione poetica settentrionale," *Omaggio a E. Fraenkel* (Rome, 1968), 136–89; see also the critique of R. Janko, *Homer, Hesiod, and the Hymns: Diachronic Development in Epic Diction* (Cambridge, 1982), 12ff.

[7] On the formulas of Hesiod's diction, see, for example, M. Parry, "Studies in the Epic Technique of Oral Verse-Making," *Harv. Stud. Class. Philol.* 41 (1930): 73–147, and 43 (1932): 1–50 (reprinted in *The Making of Homeric Verse: The Collected Papers of M. Parry*, ed. A. Parry [Oxford, 1971], 266ff. and 325ff.), A. Hoekstra, "Hésiode et la tradition orale," *Mnemosyne* 4, no. 10 (1957): 193–225, and F. Krafft, *Vergleichende Untersuchungen zu Homer und Hesiod* (Göttingen, 1963), 163ff.; on the relation of formulaic diction to the oral tradition, see E. A. Havelock, "Thoughtful Hesiod," *Yale Class. Stud.* 20 (1966): 59–72, Kirk 1962, 68ff., and G. P. Edwards, *The Language of Hesiod in Its Traditional Context* (Oxford, 1971), 190ff.

For a criticism of the consideration of formulas as a distinctive characteristic of a text in the oral tradition, see Finnegan 1977, 69ff.

[8] Cf. West 1966, 40f., and A. Dihle, *Homer-Probleme* (Opladen, 1970), 120ff.; for counterarguments, see G. Nagy, "Hesiod," in *Ancient Writers*, ed. T. J. Luce (New York, 1982), 43ff., reprinted in Nagy, *Greek Mythology and Poetics* (Ithaca, N.Y., 1990), 36ff.

[9] See, in particular, P. Friedländer, "Das Proömium von Hesiods Theogonie," *Hermes* 49 (1914): 1–16 (reprinted in *Hesiod*, ed. E. Heitsch [Darmstadt, 1966], 277–94), Maehler 1963, 36ff., and Lenz 1980, 21ff. and 127ff., without forgetting the remarks on the hymn within the proem (vv. 36–74) formulated by W. M. Minton, "The Proem-

Because they contain an invocation to a deity, the Homeric preludes were certainly intended to introduce performances of Homeric poems by *aoidoi* or rhapsodes.[10] Given their function and the way their contents are organized, the verses introducing the *Theogony*—perhaps even the whole of the *Theogony*—can no doubt be said to spring from the same tradition that produced the *Homeric Hymns*, though some of the latter are probably of more recent date than Hesiod's poem.

3. The Archaic Forms of the Spoken Enunciation

In the preceding chapter I examined the status of the utterance of the enunciation in all the collections of verses of so-called Homeric poetry that function as prologues.[11] That descriptive study shows that the marks of the enunciation appearing in the prologues of the *Iliad* and the *Odyssey* and in the *Homeric Hymns* fall into three different categories. I will summarize the results briefly.

In the first case (a), corresponding to the formula "I shall sing of Hermes who reigns on this mountain," an *I* is the grammatical subject of a verb "to sing" (in the present or future tense); shortly after the *I* is in place, we pass to an utterance in the third person; the subject of this utterance is the deity, object of the verb "to sing"; the transition from a first-person utterance to a third-person statement is brought about syntactically by means of a relative pronoun of which the deity is the antecedent.[12] The *I* is there only to "shift in" the description and narrative consisting of statements in the third person, that enumerates the qualities and exploits of the deity involved.

In the second case (b), corresponding to the formula "Muse, cele-

---

Hymn of Hesiod's Theogony," *Trans. Am. Philol. Assoc.* 101 (1970): 357–77.

As a prologue, these introductory verses form a coherent group: see K. von Fritz, "Das Proömium der hesiodischen Theogonie," *Festschrift Bruno Snell* (Munich, 1956), 295–315, and W. G. Thalmann, *Conventions of Form and Thought in Early Greek Epic Poetry* (Baltimore, 1984), 134ff. On the *Theogony* as a probable prelude to another poem, see Nagy [n. 8], 53ff.

[10] On the use of the *Homeric Hymns* as preludes for poetry competitions, see F. Càssola, *Inni omerici* (Milan, 1975), xii ff., A. Aloni, "*Prooimia, Hymnoi*, Elio Aristide e i cugini bastardi," *Quad. Urb. Cult. Class.* 33 (1980): 23–40, and M. Costantini and J. Lallot, "Le *prooímion* est-il un proème?" in *Etudes de littérature ancienne*, Vol. 3, *Le texte et ses représentations* (Paris, 1987), 13–27.

[11] There is the bare suggestion of an examination of this type in R. Janko, "The Structure of the Homeric Hymns: A Study in Genre," *Hermes* 109 (1981), 9–24.

[12] On this type of predication by means of a relative clause, see above, Chapter 1, n. 17. For the function of the different summaries of the *Theogony* embedded in the narrative of the qualities and actions of the Muses, see R. Hamilton, *The Architecture of Hesiodic Poetry* (Baltimore, 1989), 10ff.

brate Artemis who was raised with Apollo," it is a *you* that serves as grammatical subject of the verb meaning "to sing"; this *you* corresponds to the Muse, invoked in the vocative. The recital of the qualities and actions of the goddess, object of the verb "to sing" found in this example, is then introduced by the same predicative process as in the first case.

In the third case (c), "Tell me, Muse, of the man of many turns who wandered so long," the *I* and the *you* are present together; the *you* representing the Muse remains the subject of the verb meaning "to sing," while the *I* is in the dative. Because of its syntactical form, the *I* is in the narratee's place and everything occurs as though the Muse-narrator were addressing her song to the *I*. The descriptive narration is then engaged in the usual way.

If we try to relate these three types of utterance of the enunciation to the extradiscursive communication of archaic Greek poetry, we have to acknowledge that the two situations are not alike. If at some stage of the oral tradition it is legitimate to identify the *I* with the person who composed and sang the poem (the enunciator), the *you* does not correspond at all to the enunciatee of the verses, namely the public who was present at the performance of Homeric poetry. The Muse in the position of narratee/allocutee, or even of narrator/speaker, is thus a purely linguistic formula; she is merely a double of the *I* on the linguistic plane. It is thus easy to understand how the *you* of the narratee, a projection of the *I*, can easily occupy the narrator's position. [13]

Here, we witness the construction of a true semiotic entity, a "simulacrum" in Eric Landowski's sense; thus would we also understand the constitutive process of one of the essential characteristics of the "fictional" nature of literature. [14] If we pursue the semiotics of the function of this simulacrum's function in the semionarrative syntax where it substitutes for the *I* of the speaker, we see that the Muse-narratee plays the actantial role of a (semiotic) Sender in relation to the *I*-narrator; it is because of her actantial role that the Muse can substitute for the *I* by taking over the narrator's position. [15] The role of Sender confers on the

[13] On the doubling of the *I* and its probable relation to the expression of inspiration, see the brief remarks of Benveniste 1974, 85f.; on a comparable procedure in Vedic poetry, see B. Oguibenine, "Le discours et le culte dans le RgVeda," *Cahiers de Litt. orale* 4 (1978): 112–28.

[14] See Landowski 1989, 228f., and the complementary remarks of Greimas and Courtés 1986, 193 and 206.

[15] Cf. the revealing thoughts of M. Sbisà, "Actes de langage et (acte d') énonciation," *Langages* 70 (1983): 99–106; and above, Introduction, §§ 2 and 3.

Muse her superior position in the hierarchy, along with the authority emanating from it; as a result of these substitution tactics, the Muse can provide a divine guarantee for the enunciation and for the utterance that is its product. These tactics can be included among Philippe Hamon's "authority ruses in the texts"; but in this case the authority is given to the Muse instead of to the reader! In the prologue of Hesiod's *Theogony*, the divine authority is able to utter lies resembling reality as well as the truth.[16] In the same way, the *I*-narrator, whose poetic competence is guaranteed by the Muse as Sender, takes over the actantial role of Sender in relation to the actors of the third-person narrative that he delivers. Invested with the power-knowledge (*pouvoir-savoir*) of the Muse, the narrator is in a position to manipulate and sanction the actions of the protagonists of his story.

We may note, however, that in early Greek poetry the enunciatee is not necessarily completely absent from the utterance. As we have seen, the *I* of the narrator is often in the plural, as *we*, and there is every reason to believe that both the enunciator and the enunciatee are included in this *we* on the level of the utterance of the enunciation.[17] In the communication process, the linguistic existence of the *you* and the appearance of the *I* as *we* imply that the *I*-sayer is aware of communicating, not with a public, but with a god who inspires his song; as for the public, it is associated with the *I* as receiver of the song inspired by the Muse. Communication, a function of the utterance, becomes a process with religious relevance.

4. Innovations in the Utterance of the Enunciation of the *Theogony*

In the previous chapter, we saw how an analysis of the utterances in the prologue of Hesiod's *Theogony* showed certain significant deviations from the three cases described earlier (see Appendix, Texts D). On two occasions (verses 1 and 36), the *I* and the Muses both become elements combining with the verb "to sing." But in contrast to the

[16] See P. Hamon, "Note sur la référence," *Fabula* 2 (1983): 139–48. For the relation of the words of the Muses with the truth and *mimēsis*, see Pucci 1977, 11ff., with the commentary of G. Ferrari, "Hesiod's Mimetic Muses and the Strategies of Deconstruction," in *Post-Structuralist Classics*, ed. A. Benjamin (London, 1988), 45–78, and Leclerc 1993, 211ff.

[17] See above, Chapter 1, § 5. For a linguistic analysis of the pronoun *we*, see the references given above, Chapter 1, n. 22.

third case mentioned above (c), the *I* (in the plural) functions as the subject while the Muses function as the object of this verb; it is no longer "Muses, sing for me of the hero who . . ." but "let us begin to sing of the Muses of Helicon who. . . ." The narrative is then engaged by means of the process described, namely by a relative clause with a predicative value; but it is the Muses, antecedents of the relative pronoun introducing the predicative statements, who become the subject in the third person of these narrative statements. And in the narrative thus introduced, the Muses in their turn will sing the themes to be found in the *Theogony* (verses 11ff. and 44ff.); the content of the Muses' song then becomes a story embedded in the narrative describing their qualities and functions. We have here, therefore, a sort of *mise en abyme*[18] of the song of the Muses, which, from an enunciative perspective, is definitively appropriated by the *I*. This reversal of the syntactical positions of the *I* and the Muses has, as corollary, the subordination of the latter and their song to the former.

In the first description by the *I* of the Muses' activity, we see a change from the present ("they possess Helicon," verse 2; "they dance," verse 4) to the past ("they formed choruses," verse 7; "they danced," verse 8, etc.). This has been the source of considerable vexation among philologists; those who have not simply skirted the difficulty on the traditional pretext of interpolation have seen the passage as characteristic of Hesiod's style. But the syntactical event in question here is not merely a matter of stylistic quality: it has a very important semantic effect. If verses 2–4, in the present, describe the general powers of the Muses, verse 5 begins the account (in the past tense) of their qualities and includes the poet's vision of the goddesses (verses 22ff.).[19] The encounter of the *I* with the Muses thus becomes one of the possibilities resulting from their attributes; this change of tense in the syntax inserts the individual experience in the paradigm of inspiration conferred by the Muses in early Greek poetry.

The account of the vision is thus integrated into the *I*'s first descrip-

---

[18] See L. Dällenbach, *Le récit spéculaire: Essai sur la mise en abyme* (Paris, 1977), 76ff.

[19] For the commentaries of philologists on this subject, see in particular von Fritz, [n. 9], 33, and Kambylis [n. 1], 50ff.; but Maehler 1963, 36f., cites a series of parallels to the convention found in the *Homeric Hymns* (in particular, in *Hymn to Apollo* 2ff.). M. L. West, "An Unrecognized Injunctive Usage in Greek," *Glotta* 67 (1989): 135–38, sees in this process a traditional characteristic of the description of gods' activities in Indo-European poetry.

On the temporal distance characterizing the narration of the vision, see H. Neitzel, "Hesiod und die lügenden Musen," *Hermes* 108 (1980): 387–401.

tion of the qualities and actions of the Muses. And since it is a narration, the protagonist of the vision does not appear as *I* but as *he*, a *he* who bears a name: Hesiod (verse 22). It is upon him that the Muses conferred the gift of song. The identification of the *he*, who is named, with the *I* is arrived at indirectly some verses later when we return to the utterance of the enunciation through the shifting-in of the *I* form (verses 24 and 30).

The naming of the *he*, his identification as Hesiod, is a direct reference to the real communication situation; when compared with the utterance of the enunciation in Homeric poetry, this is an innovation—no similar procedure can be found either in the epic poems attributed to Homer or in the *Homeric Hymns*. The appearance in the utterance of the enunciation of communication conditions external to the discourse anticipates, as I have said, the convention of the *sphragis*, the "signature," frequent in later poetry. From now on, the speaker has a proper name: he is Hesiod.

5. The Modalities of the Enunciation in Their Social Context

The two new elements introduced—superiority of the *I* over the Muses and the partial expression of the communication situation—mark the distance that manifests itself between the poet and the authority for inspiration represented by the Muses in poems using epic diction but having a different social function.[20] This distance is seen in the process that secularizes the poet's status; in the developing city, the poet becomes less the mouthpiece of divine authority than the artisan of a song commissioned by an "employer" and presented as monumental reality to a group of assembled citizens; his signature corresponds to that of the potter now beginning to be marked on the objects he produces.[21] The signs some scholars wished to see in Hesiod of a

[20] The distance between the *I* and the Muse is seen in verse 36, where the *I* (in the form of *we*) addresses a *you* corresponding not to the Muse but to a doubling of the *I* itself; see on this subject H. Schwabl, "Zur Theogonie des Hesiod," *Gymnasium* 62 (1955): 534. If the public is possibly included in the linguistic form *we* (cf. above, § 3 with n. 17), it is certainly not indicated by the *you* as Maehler 1963, 43, thinks. R. P. Martin, "Hesiod's Metanastic Poetics," *Ramus* 21 (1992): 11–29, goes so far as to suggest that Hesiod himself in his uttered identity is a simulacrum, a mask for an Ionian poet.

[21] Cf. Detienne 1967, 81ff., and 1981, 137, as well as Svenbro 1976, 204ff., and J.-P. Vernant, "Etude comparée des religions antiques," *Annuaire du Collège de France* 78

consciousness of the poet's function and, consequently, of the development of the "individual" can only be perceived as part of this more general process.[22] Amid a growing consciousness of the objective link between the enunciator and the enunciatee, forged by a commercial contract, the invocation to the Muses, basic to Homeric poetry, tends to become a literary convention in Bacchylides and Pindar. When Pindar in the prologue of *Paean 6* (fr. 52f, 6 Snell-Maehler) proclaims himself the "prophet of the Muses," it is to affirm at length his *I* and to subordinate to it the inspiration conferred by the Muses. In the prologue of the *Theogony*, the prophetic quality manifest in the knowledge of the past, the present, and the future is still attributed equally to the Muses and to the *I* (verses 32 and 38):[23] the gift of prophecy is precisely what changes hands between the Muses and the *I* during the vision on Mount Helicon.

The use of the written word for poetic composition surely plays a part in the process of creating distance between the poet and his public, but the modifications that the social structure of the polis was undergoing in the archaic period prevent it from playing a determining role. The use of writing was one among several technologies (hoplite armor, triremes, mounted horses, coinage, and so on) in use at the time; it would take a very long essay to record the impact of those technologies on social and economic life.[24] It is nevertheless certain that the corresponding social changes had a determining influence on the definition of the poetic genres and above all of their political functions.

(1977/78): 451–65. This process of the awareness of the artisan as individual creator parallel to the development of the structures of the polis is of course also found in the representational arts: see Z. Petre, "An Age of Representation—Artifice and Image in Greek Thought in the Sixth Century B.C.," *Revue roumaine d'histoire* 18 (1979): 245–57.

Pindar, *Isthmian* 2.1ff., gives a clear suggestion of this process of making the poetic function more secular when he contrasts the dependence of poets on the Muse in olden times to the search for truth carried out on a salary; see R. Descat, "Idéologie et communication dans la poésie grecque archaïque," *Quad. Urb. Cult. Class.* 38 (1981): 7–27.

[22] See, for example, S. Østerud, "The Individuality of Hesiod," *Hermes* 104 (1976): 13–29, Nagy [n. 8], and P. Judet de la Combe, "L'autobiographie comme mode d'universalisation: Hésiode et l'Hélicon," in *La componente autobiografica nella poesia greca e latina fra realtà e artificio letterario*, ed. G. Arrighetti and F. Montanari (Pisa, 1993), 25–39.

[23] Cf. the Indo-European parallels mentioned by Dodds [n. 1], 103 n. 118. The enunciative coincidence between Muse and speaker in the *Theogony*'s proem is so strong that a probable etymological play attributes to the name of Hesiod (*Hēsí-odos*: "who utters the voice") the very function of the Muses who "utter a charming voice" (*ossan hieisai*: vv. 10, 43, 65, and 67): cf. Nagy 1979, 296f., and 1990, 372f.

[24] On the subject of new technologies, see Musti 1981, 47ff., and, in particular, G. E. R. Lloyd, *Magic, Reason, and Experience* (Cambridge, 1979), 158ff.

6. Analogies with the Homeric Proems

But it is worth noting that in the last part of the *Theogony*'s prologue, we find two utterances of the enunciation conforming precisely to the models we can define in the *Homeric Hymns*. First we find the shifting-in of a *you* that corresponds to the Muses and is the subject of a verb "to sing" (in the imperative, verse 105; cf. verse 108): "praise, daughters of Zeus, the generation of immortals who. . . ." The object of this verb consists of several "mini-stories" that take up the themes of the *Theogony* in its main genealogical stages. Next, the prologue ends with the concomitant appearance of the *you* (as subject/narrator of a verb "to say") and of the *I* (in the dative, as narratee, verses 114f.): "tell me, Muses, those births from the beginning, and narrate the first of them." This form of utterance of the enunciation results in the poem that immediately follows, namely the *Theogony* itself, being put into the mouth of the Muses: this part of the poem begins with the appearance of Chaos (the *geneto* of verse 116 takes over exactly the *geneto* of verse 115). Now, it appears that the use of two traditional forms of the uttered enunciation (b and c) corresponds to the more frequent, enlarged formulation for the conclusion of the *Homeric Hymns*: the narrator/speaker takes leave of the evoked god, addressing a prayer to him; the prayer will presumably be answered because of the pleasure the god will derive from the performance of the present song. The development of the final prayer to the gods invoked from verse 104 on thus makes the prelude to the *Theogony* a real proem, one that follows in the tradition established for us by the *Homeric Hymns*. Moreover, one should notice that when the prelude poem's speaker addresses himself to a god of the song—as in the case of Apollo accompanied by the Muses in *Homeric Hymn* 25—the composition presents a markedly reflexive character. In exchange for praising the musical qualities of the divinity evoked, the speaker requires the god's protection for his own song. Similarly, the narrator of the *Theogony*'s prelude asks the Muses, after praising their powers at length, to give him "a song that charms" (verse 104). Here as well, the *do ut des* of the prayer to the gods inserted in the shape of a proem manifests itself in and through the song. But Hesiod, through various enunciative maneuvers, takes remarkable advantage of the poetic reflexivity offered by this traditional form.

The third-person narration of Hesiod's vision represents a kind of narrativization of the Homeric forms of the spoken enunciation that address the Muses. In the course of the vision, it is the Muses who confer on Hesiod the ability to sing; they thus take the place usually given to the narrator in the utterance of the enunciation, while the poet takes what would otherwise be the narratee's place.

7. A Different Vision of the Poetic Function

The prologue of Hesiod's *Theogony* is significant in that it contains an ambiguous image of the poet's function. On the one hand, the *I* has its origins in those forms of the utterance of the enunciation in which the Muse is superior to the *I*; without the help of the Muse speaking through it, the *I* is powerless. On the other hand, the poet reveals in the text his involvement in a situation in which he communicates with the exterior by expressing the identity conferred on him by his name; he is the poet who transmits to a public, as yet unnamed, his own poem. In the utterance of the enunciation, the song of the Muse henceforth appears subordinate to the *I*, which communicates the song by taking it over completely.[25]

In short, everything happens as if the privileged relationship between the *I* and the *you* represented by the inspiring Muse gradually gave way to an expression of the relationship between the protagonists of the poem's objective communication process. The appearance of elements of this process in the spoken enunciation results in the progressive disappearance of a link between the *I* and the *you*, a *you* existing only on a purely linguistic level.

This new awareness of the objective conditions of the poet's profession is so clear in Hesiod's texts that we find in the *Works and Days* a complete description of the occasion on which the *Theogony* was probably recited. There are of course similar descriptions of epic performances in the *Odyssey*, such as the one that introduces the *aoidos* Demodocus at the court of the Phaeacians (*Odyssey* 8.46ff.), but the *Works and Days* is for us the first text in which the protagonist of the performance is the author himself. In verses 650–62 (see Appendix,

[25] The specific awareness of the poet's function, seen by us in the subordination of the Muses' song to the *I*, was already pointed out by traditional means in Schwabl [n. 20], 534, Kambylis [n. 1], 53f., and Maehler 1963, 38ff.; the last points out that, besides describing the acts and qualities of a god (in this particular case the Muses), showing the effect of these acts on himself, the poet goes beyond the generic laws at work in the *Homeric Hymns*, although his prologue conforms to them: see above nn. 9 and 10.

See also Pucci 1977, 8ff., and Lenz 1980, 199ff.

Text E), the narrator refers to the funeral competition at which he sang his "hymn," usually identified with the *Theogony*.[26]

From the perspective of the utterance of the enunciation, these verses of the *Works and Days* reveal Hesiod's view of his role as poet. In the account of the victory he won at this musical competition and of the consecration of the prize to the Muses, although the verbs describing the action are in the aorist (the principal tense of the story), they are the predicates not of a *he* but of the narrator's *I*. Moreover, the description of the victory is dependent on a verb "to say" in the present tense, whose the subject is the *I*; this verb form, with its performative meaning, explicitly subordinates the recital of the actions of the *I* to the tense of the enunciation. Finally, at the end of the description, the narrator/speaker again uses the formula of the *Theogony*, affirming that it is the Muses who taught him the song. But in this case the receiver of the Muses' knowledge is the narrator's *I*, rather than a *he* identified with Hesiod.[27] In other words, while acknowledging the debt owed to the Muses, the *I* knows and affirms out loud that the execution of the *Theogony* is a performance of which the *I* is the subject and the author.

Also significant is the narrator's remark that the games at which he won the victory took place in honor of Amphidamas, a warrior who probably fell at the battle for the Lelantine Plain; for those who would believe in the historical character of a war that was probably a ritual one, the reference to Amphidamas would give to Hesiod's story a precise temporal indicator.[28] Thus the communication situation of the

[26] The authenticity of this passage from the *Works and Days* was already put in doubt in Antiquity by Plutarch (*Commentary to Hesiod, "Works and Days"* fr. 84 Sandbach = scholion to Hesiod, *Works and Days* 650, p. 205, 22ff., Pertusi): see West 1978, 319. But modern interpreters have shown that there is no reason to reject these verses: see G. Tedeschi, "La guerra lelantina e la cronologia esiodea," *Studi triestini di Antichità in onore di L. A. Stella* (Trieste, 1975), 149–67. On this passage, see also the important remarks of R. M. Rosen in "Poetry and Sailing in Hesiod's *Works and Days*," *Class. Ant.* 9 (1990): 99–113, and of Leclerc 1993, 244ff.

[27] Note that the formula describing what the Muses have to teach is found twice in the passage of the *Odyssey* introducing the poet Demodokos: Homer, *Odyssey* 8.480f. and 488. However, significantly enough, this formula is not given to the poet to speak, but to Odysseus, who describes the poet's activity. From the point of view of the utterance, the Receiver of the Muses' teaching is therefore not the *I* but a *they* (designating poets in general), then a *you* (Demodokos). Moreover, it has to be noticed that etymologically, the term *Mousa* may be related to the verb *manthanō* 'to learn': see Càssola [n. 10], 401.

[28] As the Lelantine War appears to be one of those ritual wars fought by the Greeks in the archaic period, the historical character of this reference, defended by West 1966, 43f., and by Tedeschi [n. 26], 155ff., can be put into question: see A. Brelich, *Guerre, agoni e culti nella Grecia antica* (Bonn, 1961), 9ff.

Theogony is not only taken over completely by the *I*, it is situated in a historical rather than a legendary past.

8. Objectification of the Relationship to the Muse

Given the increasing conspicuousness of the *I*'s affirmation in the archaic tradition and of the poet-artisan's objective function, what can now be said about the authenticity of the vision described in the prologue of the *Theogony*? The awareness expressed by the *I* that he is indeed the performer of his song in the Amphidamas competition, as well as his preeminence over the Muses as stated in the first verses of the prologue, seems to speak in favor of the conventional character of this vision; in that case, the story would be simply a literary fiction. In recounting both the vision depicted in the *Theogony* and the victory described in the *Works and Days*, however, the *I/he* corresponding to Hesiod assumes the position of narratee/allocutee (enunciatee when it is the *he*) and not that of the narrator/speaker: the *I*/Hesiod is the one who receives from the Muses inspiration and the ability to sing. This situation corresponds exactly to the inverted relationship between the *I* and the *you* noted in the third type of enunciative engagement found in the Homeric poems (c); it turns up again at the end of the prologue of the *Theogony*, where the *I*, because of the case shift, takes the position of the narratee while the *you* is the narrator.

In poetry transmitted orally, as is the case here, it is naturally the Muses and their mother, Mnemosyne, or Memory, who are the guarantors of the word that the *I*-poet can only speak and sing, limited as he is to his role as intermediary.[29] If the *I* can be linguistically limited to the role of narratee/allocutee, it is owing to the effect of the central function of memory as inspiration and its incarnation in the figures of the Muses and of Mnemosyne. In this interplay of substitutions, the semantic qualities lent to the Muses and to Memory thus double the actantial role of Sender conferred on them by their syntactical position in the utterance of the enunciation. The communication process of the *Theogony* is therefore still dependent on a projection beyond the poetic *I* of the psychological faculties that for the ancient Greeks constituted inspiration—inspiration not as invention or possession but as remem-

---

[29] Concerning the role of the anthropomorphization of Memory in the Ancients' idea of poetic inspiration and in relation to oral poetry in which the poetic record takes on a religious value, see Detienne 1967, 9ff., Simondon 1982, 103ff., and Gentili 1988, 10f. Within this conceptual framework, the inspiration of the Muses is thought of as knowledge and memory, not as possession as will be the case with Plato: see P. Murray, "Poetic Inspiration in Early Greece," *Journ. Hell. Stud.* 101 (1981): 87–100.

bering, according to Eric A. Havelock, remembering what has been learned.[30]

.   The paradoxical character of the *I* as both autonomous narrator and bearer of inspiration bestowed by the Muses is found again on the level at which the objective conditions of communication are expressed. The narrativization of the relations between the *I* and the Muse, along with the reference to the pragmatic level represented by the naming of Hesiod in the *Theogony* and the description of the performance context for this poem in the *Works and Days*, is a process that objectifies those relations; in so doing, it should make us aware of their purely conventional character. But in this confrontation between spoken enunciation and real level of communication, the Muses tend to retain, as I have shown, their preeminent position in relation to the poet. Even in the precise description of the objective context of the poem's communication described in the *Works*, the *I* is shown as inspired by the Muses: there is no mention made of the public/enunciatee to which his song is addressed. And the privileged relationship of the *I* with the Muses is so strong that the (fictional) gift of song given by the Muses is reciprocated by the (real) consecration of the tripod received by the poet as the prize for his victory.[31] In this way the subjective and discursive relationship between the *I* and the goddesses is anchored in social reality.

It is here, where the inspirational authority is projected outside the poetic *I* and the *I* is transformed enunciatively into a simple narratee/allocutee, recipient of the word proffered by the Muses, that we can understand Hesiod's strategy of overlapping not only the Muses and the poet but also, and particularly, Calliope and the king administering justice (verses 80ff. of the prologue). The Muse gives life to the king's words just as she inspires the poet; and in a society in which the laws correspond to a customary right not yet fixed and codified in writing, the king is doubtless equally dependent on the Muses and their divine guarantee for the rules of his legal code, a code existing only in the memory of those who administer the law.[32] In the *Works and Days* the poet will be taking over the function of the king as judge.

[30] See E. A. Havelock, *Preface to Plato* (Cambridge, Mass., 1963), 97ff., esp. p. 100.

[31] The tripod in question here seems to have been on Mount Helicon in the second century A.D. (see Pausanias 9.31.3). The foot of the mountain was a famous cult-site of the Muses: see A. Schachter, *Cults of Boiotia,* Part 2, *Herakles to Poseidon, Bull. Inst. Class. Stud.* (London), *Suppl.* 38, no. 2 (1986): 147ff.

[32] See C. P. Roth, "The Kings and the Muses in Hesiod's *Theogony,*" *Trans. Am. Philol. Assoc.* 106 (1976): 331–38. Elaborations in M. Puelma, "Sänger und König," *Mus. Helv.* 29 (1972): 86–109, and in C. Brillante, "Poeti e re nel proemio della *Teogonia* di Esiodo," *Prometheus* 20 (1994): 14–26.

In Hesiod's description of the Muses' "gentle dew" transformed in the prince's mouth into "sweet words," the recipient of the royal discourse—that is, the people (*laoi*, verse 84), whose attention is focused on the king about to pronounce justice—is not excluded. But in the same way that the Muses' song allows the public to forget the preoccupations torturing it (verse 55), the pronouncements of the judge-king quell quarrels and calm feelings.[33] As a result, the role of the one who was supposed to carry out the function of the narratee in the text disappears in the annulment of what constitutes his identity. Moved by the poetry inspired by the Muses, the recipient, forgetting his torments, occupies a position similar to that of the poet; he also associates himself with the authority of inspiration and with the words evoked by its memory. The public forgets its own existence to remember with the poet and the Muses the facts of a different reality and thus does not appear on the level of the utterance of the enunciation. Here again, the old schema wins out over the process of objectifying the relationship between the *I* and its public, on the one hand, and the Muse, on the other.

9. On the Side of Authenticity

Much research in the area of ancient Greek literature has shown that in the archaic period the conventional character of poetic language did not necessarily preclude the reality of the experience it expressed. This is indeed the case in lyric poetry when love is described; here, the formulaic aspect of the language, far from being a sign of the absence of sincerity, is the communicative instrument linking a group and an individual. Independent of any oral tradition, formulaic language is the very means by which group feelings are collectively expressed.[34]

Similarly in the *Theogony*, a series of conventional expressions used in describing the poet's encounter with the Muses helps to include the public (probably associated with the *I* in the *we* found at the beginning of the prologue) in the authentic experience of the author. It is true that the initial connection Hesiod makes between the level of the spoken enunciation and the pragmatic plane of the communication, by relat-

---

[33] On the similarity between poet's function and king's function in Hesiod, see J. M. Duban, "Poets and Kings in the *Theogony* Invocation," *Quad. Urb. Cult. Class.* 33 (1980): 7–20, and M. B. Arthur, "The Dream of a World without Women: Poetics and the Circle of Order in the *Theogony* Prooemium," *Arethusa* 16 (1983): 97–116.

[34] See, in particular, Calame 1977, 1.436ff.

ing lived experience and alluding to the objective consequence of that experience on the performance of the poem, seems to invalidate the authenticity of the experience he describes. The original connection of the *I* with the Muses has only a linguistic existence; confronted with reality, in which this relationship normally has no place, it gradually assumes the function of a literary convention. But in Hesiod's case, the fact that the description of this reality as communication (reference to the consecration of the tripod to the Muses and the exclusion of the public) is conditioned by a privileged relationship with the goddesses proves that the influence of the Muses is still accepted as real and that the vision in the prologue to the *Theogony* can be considered authentic.

Research into the marks of the utterance of the enunciation reveals that it is not so much the syntax of these marks as the semantic values they suggest, particularly in addition to the explicit reference to the "objective" enunciative context, which allow us to judge whether the vision in which *I* and *you* are the protagonists is fictional or not.[35] It is on the basis of these qualities that the fiduciary contract is drawn up between the *I*-subject transformed into a narratee and the Muse who, as Sender, takes over the role of narrator. Faith alone is the foundation for such a manipulative strategy, a strategy characteristic of religious discourse, in which the Muse/simulacrum becomes the source of the statements that compose the poem.

As I have tried to show, however, Hesiod's *I* is not always the mere receiver of the honeyed words of the Muse; in certain passages it requires the function attached to its enunciative role of narrator/speaker. This ambiguous situation indicates the intermediary position occupied by Hesiod not only between an oral tradition and a poetry which suggests more and more that it was written down but, more important, between a society in which the influence of the gods is felt to be predominant and a civic life in which the individual takes on social responsibility, the result of which is a growing practical efficiency, even in poetry.

[35] It is significant that differences in the "deixis" bring into contrast texts of an oral tradition with texts dependent on the tradition of writing: see W. Rösler, "Über Deixis und einige Aspekte mündlichen und schriftlichen Stils in antiker Lyrik," *Würzburger Jb. für Altertumswiss.* N. F. 9 (1983): 7–28. But contrary to what Rösler thinks, the high number of deictic words should not be thought of as indicating the oral character of the text under consideration: deictic words are almost absent from Homeric poems, which are otherwise the nearest to an oral tradition! Above and beyond combining in too simple a fashion the categories' marks of deixis/absence of deixis, reality/fiction, orality/literature, it is the qualities of the possible world constructed and designed by the deictic elements that are determining as far as the problem of reference is concerned.

CHAPTER 3

Herodotus: Historical Discourse
or Literary Narrative?

1. Philology at the End of Its Rope

By force of circumstance, the contemporary classical philologist has become a specialist in scraps and fragments. It is true that even in the 1950s restoration of important, if incomplete, sections of the literary heritage of the Greeks was still going on; but for various reasons, mainly political, the era of the great revelations of papyrology in the study of ancient lyric poetry or of New Comedy seems to have come to an end. A classical scholar who does research therefore risks being reduced to such tasks as refining the great interpretations of Sophocles and Plato advanced during the last two centuries. It is no secret that it is now quite possible to write a twenty-page study of a poem by Sappho or Theocritus merely by annotating the interpretations of our predecessors: the core of such a study generally consists of a summary of these interpretations with a few corrections on some minor points tossed in.[1] Rehashes of this sort cannot be justified by respect for an interpretive tradition that has too great a tendency to regard itself as the norm, and even less by hopes of securing an academic career.

We would be on similarly shaky ground if we aspired to found a "new" or "postmodern" philology: it would doubtless meet with the

---

[1] See, for example, for Sappho, W.-L. Lübermann, "Ueberlegungen zu Sapphos 'Höchstwert,'" *Ant. u. Abendl.* 26 (1980): 51–74, and for Theocritus, N. Zagagi, "Self-Recognition in Theocritus' Seventh Idyll," *Hermes* 112 (1984): 427–38.

transient fate reserved for superficial fashions whose only claim to fame is the noisy publicity promoting them and the material gains that are their real raison d'être.

The new methods developed in the vast field of the social sciences, by contrast, can provide the stimulation needed for the renewal that has been under way during the last few decades. Anthropology can lend our understanding of Antiquity the comparative terms needed for research that focuses on the distinctive characteristics and specificity of a culture. And in return, the ancient texts, because of their extraordinary vitality and because of the astonishing openness of the processes of signification they display, offer very fertile ground for testing certain approaches developed in linguistics, sociocriticism, ethnographic inquiry, and semiotics.

2. Herodotus, "The Father of History"?

The work of Herodotus, for example, in a modern edition reduced to two volumes, generated more than five hundred studies between 1937 and 1960.[2] As far back as Cicero, the investigator of Halicarnassus was viewed as the father of history;[3] this symbolic definition, widely exploited by contemporary interpreters, has not prevented the appropriation of Herodotus by literary historians. Spurred on by the criticism of the historian Ctesias, the Ancients were particularly aware of the problem of Herodotus's credibility in his retelling of historic events. The attention of the Moderns, however, focused on the reliability of his ethnographic descriptions of countries they themselves were gradually rediscovering.[4] Was it, then, because Aristotle considered Herodotus to be a teller of myths (muthologos)[5] that he became, in addition to a historian and an ethnographer, a literary figure, a poiētēs?

[2] See L. Bergson, "Herodot, 1937–1960," Lustrum 11 (1966): 71–138.

[3] Cicero, Laws 1.1.5. Among contemporaries, note the title of J. Myres's work Herodotus, Father of History (Oxford, 1953), and the subtitle of M. Pohlenz's classical book Herodot: Der erste Geschichtsschreiber des Abendlandes (Leipzig, 1937).

[4] On Ctesias of Cnidus, successor to and critic of Herodotus, see F. Jacoby, "Ktesias," Realenc. Alt.-Wiss. 11, no. 2 (Stuttgart, 1922): 2050ff. For the Moderns, beginning with H. Estienne's Apologia pro Herodoto published in 1566, see A. Momigliano, "The Place of Herodotus in the History of Historiography," History 43 (1958): 1–13 (reprinted in Momigliano 1982, 138–55); there has been renewed interest in Herodotus as a historian, although his work is unfortunately and anachronistically judged by the yardstick of criteria valid for contemporary historical writing: see F. Hampl, "Herodot: Ein kritischer Forschungsbericht nach methodologischen Gesichtspunkten," Grazer Beiträge 4 (1975): 97–136.

[5] Aristotle, Gener. Anim. 3, 756b 6: Herodotus is a muthologos, one who reports

In spite of its Byzantine character, the question is not academic. Any attempt to answer it must define the status of Herodotus's work, not in terms of literary genres, since we know that the definition of literary genres is highly relative and varies according to the criteria used to distinguish them, but as a textual object; this will enable us to grasp the essential elements of its construction and, as a result, know how to use it. The question is, in short, how to make good use of the work of Herodotus. That is the central problem for the critic, as well as for the teacher.

3. Before Herodotus, the Muse as Inspiration

In the whole of archaic Greek literature, from Homeric poetry to Pindar, the utterance of the enunciation is characterized—as I have shown—by the projection of the *I* of the narrator onto a higher authority, an authority assumed by the figure of the Muse or the Muses, daughter(s) of Memory, an authority endowed with poetic power and knowledge. The Muses appear as the guarantors of the competence of the narrator/poet, who merely lends his voice for the exercise of their omniscience.

The privileged position of the Muses is expressed first on the linguistic level—as I have tried to explain—by the use of cases to change the position of the pronouns *I* and *you*, which represent the narrator and narratee. In the dative case, the *I* of the narrator/speaker takes the place of the Receiver, the narratee/allocutee, and then it is the Muses who communicate to the poet the great deeds of the courageous Greeks or the cunning exploits of Odysseus. From a narrative point of view, the power-knowledge (*pouvoir-savoir*) attributed to the Muses is acknowledged in the actantial position of the Sender, occupied by the Muses, in opposition to a Subject (the narrator turned narratee), who takes over the act of reciting/singing. Thus the Muses contribute to establishing the Subject's competence, and the Subject is then involved in the achievement, represented by the actual performance of the poem before the public. Even if the Muses are a purely fictitious authority, the utterance of the enunciation leads to the process whereby the text is communicated, and to the specific circumstances in which poetic communication can occur. In other words, the power-

---

(2.93), concerning the conception and reproduction of fish, an ingenuous logos repeated by everyone.

knowledge lent to the daughters of Mnemosyne can only be explained in terms of an essentially oral tradition. In the absence of a mnemonic technique backed up by some system of writing, the production of the text must depend solely on the poet's memory, which is made divine by inspiration.[6]

Together with a series of social changes and technical acquisitions, among which is the transformation that took place in poetic genres when the writing system borrowed and adapted from the Phoenicians became more widespread, we have seen how the narrator-Muse connection can become objectified in the utterance of the enunciation and how the *I* assumes an ever more autonomous position. Autonomy also increases in relation to the product of the poetic activity, which becomes regarded as an object of skill to be placed before a public that henceforth makes its appearance on the level of the spoken enunciation. At the beginning of the fifth century, Bacchylides can boast of being "the divine prophet of the violet-lidded Muses."[7]

4. Herodotus Names Himself

But what happens to the utterance of the enunciation when we leave the poetic forms of the Greek culture of the eighth, seventh, and sixth centuries B.C. and look at the prose works of Herodotus in the century of Pericles?

The Prelude to the Inquiry

Like the *Iliad*, like the *Odyssey*, like any poetic composition of the archaic period, the work of Herodotus starts out with a prelude (see Appendix, Text H). In it the narrator expresses his intention not to let what has been accomplished by men (*ta genomena tōn anthrōpōn*) be effaced by the action of time. More precisely, he will see to it that "the fame of the wondrous deeds of the Greeks or of the barbarians will not die without fame, without *kleos*." This short preamble seems to be in keeping with the aim of the Homeric *aoidos*, who celebrates, with the help of the Muses, the *klea andrōn*, the glorious deeds of the heroes; or, more exactly, it seems to embrace the intent of the lyric poet, who

[6] On the role of the Muses as custodians of literary memory and as the inspiration of poets in a mainly oral tradition, see above, Chapter 2, § 8.

[7] Bacchylides 9.2f.

praises the great accomplishments of the men of the present.[8] The glorious deeds of the Greeks against the Persians in the Persian Wars have been substituted for the exploits of the Hellenic heroes before the walls of Troy or the victories of the athletes in the Panhellenic games. The theme central to the work of Herodotus is indeed the conflict between the Greeks and the barbarians at the beginning of the fifth century.

But beyond this similarity, it is the differences that are striking; they set Herodotus's prelude at a distance from the poems of epic and lyric poetry:

—The *I* of the archaic narrator/speaker, which sometimes took on the role of the narratee/allocutee as a function of the syntactical interplay of the cases, has given way to a *he*.

—In contrast to the epic *I*, which is never explicitly linked to a proper name but which can be adopted by the person who utters the poem in the present tense of each enunciation, this *he* is given the identity conferred by a proper name; in this case the *I*'s name is Herodotus, who comes from Halicarnassus.

—There is no question of an invocation to the Muses; the *sphragis* has replaced the appeal to the source of inspiration, previously the explicit Sender of the literary achievement.

—If the aim is indeed to protect men's glorious deeds from the continuous predations of time, in Herodotus's prelude there is no longer any thought of recalling them, as was often the case in the *Homeric Hymns*, for example. Remembering is now the concern of the work's postscript and not its prelude. In an almost completely oral tradition, the literary composition could only have been the recollection, the remembrance of previous achievements, under the divine guarantee of the Muses and their mother Mnemosyne, Memory;[9] things have changed, it seems.

---

[8]See, for example, Homer, *Odyssey* 8.73, in which the Muse inspires Demodokos and invites him to sing the glories of heroes or *klea andrōn*, corresponding in this case to the quarrel between Achilles and Odysseus; see also *Iliad* 9.189, and *Odyssey* 1.338. The idea of the song saving the great deeds of men from oblivion and making monumental works out of them was developed in the poetics of Pindar: see, for example, Pindar, *Pythian* 3.110ff., and the commentary of H. R. Immerwahr, "Ergon: History as a Monument in Herodotus and Thucydides," *Am. Journ. Philol.* 81 (1960): 261–90.

[9]For the *Homeric Hymns*, see, for example, the use of the verb *mimnēiskomai* in *Homeric Hymn to Apollo* 1 and *Homeric Hymn* 7.2. On the function of Memory in early poetry, see above, Chapter 2, n. 29. For the change introduced by Herodotus in the recollection of the past, cf. H. Pelliccia, "Sappho 16, Gorgias' Helen, and the Preface to Herodotus' *Histories*," *Yale Class. Stud.* 29 (1992): 63–84.

—To the concern to save the heroic deeds of the Greeks and the Persians from the destructive action of time is now added a questioning of the *aitiē*, the "reason" for the differences that set Greek and Persian against each other; and this *aitiē* is to be understood as a determining cause as much as a moral and legal responsibility that engages the protagonists of the narrative in a series of faulty actions and interventions in an attempt to atone and compensate for the wrong committed.[10]

But if the nature of the subject (*he*) that takes over the prelude's utterances places it on the narrative plane of Herodotus's story, the use of the present and of the deictic *hēde* points to the work which follows the prelude and, at the same time, situates this introductory phrase in the very moment of the text's utterance; thus we have enuncive shifting-out and enunciative shifting-in with respect to the utterances that make up the narrative. Herodotus thus presents his work, in the immediacy of the utterance indicated by the present tense and the demonstrative adjective, as the presentation/demonstration (*apodexis*) of his investigations (*historiē*).[11] The intention to communicate is thus made obvious in the present tense of the enunciation; but the method of communicating—a public reading or recitation—is not referred to. There is also no *you*, and therefore no mention of the narratee of the text. The *I* withdraws behind the distant *he* of an author referred to in the third person.

Enunciative Interventions

The partial withdrawal in the prelude of the *I*-narrator behind a *he* by means of an incomplete process of enunciative shifting-in does not,

---

[10] If for F. Jacoby, "Herodotus," *Realenc. Alt.-Wiss., Suppl.* 2 (Stuttgart, 1913): 235, establishing the cause of the war is based only on the short legendary account of the confrontation between Greeks and Persians immediately following the prologue, F. Bornitz, by contrast, has shown, in *Herodot-Studien: Beiträge zum Verständnis der Einheit des Geschichtswerk* (Berlin, 1968), 139ff., the value of moral and juridical responsibility implied in the use of the term *aitiē*. But he does not sufficiently emphasize the fact that this meaning of "responsibility" is not at all incompatible with the term "cause": cf. Pindar, *Olympian* 1.35, with *Nemean* 7.11, and see Nagy 1990, 228ff. The initiator of the conflict is the one responsible for it: M. Giraudeau errs concerning this, in *Les notions juridiques et sociales chez Hérodote* (Paris, 1984), 93ff., by anachronistically tying the idea of responsibility contained in *aitiē* to the idea of the individual's will, without seeing that in Herodotus "will" is generally strongly affected by the intervention of the god. See also n. 22 below.

[11] For the meaning of *apodexis* and *historiē*, see the analysis of H. Erbse, "Der erste Satz im Werke Herodots," in *Festschrift Bruno Snell* (Munich, 1956), 211: "Der (im

however, prevent the *I* from intervening on several occasions during the report of his investigations in the nine books containing them. The various interventions of the narrator/speaker, indicated by an enunciative shifting-in involving both the subject of the statements (*I*) and their tense (use of the present), can be divided into four different categories: (1) references to the way in which the information contained in the investigation was communicated to the narrator (seeing, hearing, examining); (2) judgments about the "truth" value of this information and how much credibility should be accorded to it; (3) remarks (infrequent) about the construction of the work itself (introduction of a digression, resumption of the story line, etc.); (4) on rare occasions, value judgments concerning the content of the accounts or the information reported.

Since our topic here is the narrator's attitude toward the creation of his discourse, toward his act of enunciation, only the first two enunciative interventions are noteworthy. Remarks about the form and content of the discourse are, for our purposes, of secondary value.

From the perspective of the utterance of the enunciation and its indices, we can distinguish two ways in which the narrator/speaker approaches narrative throughout his work; these two modes are distinct but capable of being combined. In the beginning of his inquiry, the narrator identified in the prelude with Herodotus of Halicarnassus reports, as he examines the reasons for the conflict between the Greeks and the Persians, the *logoi*, or discourse, of the barbarians: "This is what the Persians and the Phoenicians say [*tauta men nun Persai te kai Phoinikes legousi*]." This anchoring, or enunciative shifting-in, involves the temporal level (use of the present tense) and the deictic level (indication of the utterance) but not the subject of the utterance (perpetuating the *he*) or space (the reference to the Persians and Phoenicians creates a space that is shifted out in relation to the space of the *I*); such a partial anchoring/enunciative engagement allows the pretense of a faithful transmission/transcription of the words of the source quoted and used by the narrator. In the same way, for example, throughout the Egyptian accounts, particularly in the section concerning the history of Egypt, the narrator distances himself to a degree and appears only to transcribe what the priests he consulted say or have said. The subor-

vorliegenden Buch realisierten) Darlegung der Erkundung"; see also Nagy 1990, 217ff. and 250ff., who shows that the public display by Herodotus of the deeds of the heroes of his *Inquiry* is a speech-act.

dination of the statements to the moment of this enunciation mediated by the priests is so strong that the narration is often reported in the infinitive, a form of indirect discourse, depending on a form of the verb *legō* in the plural.[12]

It must be added that in this partial form of enunciative shifting-in, the *he* that takes over the narrator's story only rarely corresponds to a named individual; as specific sources, Herodotus recognizes only Homer, Hecataeus, and Aristeas of Proconnesus; and the work of the latter two is cited only once, whereupon its content is hastily refuted by the historian.[13] Elsewhere Herodotus confines himself to identifying the *he* of the narrator whose account he is following with a group—Egyptian priests, priestesses of Dodona, or people from the region (*epikhōrioi*) such as Athenians, Samians, or Scythians—or he uses an impersonal formula corresponding to "they say that" (*legetai, legetai logos*).[14] At first sight it is thus the logos of others—an impersonal logos, scarcely identified, rarely individual—that speaks through the logos of Herodotus.

Herodotus's narrative is not entirely transparent, however. To the tales he has heard, introduced by an unfinished enunciative shifting-in that retains the third person, Herodotus strongly opposes his own accounts, drawn from what he has seen. Information obtained by way of visual perception appears in utterances given by the narrator's *I* in a complete enunciative shifting-in. If the *he* (*they*) is the hearing (or auditory) witness, the *I* is the visual witness. In a well-known passage of Book 2, concerning Egypt, the narrator clearly portions out narrative authority between, on the one hand, *logoi* based on his own visual experiences (*emē opsis* 'my sight') and on his own research (*historiē*)

---

[12] Herodotus 1.5.1 and 3; 2.99.2; 2.107.1; 2.136.1 and 2, etc. Not referring to the texts, I. de Jong, in her review of the French edition of this volume, *Mnemosyne* 83 (1990): 166–68, has not grasped the meaning of that remark.

[13] Homer cited as source: Herodotus 2.116, and 4.29; Hecataeus: 6.137; Aristaeus: 4.13 and 16. In 4.32f., one finds a tradition attributed to Hesiod and the *Epigonoi* concerning the Hyperboreans.

[14] See, for example, Herodotus 2.52; 5.63.1; 3.46.16; 4.2.20; 1.96.6, etc.; in Jacoby [n. 10], 395ff., there is an exhaustive list of the various subjects (generally collective) that Herodotus attributes to the stories he says he is reporting. D. Fehling, *Die Quellenangaben bei Herodot: Studien zur Erzählkunst Herodots* (Berlin, 1971), 179ff. (also published in English as *Herodotus and His "Sources": Citation, Invention and Narrative Art* [Leeds, 1989]), thinks that the indications given by Herodotus concerning his sources are fictitious. Speaking of the "delegation of speech," Darbo-Peschanski 1987, 113ff., is certainly closer to the poetic reality of the *Inquiry* (see also 86ff.).

and, on the other hand, things he has heard (*ēkouon*) being said. The former are often compatible with the latter. A visual account can complete an auditory account, as in the case of the description of the Labyrinth built by the "twelve pharaohs." And this procedure is not confined to ethnographic investigation; it is just as viable for history: for example, Herodotus's own updated history of Egypt, in which the priests' account and the account of others in agreement with the priests are complemented by the researcher's own visual experience (*tēs emēs opsios*).[15]

The *I* of the visual witness is extremely discreet, however, often renouncing his opinions to efface himself—without recourse to an (enuncive) shifting-out/(enunciative) shifting-in—behind the *he* of the description and the narration. In fact, we see that in enunciative interventions concerning his sources of information, the narrator's *I* does not appear with a complete pronominal, temporal, spatial, or deictic engagement (indicating the utterance he introduces), except in one instance: when it is a matter of the *I*-narrator passing the baton, so to speak, to a *he*-narrator who takes over the narration. This occurs in the anecdote of the banquet offered to the Persians by the Thebans before the battle of Plataea, a story Herodotus transcribes after indicating that he received it from a certain Thersandros of Orchomenus: "What follows [*tade*] I have heard [*ēkouon*] from the mouth of Thersandros . . . ; Thersandros said [*ephē*] that he had been invited," and so on.[16] We find here, therefore, a combination of the two shifting-in procedures—one complete and one partial—used to introduce Herodotus's narration.

But, as I have said, the narrator can also express his opinion on the credibility to be accorded the account he has received. His attitude,

---

[15]Herodotus 2.99.1f.; see also 2.29.1, in which the autopsy is compared with evidence heard: it is clear that the activity of *historein* also includes visual evidence as well as hearsay. On the compatibility of these two modes of information, see 2.147.1, and 148.1ff. For more on this antithesis of hearing and seeing, see the commentary by Hartog 1992, 271ff., and that of G. Schepens, *L' "autopsie" dans la méthode des historiens du Ve siècle avant J.-C.* (Brussels, 1980), 54ff., as well as the contributions of J. Marincola, "Herodotean Narrative and the Narrator's Presence," and of C. Dewald, "Narrative Surface and Authorial Voice in Herodotus' *Histories*," in *Arethusa* 20 (1987): 121–38 and 147–70.

[16]Cf. Herodotus 9.16.1; cf. 3.55.2, and 4.76.6, passages in which Herodotus cites an (oral) source corresponding to an individual; the historian identifies him by his proper name.

when expressed enunciatively, can be implemented in many ways. It can take the form of a simple refusal to give credit to the account: when the Chaldaean priests tell Herodotus that the god comes to his temple in person to sleep with a chosen woman, Herodotus considers their words untrustworthy (*emoi ou pista legontes*).[17] But the narrator often backs up with proofs his refusal to believe an account he has heard. He confronts the accusation that after the Battle of Marathon, the Alcmeonids invited the Persians and Hippias by way of a prearranged signal to sail around Cape Sounion and capture Athens. In a complete enunciative shifting-in, he takes a definite stand: "I find this a surprising statement and I do not accept this account [*thōma de moi kai ouk endekomai ton logon*]." His refusal is founded on two arguments. One concerns probability: as declared and recognized enemies of the tyrants, the Alcmeonids could not possibly have favored a return of Hippias to Athens. The other concerns a moral judgment: to accuse the Alcmeonids is to slander them. The narrator concludes, "I say no more; reason [*logos*] refuses to accept this act."[18] Thus logos must receive the baton from an *I* in order to allow the *I* to suspend judgment. Rejecting an account out of hand and refusing support after a demonstration with proof can work in combination, however, as we see at the beginning of Book 3, where the motives for Cambyses' attack on Amasis, the pharaoh of Egypt, are recounted. The Persian version is reported without any enunciative intervention by the narrator, who delegates his narrative power to the Persians themselves (*houtō men nun legousi Persai*). The Egyptian version is not exact (*legontes tauta ouk orthōs legousi*); it contains allegations contrary to Persian customs. A third version (*legetai de kai hode logos*) is simply referred to as *ou pithanos*: it is not credible.[19]

---

[17] Herodotus 1.182.1. Other passages in which the story reported is said to be *ou pithanos* are also cited by Hartog 1992, 303f.; but Hartog need not associate with the Greek term *muthos* the story Herodotus refuses to trust: that is an anachronism. See my study "'Mythe' et 'rite' en Grèce: Des catégories indigènes?" *Kernos* 4 (1991): 179–204.

[18] Herodotus 6.121.1; 123.1, and 124.2. I must also point out the passage, unique of its kind, in which the narrator, in a full enunciative shifting-in, pronounces a personal opinion (*gnōmē*) about certain events, in spite of the enemies such an opinion might bring him; nevertheless, the narrator adds, this opinion corresponds to the truth (*alēthes*): 7.139.1. This statement, very unusual for Herodotus, is not fortuitous: it was made on the eve of Xerxes' invasion of continental Greece, at a time when it was necessary to prove the hypothesis, central to Herodotus, that the Athenians were the saviors of Greece. The historian for once personally undertakes to uphold a definite thesis, probably in front of a specific audience.

[19] Herodotus 3.1.5; 2.2, and 3.1.

But in the majority of cases the narrator refuses to guarantee the validity of the account he renders in the presence of the narratee/enunciatee (the latter himself being referred to in an impersonal form); he abstains from involving himself in the veracity contract that characterizes most narrations:[20] it is up to the narratee/enunciatee to decide whether he will agree to believe the content of the report. The narrating *I* indicates in a complete enunciative shifting-in that he, for his part, suspends belief and confines himself to transcribing (*graphō*), as is, the logos in question. One recalls the famous passage in which the narrator leaves it up to the narratee, "whoever he may be," to trust or not to trust the *legomena*, the words of the Egyptians. This very rare address to the narratee in a third-person imperative is used by the narrator to define his role more clearly, by way of contrast: as for himself, he just writes down what he has heard said by this one and that one (*ta legomena hup' hekaston akoēi graphō*). Less well known is the moment when the same narrator, concerning the different accounts circulating about the attitude of Argos toward Xerxes, affirms the role he plays in an unusual way: "As for me, I owe it to myself to report what is said [*legein ta legomena*], but I am in no way constrained to believe it; let this principle be applied to the whole of my narrative!"[21] Here the narrator intervenes as *I* to affirm his function as simple transcriber, his role as simple intermediary between the *legomena*, the words that are spoken, and the (implied) narratee, receiver of his work of transcription; the latter represents the only authority able to judge the veracity of these accounts put down in writing.

It goes without saying that the different enunciative interventions concerning veracity generally follow the account in question, whereas the interventions concerning the nature of the source used precede it: the former correspond to the latter in the same way that the sanction phase corresponds to the manipulation phase in the canonic structure of the narration. I should add that the final suspension of belief by the *I*-narrator generally coincides with an admission of the impossibility of personal verification by sight; verisimilitude is reached by way of

---

[20] See Darbo-Peschanski 1987, 123ff. Concerning the idea of narrative truth-values, see Greimas and Courtés 1979, 417f.

[21] Herodotus 2.123.1, and 7.152.3; see also 4.16.2; 4.195.2; 6.53.1, etc. The enunciative interventions of the narrator in Herodotus's work have been counted and analyzed by A. Beltrametti, *Erodoto: Una storia governata dal discorso: Il racconto morale come forma di memoria* (Florence, 1986), 35ff.; see also Darbo-Peschanski 1987, 107ff., and D. Lateiner, *The Historical Method of Herodotus* (Toronto, 1989), 64ff.

akoē, by hearing; truth, or better, accuracy, is arrived at by way of (*aut*)*opsis*, (personal) examination by seeing.

We know that the terms *historiē* and *historeō* used by Herodotus in giving an exact description of his work as an investigator share with the verb *oida* 'I know' a common etymology. In the same way that *eidenai* is to know because of having seen, *historein* is, etymologically at least, to examine by looking. *Oida*, like *historeō*, comes from the root *wid-* (as in Latin *videre*); thus these two words are connected with the visual act. And the semantic result of the etymological analysis is confirmed by Homer's use of a substantive such as *histōr*; this juridical term, used in the formulation of a judgment or the conclusion of a bet, refers to the arbiter, an arbiter appealed to because he will serve as eyewitness to the juridical act or, more generally, because he is able, through his speech-act, to let his hearers see and to bear witness, even to be a guarantee. Contrary to what might be expected in a culture still closely linked to an oral tradition, seeing invokes more confidence than hearing. What this means is that, beyond the reports or *legomena* of others and beyond reliance on their witnesses, Herodotus presents himself as an arbiter of history, as a judge of the actors of history, committed to the restoring of the balance of *dikē*, of justice.[22] Seeking to establish causes and assign responsibility by means of his investigation, he is himself establishing justice, through his speech and through his writing; he is, so to speak, pronouncing a sentence. But let us return to the way in which Herodotus speaks of himself and to the attitude he adopts toward his own words.

5. Creating Heroes from the Discourse of Others

In the Tradition of Archaic Poetry

In spite of appearances, the utterance of the enunciation in Herodotus is hardly different in its general structure from the procedures used

[22] For an analysis of the terms *historein* and *oida*, see E. Benveniste, *Le vocabulaire des institutions indo-européennes*, vol. 2 (Paris, 1969), 173f., P. Chantraine, *Dictionnaire étymologique de la langue grecque*, vol. 3 (Paris, 1974), 779f., and B. Snell, *Der Weg zum Denken und zur Wahrheit: Studien zur frühgriechischen Sprache* (Göttingen, 1978), 26 and 36ff., with, for Herodotus, the remarks of Hartog 1992, 272ff. We may compare Herodotus 2.99.1, where the activity of the *historiē* is explicitly connected to the *opsis*, and 2.118.1, where the result of the questions put by the Egyptians to the protagonists of the story themselves corresponds to knowing (*eidenai*).

For the more general sense of *historeō* as "testify," see Herodotus 1.56.1 (Croesus); 2.19.3, and 29.1 (sources of the Nile); 2.44.1ff. (the antiquity of Herakles is shown

in epic or lyric poetry. From a narrative standpoint, the subject of the enunciative act sets up outside himself, as does the archaic poet, the authority that requires him to speak, that is, his Sender: Muses, on the one hand, storytellers, on the other, almost always in the plural. The archaic poet lends the Muses his voice; the historian transcribes what he has heard from the *logioi andres*, specialists in narrative whom he has seen and listened to attentively. The linguistic embodiment of the Sender in the utterance of the enunciation shows, however, that his semantic position has been modified; this change is marked most frequently by an abandonment of the use of the second person and of the Subject-Receiver's direct address to a divine entity whom he feels present and active in himself. One also encounters the occasional use of the imperfect—the norm is to use the present—in referring to the account placed in the mouth of the *they* who occupy the position of the Sender. When the *you* changes to *he* and the past is substituted for the present (*elegon* instead of *legousi*), the marks of enunciation tend to become confused with the person and tense of the narrative statements, of the story.

Other than in his use of different enunciative programs, the narrator Herodotus seems not to differ fundamentally, at first glance, from the archaic poet; like the latter, he provides himself with a Sender in a manipulation phase in which the *they* of the *logioi andres* takes the place of the *I* of the narrator, guaranteeing with respect to the cognitive performance the coherence of the narrative and the transmission of the knowledge it conveys. At the end of the account, by contrast, when it is a matter of sanctioning the narrative's truth value (sanction phase), the *I* of the narrator often takes the place of the Sender to confirm or reject the temporary credit attributed to the *they*-narrator in the manipulation phase. And when the narrator prefers not to give his opinion, he assigns the role of Sender-judge to the narratee, that is, to his listener or reader. The partial character of the enunciative shifting-in, or anchoring, that introduces the narrative thus suggests a sort of respite, one which gives the narrative credibility before the *I* sanctions it in a full enunciative engagement—unless, of course, this sanctioning, in the same sort of procedure, is left up to the narratee/enunciatee.

Should we view this projection of the *I* as Sender of its own narrative

---

from a combination of eye witnesses and oral statements), etc.; this meaning of *historeō* has been explored by A. Sauge, *De l'épopée à l'histoire: Fondements de la notion d'*historiē (Frankfurt a.M., 1992), 251ff. The juridical aspects of the activities of inquiry, indictment, and publication carried on by Herodotus have been shown by Nagy 1990, 233ff. and 255ff.; on *historiē* as law-court, see Darbo-Peschanski 1987, 43ff.

onto a *they* rather than a *you* as an effect of the transition from oral to written composition? Or is it the effect of the substitution of prose for verse? In Herodotus the notion *graphein* 'writing' is indeed substituted for that of *aeidein* 'singing'; the inscription has replaced the song. But in the *Theogony* of Hesiod we have already noted an enunciative reversal similar to that used in Herodotus; the poet is no longer a medium through whom the Muses sing but an *I* who describes these goddesses, goddesses spoken of in the third person and set apart in space and time when they teach the poet his song on the heights of Mount Helicon. Among the lies and truths that the daughters of Zeus recount, it is the poet who emphatically opts for the truth.[23] It must not be forgotten that in the fifth century writing appears only as a technical and mnemonic means—indispensable though it had become—of giving material support to a logos, the communication of which is essentially oral. The work of Herodotus was rarely read; it was written, to be spoken in public "discussions" on the occasion of the great Athenian or Panhellenic gatherings.[24] Under these conditions, the astonishing development of the autonomy of the *I* in relation to the (supposed) source of the poetic word is far from dependent on the progressive use of writing alone.

Assimilating Others' Words

The substitution, between the end of the eighth century and the fifth, of the *they*/logos for the *you* of the Muses seems much more significant as evidence of a breakthrough to the written document, even if it was not yet defined as such. Discourse in this case is assumed by a collective *they*, despite the sanctioning acts of which the *I* some-

[23] Hesiod, *Theogony* 22ff.; cf. above, Chapter 2, § 4.

[24] See, in particular, the reports of Eusebius, *Chronicon* Ol. 83, 4 (I, p. 106 Schöne), and Lucian, *Herodotus* 1 and *Suda, s. v. Thoukudides* (Θ 413 Adler); on the different modes of communication of the first "historical" Greek works, see A. Momigliano, "The Historians of the Classical World and Their Audience," *Ann. Scuola Norm. Sup. Pisa* 3, no. 8 (1978): 59–75 (reprinted in Momigliano 1982, 106–24), and B. Gentili and G. Cerri, *Storia e biografia nel pensiero antico* (Rome, 1983), 9ff. (with numerous bibliographical references to studies on the diffusion of books and reading in Athens in the fifth century). Rösler [Chap. 1, n. 7], 20ff., even suggests that a written version would have appeared only after oral lectures given by Herodotus had taken place. This rejection of the use of writing toward the final phase of composition of the work stands in contradiction to the statement in the same article whereby the numerous criticisms offered by Herodotus would constitute one of the major signs of a written literary production; see also Rösler, "Die 'Selbsthistorisierung' des Autors: Zur Stellung Herodots zwischen Mündlichkeit und Schriftlichkeit," *Philologus* 135 (1991): 215–20.

times makes it the object. This *I*, while showing signs of autonomy, is constructed in and by the *logoi* of others and is ready to distance itself when necessary. We must not forget that most of these discourses are oral, passed on from mouth to ear.[25]

The permanence, within the narrative syntax of the uttered enunciation, of an exterior Sender and of the guarantee such a Sender represents allows Herodotus's investigations to substitute for the epic poem while accomplishing the same objective, namely that of preserving the memory of the great deeds of men. This Sender is no longer defined semantically, however, in Herodotus by a figure that is merely a projection of the *I* onto a divine *you*; it receives instead the features of the *they* of the narration specialists, a *they* we would be wrong to equate with a *them* external to the *I*, the would-be incarnation of its otherness.[26] Because of the partial enunciative shifting-in procedures described above, the *they* is announced through the *I*, and the explicit intervention of the narrator/speaker is needed in one of his rare acts of sanctioning the truth value of the *logoi*, in order for the *they* to migrate to the side of the differentiated, of the "other."

The *I/you* (*we*) of epic poetry, later of lyric poetry, invested the ethical rules underlying a narrative with a validity limited to the community the poem addressed. The *I/they* of Herodotus widened the field of application of this validity and gave it a sort of universality; Greeks and barbarians alike are subject in their actions to the same unwritten laws: the limits imposed by fate, ill luck, the jealousy of the gods, blindness to the point of injustice. In ethnographic accounts, only those populations on the margins of the *oikoumenē*, at the boundaries of the inhabited world, are dismissed as other. Should we need to be convinced of how thoroughly the other and the self were assimilated, at least as regards the motivation for action and the meaning attributed to historic events, we need only listen to Cyrus the Persian in his speech at the end of Herodotus's work: the rougher the ground, the braver the warrior; the desire for riches leads straight to slavery.[27] Can a barbarian speak Greek any better than that?

[25] On the often oral nature of Herodotus's sources, see J. A. S. Evans, *Herodotus* (Boston, 1982), 145ff., Waters 1985, 76ff., and Simondon 1982, 260ff.; Simondon bases her proof mainly on the passages in which the narrator refers to his own memory: Herodotus 6.55; 7.96.1; 8.85.3, etc.

[26] Thus it is difficult to state that Herodotus is "the only subject of the enunciation," as Hartog 1992, 368 and 372, suggests, or that he is just "the translator of the difference" (ibid., 369).

[27] Herodotus 9.122.3.

6. Herodotus, Historian and Poet

At the very moment, therefore, when the narrower confines of the city were expanding into the Athenian "empire," it is likely that history was made in the enunciative transition from the *I/you/we* to the *they*, in the passage from the limited collective, focused on the source of the enunciation, to the quasi universal. Here indeed—it seems—is historic discourse in its canonic form, a "discourse in the third person" creating an exchange between the dead and the living, according to Michel de Certeau's definition, a discourse that is "knowledge from documents," to complete the latter with Paul Veyne's formulation:[28] by limiting the interventions of the *I*, historic discourse dispenses with the full enunciative shifting-in of the narrator in order to concentrate on the partial engagement represented by quoting a "document." Although the narrative in Herodotus's *Inquiry* remains faithful to the aims of epic by continuing to have an external guarantee, the linguistic form and the enunciative role adopted from now on by the Sender move the narrative into the realm of historic discourse.

It is therefore not surprising that in the prologue of the *Inquiry* the narrator/speaker appears in the third person, taking on in its nonpersonhood the nonpersonhood of his sources; in this way the universality of history, a universality independent of the person who creates and enunciates it, is established. Perhaps it is his third-person status that explains why Herodotus adopts a wait-and-see attitude throughout his logos as regards its credibility; he leaves it up to the receiver, the enunciatee, to judge the trustworthiness of his tale. By using the present tense and the deictic *hēde* (equivalent to *here is*), by contrast, the historian of Halicarnassus removes from the discourse he has heard its distance in time and space, turning it instead into a logos-object he presents in the here and now. These things (*tauta*) they told him (*elegon*, imperfect) back there (in Egypt or on the coast of the Black Sea) are presented (*apodexis*) before our eyes, or rather for our ears. And this narrative, attributed to Herodotus by the narrator, is, in the last analysis, "my" story, the story of an author who speaks and

---

[28] De Certeau 1975, 60f. Note that in Herodotus, contrary to the definition of traditional history given by de Certeau (following Barthes 1967), the utterance is assumed by a "subject," but by a subject-*they* that is not the same as the narrator; still, someone is there "to assume the utterance" (Barthes 1967, 71)!

On writing a scholarly history based on "documents," see de Certeau 1975, 84ff., and P. Veyne, *Comment on écrit l'histoire* (Paris, 1971), 14f.

utters with the same intention of remembering as Homer and his fellow rhapsodes or Pindar and the other singers of Olympic exploits.

To summarize, from Homeric poetry to Herodotus we see a double movement in the utterance of the enunciation in Greek literature. On the one hand, the *I* attains a certain autonomy, probably corresponding to the identification of the self of the narrator as he begins to name himself in a *sphragis*. If the *I* in epic poetry, insofar as it has no proper name, can be adopted by any *aoidos* who recites a given poem, the *I* in lyric poetry is dependent on a more precise communication context, one that has an enunciative character in the poetic utterance. The narrator then names himself at will in the third person in the margins of this lyric context, allowing the poem, in the performance of which he does not necessarily participate, to take on the appearance of an artisan's creation offered to a purchaser and a well-defined public. On the other hand, in the passage from the *you*-Muses to the *they* of the *logioi andres*, Herodotus reconnects, in a way, with the more universalist tradition of epic poetry: the enunciative scope of literary discourse is expanded, but on an entirely new, "documentary" basis. This expansion is mainly seen in the relative disappearance of the enunciation source in the utterance:[29] the objectification of the lyrical *I* finds its correlate in the objectification of the entire discourse. There is therefore no linear development from an impersonal *he/she* to an autonomous *I* in the history of archaic Greek literature.

Hence the numerous hesitations of the literary historians in classifying Herodotus and his work. Herodotus is perhaps the father of history, but he is also a poet in the etymological sense of the word, a *poiētēs*.[30] His historical work fulfills the epic aims of the *Iliad* and, in its "ethnographic" developments, the *Odyssey*'s quest to explore the boundaries of the *oikoumenē*.

[29] It is only in this sense that it is possible to reply to the question recently posed by Rösler [Introd., n. 35]. The *I* cannot be considered to be the only sign of the correspondence of an author with the narrator who is making an utterance himself. Relying particularly on Pindar (*Pythian* 1.92ff.), who associates *logioi* and *aoidoi* in the glorification of heroes, Nagy 1990, 221ff., has convincingly shown the epic function of Herodotus's work; see also Hartog 1992, iv ff. H. Erbse, *Studien zum Verständis Herodots* (Berlin, 1992), 122ff., has found in Herodotus's modes of exposition many traits of Homeric narrative.

[30] For the literary aspects of the narrative fiction created by Herodotus, see the remarks of Waters 1985, 61ff., and for some of the larger categories that organize the historical and anthropological structure in Herodotus, see J. Redfield, "Herodotus the Tourist," *Class. Philol.* 80 (1985): 97–118. The illusion of the historical discourse trying to combine the signified and the referent in "an effect of reality" was denounced by Barthes 1967, 72ff.; see also the preliminary remarks of Ricoeur 1983, 122ff.

7. Between Hecataeus and Thucydides

Herodotus is not the only poet to turn into a historian during the century of Pericles. Hecataeus, whom Herodotus does not hesitate to cite and criticize, is considered to be the predecessor of the logographer of Halicarnassus. His placement at the beginning of the collection of fragments of the Greek historians put together by Felix Jacoby makes him the first historian in the eyes of the scholarly world. Hecataeus, like Herodotus, announces himself at the outset of his *Genealogies*, a work also entitled *Inquiries* by the Ancients, or else *Heroic Stories*. "Hecataeus of Miletus declares [*mutheitai*] this: *I* transcribe [*graphō*] what follows [*tade*] according to the criteria of verisimilitude [*hōs moi dokei alēthea einai*]; the stories [*logoi*] of the Greeks are many and often, it seems to me, laughable."[31]

Here we have a direct reference by Hecataeus at the beginning of his work to the transcription of the logos. But, paradoxically, the moment of communication, the (oral) enunciation of the narrative, is objectified by the use of the third person in the form of a *sphragis*, a preliminary signature, whereas the moment of the (written) composition of the logos is taken on by the *I* of the narrator in a complete enunciative shifting-in. This enunciative polyphony is less surprising when we take into account the text's reference to the verisimilar truth that Hecataeus intends to consign to writing and when we recognize that in respect to questions of truth, the position of the historian of Miletus is not so different from that of Hesiod. Hesiod's Muses can say many true things (*alēthea*), but they also know many untrue things (*pseudea*) that are similar to reality; as for me, Hesiod, inspired by the daughters of Mnemosyne, I shall celebrate the past and the future of the gods.[32] In Hecataeus, as in Herodotus, the words inspired by the Muses have been replaced by the *logoi* of others, in this case, of the Greeks; but in contrast to his colleague from Halicarnassus, the logographer of Miletus does not write down everything he collects: conscious of his knowledge in the manner of a poet of the end of the archaic period, he takes on when he utters the *I* a true logos, a discourse that has made a choice among the stories of the Greeks. Hecataeus is thus closer to the poetics of the archaic period than is Herodotus.

---

[31] Hecataeus, *FGrHist*. 1 F 1a; cf. Detienne 1981, 135ff., who does not comment on the paradox of this "oral" *sphragis*!
[32] Hesiod, *Theogony* 27ff.; on the verses discussed here, see above, Chapter 2, § 4.

In addition, in Hecataeus we are present at the enunciative inclusion of the moment of the written composition, a moment with which the *I* engages by way of a complete enunciative shifting-in (*tade graphō*: I, present, here), in the context of an oral discourse introduced by a partial shifting-in (*Hekataios hōde mutheitai*: *he*, deictic mark of the *here*). This inclusion, whose impact is diluted by the presence of the same deictic in the description of two different moments, is significant not only for the relative importance given to oral communication as opposed to the process of written composition but particularly for the detachment of the narrator in relation to his logos at the moment of naming himself, at the moment of enunciating himself. This point brings us back to Herodotus the historian.

So much for the time preceding the work of the logographer of Halicarnassus. At a later point, Thucydides speaks of himself all through his history of the Peloponnesian War, beginning with the prologue of his work, in which the distancing is complete in relation to the usual marks of the enunciation: "Thucydides the Athenian has written of the war that brought the Peloponnesians face to face with the Athenians."[33] With this use of the third person and the aorist, and in the absence of the deictic, history has become narrative, and a written narrative at that. It no longer needs an external Sender, be the latter a projection of the *I* onto a divine figure of inspiration or the spoken words (*legomena*) of a *they* speaking through the author's mouth and his pen.

But let us make no mistake; as Nicole Loraux warns us with good reason, "Thucydides is not a colleague of ours." True, in the manner of a good historian, Thucydides distances himself and removes himself as editor and narrator of history by speaking of himself in the third person and in an act recorded in the past tense; but he also frequently intervenes in the first person and in the present tense to make judgments on the course of the events his account describes. The historical work is not created for the immediate gratification of the ear; it is useful as an example of the past that allows the city to judge the future—it is "an acquisition forever."[34] Ultimately, the relationship of the narrator with his work is objectified in order to reinforce the relationship of the logos with its civic consummation. And to accomplish this, the narrator intervenes as a poet, as the creator of the examples offered by the historical work.

[33] Thucydides 1.1.1; see Hartog 1992, xiv ff.
[34] See N. Loraux, "Thucydide n'est pas un collègue," *Quad. Storia* 12 (1980): 55–81, with the complementary remarks of Detienne 1981, 105ff. See also Thucydides 1.21.1, and 22.2ff., as well as 1.20.1; 1.23.6; 1.97.2, etc.

8. Marathon: A Literary Creation

For many decades the Thucydidean model was considered the norm for the modern way of "making" history. History thus became an account of events, the political-military history that still appears in schoolbooks today. Within this framework, Herodotus's work has been used as a historical source. And, indeed, for an episode such as the Battle of Marathon—the perfect "historical" event according to the traditional concept of history—his account is the oldest document we have and, with the exception of a few epigraphs, our only source.

Every effort to reconstruct the progress of the battle has proved fruitless, however, following the criteria of modern historical description. How many soldiers fought on each side? What role did the Persian cavalry play after having been mentioned several times before the account of the battle? Where in classical times were the swamps in which the Persians became bogged down? How did the Athenian hoplites, heavily armed, run nearly two kilometers and then engage in hand-to-hand fighting?[35] Such questions lead to skepticism; and for good reason! What Herodotus gives us is neither the description of a military event nor that of a strategy; it is, rather, a carefully balanced scenario. The Athenian army is arranged, according to the rules, with two strong contingents on either wing, the polemarch on one side, the Plataean corps on the other. The line along which it is deployed is exactly the same length as that of the Persian forces, which are, however, much more numerous. As foreseen, the moment the two armies clash, the center of the Greek line gives way, allowing the two wings to encircle the enemy. This maneuver is all the more opportune because at the center of the barbarian army is a contingent of Persian soldiers. The madness (*maniē*) the Persians ascribe to the Athenians when they see them prepare to attack is counterbalanced by the feeling that in fact inspires the Athenians at that same moment: there is no *phobos*, no

[35] Herodotus 6.111–14. For questions posed by modern historians, see R. W. Macan, *Herodotus: The Fourth, Fifth, and Sixth Books,* vol. 2 (London, 1895), 149ff., W. W. How and J. Wells, *A Commentary on Herodotus,* vol. 2 (Oxford, 1912), 353ff., and more recently, W. K. Pritchett, "Marathon," *Univ. of Calif. Publ. in Class. Archaeol.* 4, no. 2 (1960): 137–90, and "Marathon Revisited," in *Studies in Ancient Topography,* vol. 1 (Berkeley, 1965), 83–93, as well as N. G. L. Hammond, "The Campaign and the Battle of Marathon," *Journ. Hell. Stud.* 88 (1968): 13–57 (reprinted in *Studies in Greek History* [Oxford, 1973], 170–250).

For the difficulties faced by contemporary critics in making Herodotus a modern historian, see Hampl [n. 4].

panic, but rather, exactly the opposite of what the Greeks usually felt when there was mention of barbarians. Then comes the flight of the Persians back to their vessels. On the Greek side the only casualties were *agathoi* and *onomastoi*, brave men whose death on the field of battle brought them honor; "beautiful deaths" which correspond to the "beautiful" sacrifices inaugurating the engagement.

Apart from the idealization of the great deed at Marathon and its ideological and political uses during the fifth century, the engagement of the Greeks and the barbarians as related by Herodotus becomes a choreography in the epic mode with well-balanced movements worthy of the finest performances of the tragic choruses in the *orchestra* of the theater at Athens.[36] Herodotus, designer of the recent past of the city and of all Hellas, is indisputably a shrewd poet.

9. History as a Process of Symbolic Construction

But why, one might ask, should we continue to bother about our classical past if the reality of the Persian Wars is not to be obtained from those who were its closest witnesses? Of what use is our prolonged attempt to resurrect an ancient culture that escapes us in the most basic vicissitudes of its history? To answer these questions, we may say that just as we searched long and in vain among the great Greek myths for traces of the early history of Hellas, for a realistic history quite foreign to the function of the myth, so too do we continue to ask questions of the literary texts handed down to us in fragments, questions that they are in essence unable to answer. It is as vain to seek to force the abundant production of ancient Greek texts into our particular generic categories as it is to pretend to see in the tragedies of Euripides the condition of Athenian women in the fifth century. Herodotus is neither a career historian nor a modern author. When he rescues the

---

[36] For the progressive idealization of the Battle of Marathon, see P. Vidal-Naquet, "La tradition de l'hoplite athénien," in *Problèmes de la guerre en Grèce ancienne*, ed. J.-P. Vernant (Paris, 1968), 161–81 (reprinted in *Le chasseur noir: Formes de pensée et formes de société dans le monde grec* [Paris, 1983], 125–49), and N. Loraux, *L'invention d'Athènes: Histoire de l'oraison funèbre dans la cité classique* (Paris, 1981), 157ff.; for the difficulty of reconstructing the battle, see P. Ducrey, *Guerre et guerriers dans la Grèce antique* (Paris, 1985), 75ff.

For the art of the tragic in Herodotus, see the suggestions of Myres [n. 3], 76ff. A similar example, based on narrative technique, has been given by A. Hurst, "La prise d'Erétrie chez Hérodote (6.100–101)," *Mus. Helv.* 35 (1978): 202–11.

glorious past of Greece from the destructive effects of time, he up-grades the acts of men, as does Homer, to the rank of high deeds worthy to be remembered. The work of making heroes—which applied to the Persians as well as to the Greeks—corresponds to an ideological appropriation that is to be found as well in the "ethnographic" description of the peoples near or afar who took part in the events. Beyond anachronistic projection, it is the long symbolic process of reformulation and elaboration, meaningful in the sense that imaginative and speculative fiction is meaningful, that the historian of classical literature can take the risk of bringing to light. Like the anthropologist in the presence of mythical and ritual performances, the historian is confronted with one of world literature's most complex products of the process of symbolic construction and its subtle game of metaphorical echo, reverberation, and repetition.[37] It is up to him or her to disentangle the strands!

[37] For what I mean by "symbolic process," see my contribution of 1990, 36ff.

CHAPTER 4

Tragedy and the Mask: To Stage the Self and Confront the Differentiated

1. Does the Mask Represent an Identity?

Anthropological Approaches

As we know, anthropology has long dealt with the problem of the mask in terms of identification and dissimulation/representation. Let us begin with identification. The mask is often seen as a way for the wearer to abandon his own identity and enter a new, radically different reality, a mythological reality, in which he embodies one of the figures. It is on such a notion that Claude Lévi-Strauss bases his analysis of the "double image" that inspires the customs of face and body painting in certain civilizations, often at a great distance from one another in space and time; the "split representation" would then be predicated on the need of the painted person to destroy his original individuality in order to identify with the social persona he adopts. The double image, as it appears in societies with a complex social hierarchy, would thus signify, through a process of projection, the individual's identification with his social role, and his integration into the world of myth.[1]

The identification function widely attributed to the mask has quite naturally been linked with its representative function: the wearer of

---

[1] For the "identification" process, see, for example, R. Caillois, *Les jeux et les hommes: Le masque et le vertige* (Paris, 1958), 136ff.; M. Eliade, *Le chamanisme et les techniques archaïques de l'extase* (Paris, ²1968), 153ff.; Lévi-Strauss 1958, 288ff.

the mask would take on for the other the identity his disguise confers on him. Giving up one's own identity and dissimulation of the self would go hand in hand with the actualization of the identity implied by the mask (and by the costume that generally accompanies it). From the perspective of Mircea Eliade, the mask becomes the representation of the mythological and sacred reality on which the order of the community is founded.[2]

If it is premature to judge the validity of the representative function of the mask, it is in any case clear that an analysis of the mask cannot avoid examining the way it is used, and the role it plays in the enunciation procedure of which it is a part. In *La voie des masques*, Claude Lévi-Strauss has applied the principles of structural analysis to show that any given mask is part of a system of masking elements and that its particular position in the whole system can be defined by a series of distinctive characteristics arranged in binary oppositions. This semantic organization in pairs of opposing traits finds an echo in the system of myths with which the masks are connected and with which they share the same potential for transformation.[3] But beyond the indispensable structural and semantic approaches that should also relate the mask to the whole of the wearer's costume, the study of the conditions under which it is used and "activated" should at least modify the traditional ideas of its identificatory and representational functions. In any case, the mask can only be considered as part of the enunciation process that stages it.[4]

The Enunciative Hypothesis

I would like to propose a working principle at this point: As we have seen in the previous chapters, according to the studies of the indices of the production of discourse done by Benveniste and later extended by Greimas and Courtés, a distinction has to be made be-

---

[2] See, for example, J. Cazeneuve, *Les rites et la condition humaine d'après les documents ethnographiques* (Paris, 1957), 314, or M. Leenhardt, *La structure de la personne en Mélanésie* (Milan, 1970), 26ff.; Vernant 1985, 80ff., has the same idea about the alienating function of the mask.

[3] C. Lévi-Strauss, *La voie des masques: Edition revue, augmentée, et rallongée de trois excursions* (Paris, 1979), 88ff.

[4] See H. Pernet, "Masks and Women: Towards a Reappraisal," *History of Religions* 22 (1982): 45–59, and *Mirages du masque* (Geneva, 1988), 123ff., showing that the identity of the mask, an object of belief ("croire"), is created as much by the wearer as by those who are present at the ritual in which it plays a part.

tween the "real" circumstances and process of communication of a text (the protagonists of which are the enunciator and the enunciatee) and its enunciation in the utterance (narrator-narratee). Particularly in the utterance, it has been shown that the *he*, the actant-Subject of the statements that constitute the narrative, and the linguistic markers of the space-time context within which the story evolves stand in opposition to the *I* (or *you*), the actant-Subject who enunciates the statements, and to the spatial and temporal signs that refer to the here and now's enunciation. On the tail of this second distinction comes the description of the procedures of shifting-in/anchoring and of shifting-out which lead to the transition, by means of the signifying system referred to earlier, from *I* statements (spoken enunciation) to *he/she* statements (description/narrative), and vice versa.[5]

Within this framework, we can say that the mask, when it is worn, always corresponds to an "actorial role," to the role of an actor engaged in a ritual sequence, itself considered as a somatic and gestural utterance. If the mask can be seen as a (partial) manifestation of the actor of a ritual sequence, it clearly contains within it more than one actantial position. If the mask is endowed, in addition, with the same inherently fictional character as that of the protagonists of a story, by analogy the wearer of the mask (distinguished from the actor the mask "represents") can be compared to the enunciator of a ritual and thus of its corresponding narrative. The hypothetical presence in the ritual (considered as narration) of the self of the mask's wearer then corresponds to the presence of the enunciator in the utterance (i.e., as narrator); and the actor represented by and personified in the mask can be compared to the subject of the narrative: he is a being as fictional as this "paper," textual subject. The narrating *I*, wearer and enunciator of the mask, is thus added to the *he*, subject of the ritual. By means of a subtle play of successive shiftings-in and shiftings-out, the *I* of the mask's wearer and the *he* of the mask involved in the ritual action become one within the mask. It is doubtless at the price of this coming together that the contract of veridicality is drawn up with the enunciatee to guarantee the "reality" of the fiction of the mask. To complete these remarks, I will have to include, for tragedy, the *I* of the tragic text's author: tragedy is indeed not only played/acted ritual but spo-

---

[5] See above, Introduction, § 1. As for the mask, the enunciative approach was introduced by D. Bertrand in an unpublished paper entitled "Masques, sujet et représentation" given at the Conference at Montecatini on the mask (October 1981).

ken acting as well. The discourse spoken by the wearer of the mask is itself submitted to the process of spoken enunciation described in the previous chapters. And I will have to recall that in a play the *he* of the actor is linguistically expressed by the first-person *I*. It is nonetheless a fact that the problems of the mask's "identifying" and "representing" functions can be understood only when we examine the enunciative process, the modalities of its "pronominal" syncretism, and the degree of authority it confers on the action depicted.

2. Characteristics of the Tragic Mask in Greece

Setting aside theoretical thoughts for the moment, let us consider a more concrete subject: the mask of classical Greek tragedy and of its complement, satyr drama. Ancient Greece was a civilization rich in masked expression: there were masquerades and animal masks used in the cult of Demeter, bear masks for Artemis at Brauron, the cult masks of Dionysus, the grimacing mask of the Gorgon, not to mention the masks worn in the various forms of comedy and their countless performances. Why, then, choose masks in particular for tragedy? Because the tragic Greek mask offers, where its supposed functions of identification and representation are concerned, a series of significant "deviations." A study of the mask will enable us to take a critical look at the anthropological perspectives mentioned above, perhaps even to contest their merits.

I must first point out that our knowledge of the Greek tragic mask is obtained from representations of masks on vase paintings and from texts of a fairly late period; it is thus always subject to the manner in which each of these sources interprets reality; given the destructible nature of the materials out of which the mask was made, no example in its original form has come down to us. But the earliest indigenous ways of interpreting the mask separate us from our own viewpoint and may serve to establish a critical perspective.

A "Masking" Mask

If our sources are to be believed, the tragic form has been associated with the mask since its appearance during the sixth century B.C. The first examples of the tragic mask, far from allowing any sort of identification or representing anything, were still part of the burlesque procession celebrating Dionysus and were used basically to hide and dissemble. Prior to the introduction of the mask proper, faces were completely covered, as the text of the *Suda* makes clear, with fig leaves, the fig tree being sacred to Dionysus. Thespis, by contrast, who was supposed to have given the first authentically tragic performance, covered his face with white lead; both author and actor, he began by using purslane flowers or leaves to hide his face and ended by inventing a mask of fine linen. The members of the chorus who accompanied this single actor daubed their faces with wine sediment or even plaster.[6] It is probable that the actor, as he grew in importance, borrowed from the chorus the habit of wearing a mask.

Except for the female protagonist (but not necessarily the mask) introduced by Phrynichos, we have to wait for Aeschylus to introduce masks that perform, on the level of the so-called thymic, or affective, modalities, a purely expressive function; by using colors, Aeschylus is credited with having introduced at the beginning of the fifth century masks aimed at inciting feelings of fear.[7] The material used continued to be cloth. Thus, at the beginning of the classical period at any rate, the mask wearer (its enunciator) does nothing more than veil, in the literal sense of the term, the civic identity his face represents. The simple features that were probably drawn on the early tragic veil do not yet indicate the type of existence the dramatic actor is supposed to "embody" on the stage; the features are not intended to impose a new persona on the *I* of the enunciator.

A Formal Classification

In the second century A.D., the lexicographer Pollux drew up a classification of masks used on the tragic stage, the model for which probably goes back to the taxonomic passion of the scholars of the Alexandrian period.[8] The classification's applicability extends to the end of the classical period, at least for certain of the masks described.

---

[6] *Suda, s. vv. thriambos* (Θ 494 Adler) and *Thespis* (Θ 282 Adler) = Thespis, test. 1 Snell, Horace, *Ars Poetica* 275ff. = Thespis, test. 14 Snell, *Anthologia Palatina* 7, 410 = Thespis, test. 8 Snell, Plutarch, *Prov. Alex.* 30; see also Athenaeus, 14, 622c. Cf. A. Pickard-Cambridge, *Dithyramb, Tragedy, and Comedy* (Oxford, 1966), 69ff. and 79ff.

[7] *Suda, s. vv. Phrunichos* (Φ 762 Adler) = Phrynichus, test. 1 Snell, and *Aiskhulos* (Αι 367 Adler). Cf. the commentary of Pickard-Cambridge 1968, 190ff.

[8] Pollux, *Lexicon* 4, 133ff.; commentary by M. Bieber, "Maske," *Realenc. Alt.-Wiss.* 14, no. 2 (Stuttgart, 1930): 2077ff.

Far from defining stage protagonists by their individual identities, however, Pollux's taxonomy classifies human types according to sex and rudimentary distinctions of age. Without going into the details of a classification system the criteria of which are not at all homogeneous, it is evident that the most frequently mentioned characteristics defining category types indicate the style and color of the mask's hair. We are thus in the presence of a taxonomy that uses formal criteria and gives no indication of the substance of the role played by the dramatic persona represented by the mask or of the passions he might feel.

Although not totally absent, the few notations referring to a characteristic defining the identity of a particular protagonist have a very marginal place in Pollux's classification. Among the masks denoting young men, skin color is used to represent a physical or "moral" condition: illness, gaiety, sadness, love. And Pollux carefully lists in a special category masks designating a "person" (Actaeon and his horns, Phineus the blind man, Tyro with his cheeks bruised by his mother Sidero) or designating anthropomorphized entities such as Justice, Death, or the Furies, or monsters such as the Centaurs, the Titans, and the Giants. If Pollux's taxonomic criteria are to be believed, the Greek tragic mask was not used in any way to identify someone with a name. With rare exceptions, it does not signify individuals or stage personae but corresponds only to formal classes limited to indicating sex and age.[9] The few pictures representing masks that have come down to us from the fifth century B.C. confirm this observation.[10]

An Actor Projected into His Actions

From Pollux let us go back to Aristotle. The first surprise we find is that in his *Poetics*, the philosopher alludes briefly to the mask but dispenses with it entirely in the otherwise detailed definition he gives of tragedy.[11] Central to this definition is the idea of action (*praxis*) and representation/imitation (*mimēsis*), the latter being of paramount importance to those studying the mask; thus tragedy, in the famous Aristotelian definition, is the imitation by "actors" (*drōntes, prattontes*)

[9] Under these conditions it is not surprising that modern attempts to identify masks worn in classical tragedy are for the most part arbitrary: see, for example, the attempts by Bieber [n. 8], by Pickard-Cambridge 1968, 192, and especially by Webster [Chap. 5, n. 10], 45ff.

[10] References and reproductions of iconographic sources cited by Pickard-Cambridge 1968, 191f.

[11] Aristotle, *Poetics* 1449b 21ff.; for the mask in comedy, see 1449a 35 and 1449b 4.

of an action that aims at a no less famous *katharsis*, the "purging" of pity and fear by means of these passions themselves. When describing the various elements of tragedy, Aristotle focuses on the visual aspect of the drama (*opsis*) and on what motivates the action and the actors. Two causes are assigned to the action: the ensemble of dispositions (*ēthos*) corresponding to the actor's persona insofar as they move him to act and the actor's intention (*dianoia*), which amounts to the actor's justification for his actions.[12]

The second surprise we encounter is that if, to begin with, Aristotle as anthropologist sees the causes of dramatic action in disposition and intention, he reverses this causal link where tragedy is concerned: in tragedy, those involved in the drama are created by the action shown on stage; their respective ways of being, their "characters," are determined by "inclusion," as a result of their actions (*praxeis*).[13] In tragedy, according to Aristotle, the utterances of doing precede and create those of being; the performance thus seems to give birth to the competence of the actor. Hence Aristotle's conclusion that "without action there can be no tragedy, but without dispositions, it can exist." Hence also the importance of the plot (*muthos*), viewed as a composition of actions (*sustasis tōn pragmatōn*). So tragedy, like other forms of poetry, is the representation or "imitation" of action; but, considering the means tragedy uses—unity of action, music, spectacle (*opseis*)—it goes one better than epic.[14] Although here we are overstepping the bounds of this study, this value judgment firmly embeds tragedy in the framework of narrative, of a narrative centered on the idea of action and one in which the role of the mask is strangely not mentioned.

Representations of the Mask

The iconographic representations we have of the Attic stage and, consequently, of the tragic mask are not numerous as far as the fifth

---

[12] For *ēthos* and *dianoia*, see ibid., 1449b 36ff., with the numerous parallels given for these two essential concepts of Aristotelian anthropology by Lucas [Introd., n. 7], 64, 106, and 107f.

[13] Dupont-Roc and Lallot 1980, 202ff., have shown that we move from the plane of reality (the realm of ethics) to the plane of fictional characters in tragedy (the realm of poetry and *mimēsis*). For the mimetic status of tragic action, see the reflections of Ricoeur 1983, 58ff. For the ambiguity of the terms *ēthos* and *praxis*, referring both to the real, intrinsically moral action of man and to its performance on stage, I refer to the remarks of D. Lanza, "Aristotele e la poesia: Un problema de classificazione," *Quad. Urb. Cult. Class.* 42 (1983): 51–66.

[14] Aristotle, *Poetics* 1450a 15ff. and 1461b 26ff.

century goes.[15] Anyone examining the masked figures, however, has his attention immediately drawn by a remarkable feature: while the strictest respect is normally given to the face in profile, masks are the exception and show a full frontal face.[16] On closer inspection, it can be seen that frontal representation is not reserved for the mask worn by the actor but for the mask carried as an object, as part of the costume; as soon as the mask is placed on the face, it is again represented in profile. In fifth-century iconography, the masked actor on the dramatic stage is generally not distinguished by the way his face is represented from the protagonists in a scene taken from legend or daily life. With one exception,[17] no special feature of the mask distinguishes the dramatic actor from the actor in a mythological scene; as for the satyrs, who are quite often subjects of iconographic representation during this period, they are identified as protagonists, if need be, by the phallic belt they wear rather than by a mask.

The famous crater of Pronomos, dating probably from the end of the fifth century or the beginning of the fourth, illustrates this elementary point of semiotics perfectly.[18] On one side of the vase, a member of the satyr chorus dances the *sikinnis* amidst the chorus and actors probably celebrating their victory in a competition of satyr drama. The only difference between him and the satyrs in the Dionysiac scene decorating the other side of the vase is the fact that the former wears a phallic loincloth. At the same time, nothing in the drawing indicates that the chorus member wears a mask, in contrast to the satyrs of myth.

Further analysis of this exceptional artifact can lead us to what will become a definite scheme in the representation of the mask: when not shown full front or in three-quarters profile, the tragic mask is treated as an object separate from its wearer and often faces him. The mask is thus seen in two modes when not worn on the face: frontally, facing

[15] In addition to the standard works of M. Bieber, *Die Denkmäler zum Theaterwesen im Altertum* (Berlin, 1920), 87ff., and *The History of Greek and Roman Theater* (Princeton, 1961), 8ff., see, in particular, Pickard-Cambridge 1968, 180ff.; and T. B. L. Webster, "Monuments Illustrating Tragedy and Satyr Play," *Bull. Inst. Class. Stud. (London), Suppl.* 39 (1979): 10ff.

[16] For the significance of the exceptions to the rule of the profile as seen in classical iconography, see Frontisi-Ducroux 1984, 152ff.

[17] This exception is represented by the image on the bowl of Valle Pega, Ferrara T. 173 (Fig. 33 in Pickard-Cambridge 1968); the edge of the mask can be quite clearly distinguished on the actor's face.

[18] The vase called "of Pronomos," volute crater, Naples MN 3240, *ARV²* 1336, 1 (pl. 31–33 in Bieber, *History* [n. 15]). See below, Chapter 5.

the person looking at the vase, or by virtue of a ninety-degree turn, facing the actor who holds it in his hand. As long as the rule for representing the human face in profile is respected, the mask is distinguished by its facial angle; this is not so when the mask is worn on the actor's face. The absence of any distinguishing mark between the human face and the mask when worn, in either form or color, could be considered a confirmation of the much vaunted identification between the wearer of the mask and the "character" he portrays, between enunciator-narrator and actor of the ritual "narration," when speaking in terms of the enunciation.

The Mask's Ritual Sphere

Ignoring the nuances of local variations in defining the field of action appropriate to each of the protagonists of the Greek pantheon, we see that the ritual use of the mask in Greece is confined to three divinities: Artemis, Demeter and, especially, Dionysus.[19]

Let us first turn our attention to Artemis. The best-known masked events took place in the Spartan sanctuary of Orthia, located in a swampy area on the edge of town just inside the town wall. A few of the terra-cotta masks offered ex-voto to the goddess have been found; dating back to the seventh century B.C., they depict either old women or young children. They provide us with tangible proof of the wooden masks worn in the cult, according to written sources, and used in tribal initiation rituals for adolescents at the sanctuary of Artemis Orthia. Elsewhere, at Lykosoura, in the land of Arcadia to which the Greeks attributed all the characteristics of an almost primordial savagery, the cult of Demeter and Despoina, the "Mistress" who was assimilated with Kore, was the occasion for masquerades with animal figures. As for Dionysus, masked celebrations of his cult, without counting the dramatic representations in Athens, were found throughout Greece. Suffice it to mention the troupe of farcical satyrs and the innumerable images of the god himself in masked form.[20]

[19]Cf. H. Jeanmaire, "Antiquité hellénique," in Le masque (Catalogue du Musée Guimet) (Paris, 1959), 67–78, W. Burkert, Greek Religion (Cambridge, Mass., 1985), 103ff., as well as Frontisi-Ducroux and Vernant [Chap. 5, n. 28], 60ff.

[20]For the masks discovered in the sanctuary of Artemis Orthia, see G. Dickins, "Terracotta Masks," in The Sanctuary of Artemis Orthia at Sparta, Journ. Hell. Stud., Suppl. 5 (1929): 163–86, J. Burr Carter, "The Masks of Orthia," Am. Journ. Archaeol. 91 (1987): 355–83, and J.-P. Vernant, "Entre la honte et la gloire," Mètis 2 (1987): 264–99; for other references to this cult, see Calame 1977, 1:276ff. The cult of Lykosoura is

At the risk of oversimplifying, each of these gods, according to his personal mode and the image derived from it, guards the passage between the savage and the civilized worlds: Artemis, because she protects the domain of uncultivated nature inherent in the initiate's transition from adolescence to adulthood; Kore and Demeter, as guarantors of the mystical mediation between above and below implied in the process of grain production and agriculture; and Dionysus, because he allows an individual to navigate, within himself, by means of products with ambiguous qualities such as wine, the passage between submission to a civilized order and the liberation of natural forces leading to otherness. If I may be permitted to simplify, the use of the mask seems to have been reserved in ancient Greece for cults that define and guarantee the various limits of the concept of civilization, cults of the periphery, of the passage from interior to exterior, from the self to the different—and vice versa!

3. Meaning Effects of the Tragic Mask

The strange intersections we find among the data mentioned above, heterogeneous and scattered in time though they are, offer us an opportunity to define the tragic mask based on the categories of the culture that used it. The early dissembling mask, a simple linen cover for the face, and the formal criteria of Pollux's classification help us determine a distinctive trait: the tragic mask of the Greeks does not "represent" any individual identity; it is therefore not comparable to a proper name, and it seems, moreover, to have had no modal function. This observation is extended by Aristotle's reflections on the tragic actor, who has no specific status at the outset but acquires modalities and modes of existence as the action unfolds.

But if the Greek tragic mask initially tended to efface the identity of its wearer to allow for the emergence of a new "character," one with

mentioned by Pausanias 8.37.1ff.: see the archaeological references given by Burkert [n. 19], 280. On Dionysus, see, in particular, H. Jeanmaire, *Dionysos: Histoire du culte de Bacchus* (Paris, 1951), 6ff., and W. F. Otto, *Dionysos: Mythos und Kultus* (Frankfurt a.M., 1933), 81ff.; although his work is based on the interpretation of the mask as a representation and incarnation of the god in question, Otto nevertheless notes the duality of the mask as an expression of both the nearness and the distance belonging to Dionysus, a subject subsequently clarified by M. Detienne, *Dionysos à ciel ouvert* (Paris, 1986), 21ff., and by A. Henrichs, " 'He Has a God in Him': Human and Divine in the Modern Perception of Dionysus," in *Masks of Dionysus*, ed. T. A. Carpenter and C. A. Faraone (Ithaca, N.Y., 1993), 13–43.

no a priori image or specific status, its main role is to reverse the way the action is represented by setting it face to face, so to speak, with its enunciatee, if not with its enunciator. The Greek tragic mask is thus, in its iconographic aspect at any rate, the instigator of a confrontation with the person who watches the action on stage and with the wearer of the mask himself. It is not surprising that such a dual function obtains only in the cults of those divinities who, on the margins of civilization, guard the path between the interior and the exterior, between the self and the other.

These few observations lead us to a vision of the mask as merely a prerequisite for constructing a fictional identity and competence by way of a representational reversal, but they are far from solving the problem of the nature of the enunciation that the mask allows. We must investigate further.

The Mask as Enunciation

In Greek tragedy, it is thus the action that makes the actor.

From the standpoint of the enunciative analysis mentioned above, wearing the mask corresponds to the procedure of enunciative shifting-out and enuncive shifting-in; it allows the *I* of its wearer to hide behind the not-*I*, the *he/she* of the protagonist on stage. But in the case of the Greek mask worn in tragedy, this shifting-out/shifting-in procedure assumes a singular form. In the spoken ritual of the dramatic festival at Athens, wearing the mask meant effacing the *I* of the enunciation without conferring either identity or competence on the *he/she*, the subject of the utterance of the dramatic action. The tragic mask does not grant magic power to its wearer, nor does it add to the modal status of the ritual's subject. In the enuncive shifting-in it occasions, the only modality it confers is the ability of its wearer, not to be, but to become another. Therefore the *I* of the enunciator/wearer of the mask continues to exist, while the *he/she* is created step by step by the action; in other words, the mask plays a supporting role. This imperfect bonding of enunciator and narrative actor, this confusion with regard to identity, leaves a margin of opacity wherein the enunciator can appear as narrator in the utterance. The enunciative mark of the narrator's role is probably materialized in the gaze emanating from behind the two holes of the mask, the gaze of the enunciator.

It was also no doubt on account of this only partial assimilation process, and of the corresponding enuncive shifting-in, that the same enunciator was able to embody several protagonists of either sex on the Attic stage, one after the other.[21] The ability of men to portray even female characters confirms how great was the distance created by the tragic mask between enunciator and actor; realistic fiction was certainly not the main preoccupation of classical tragedy!

It is possible to contrast the incomplete shifting-out effected, for the enunciator, by wearing the mask, with the complete assimilation seen on the vases between actors wearing the tragic mask and characters in a mythological scene. This contrast would suggest a contradiction, but only if we forget that in the case of the vase, it is the iconic illustration that creates the distance from "reality," while in the dramatic presentation, "reality" is represented by flesh-and-blood actors. I shall return later to the basic difference between a semiotic object involving paper actors, if not picture actors, and an event that gives the effect of reality by having recourse to body language and gesture. In the second situation, at any rate, it is clear that the shifting-out caused by the mask can play an essential role.

I must point out, however, that the indicators which mark the presence of the enunciation in the utterance do not correspond for dramatic performance to the criteria defined by Benveniste. Linguistically speaking, the deictic markers of the play's action correspond exactly to those of the presence of the enunciation: *I* (and not *he/she*), *here* (and not *there*), *now* (and not *then*). The action of the tragedy unrolls in the here and now of the dramatic presentation, while the actors say *I*. The mask and the costume accompanying it have the function of shifting out the *I* of the enunciator/narrator and creating the distinction between the level of the simple utterance and that of the uttered enunciation. And yet the tragic Greek mask's dissembling and nonrepresentational face allows a great deal of ambiguity to creep into the shifting-out process: the substitution of the *I/he* (or *she*) of the actor for the *I* of the enunciator/narrator is blurred.

The Mask as Modalizer

What explains the opacity we have noted in the disengagement process of enunciation? What, then, accounts for the restraint we have

[21] One recalls that the first tragic performances involved only one actor, the author himself; the second actor is supposed to have been introduced by Aeschylus: see Themistius, *Orationes* 26.316d, and Diogenes Laertius 3.56. It was not until Sophocles that a third actor appeared: *Suda, s. v. Sophoklēs* (Σ 815 Adler); see also A. Lesky, *Die tragische Dichtung der Hellenen* (Göttingen, ³1972), 52ff., and N. W. Slater, "The Idea of

observed with respect to the numerous modalities that wearing the mask should create for its wearer, as well as for the figure super-imposed on the wearer? To stress the different relationships between enunciator and actor would be to ignore the fundamental tie that connects the enunciator with his enunciatee, the second actant of the communication relationship. And if we are to believe the classical analyses of Greek tragedy, this enunciatee might even be present on the stage, represented by the members of the chorus, and thus appear-ing as narratee.[22] But the Moderns hesitate over the ambiguity sur-rounding the linguistic marks of this narratee and, consequently, over the identity attributed to the choral *I*: is this *I* the incarnation of the choral group as actor and protagonist in the action (thus correspond-ing to a *he/she*) or the incarnation (as narratee: *I/you*) of the enunciatee, that is, the public for whom the tragedy is meant? And the fact that the members of the chorus are masked, like the actors, does not allow us to differentiate. Here again, the pronouns and space-time deictics fail to define the level on which the dramatic discourse takes place. Are we dealing with simple utterance or spoken enunciation? To distinguish between what the chorus says as protagonist of the dramatized action and what it says as narratee representing the enunciatee, or public, it is necessary to resort to content criteria.

Independently of the role played by the chorus and the thorny problems its enunciative analysis raises, the enuncive shifting-in ef-fected by the wearing of the mask puts the action of the play, and thus the utterance, face to face with the enunciatee/public. In this confron-tation—in the literal meaning of the word—with the enunciatee, the partial aspect of the enuncive shifting-in allows the enunciator to appear as both different and the same: different, since the mask covers his face and gives him an actor's authority; the same, to the extent that his own person is still visible beneath a mask that does not lend him an identity. If the mask, by "shifting-in" the actor, confers on him the capacity to allow the enunciator to acquire a second identity through the action, the masked enunciator owns a cognitive competence (*faire-*

the Actor," in Winkler and Zeitlin 1990, 385–95.

For the various modern attempts to stage a classical tragedy with only two or three actors, see Pickard-Cambridge [n. 6], 130ff.

[22] See M. Kaimio, *The Chorus of Greek Drama within the Light of the Person and Number Used* (Helsinki, 1970), 36ff. and 239ff., but also W. Rösler, "Der Chor als Mitspieler," *Ant. u. Abendl.* 29 (1983): 107–24, with the hypothesis developed by J. J. Winkler, "The Ephebes' Song: *Tragōidia* and *Polis*," *Representations* 11 (1985): 26–62 (reprinted in Winkler and Zeitlin 1990, 20–62).

savoir) and then takes on an instructive role with respect to his enunci-atee. The enunciator's role in the communication of knowledge is then added to his role as (partial) guarantor of truth, and the enunciator is then a true Sender for the enunciatee/public, which he can confront from behind the mask. Thus the dramatic action becomes the source of an event, of an "act". Fictional and cognitive, in spite of the gestures and body language used in performance, the dramatic action leads the receiver/enunciatee of the tragedy himself to action, social and politi-cal action, which of course takes place beyond the stage and outside fiction. Because it instructs, the dramatic action contributes to the cognitive development of the enunciatee. The enunciatee/public, in turn, by way of its pragmatic action in society, is part of a performance that will depend partly on the status it acquired during the play. Hence the civic value of Greek tragedy and its role as a model, not a mirror, since it operates only through the transpositions and deformations that the mask creates.

It is onto the drama's educational element that the emotional ef-fects—terror and pity—spoken of by Aristotle are grafted. (And let us not forget that the biographer of Aeschylus attributed to the mask in its new guise the task of inspiring terror in the public at the theater.) These effects appear in ancient theory as the conditions under which the masked enunciator imparts knowledge; they are the guarantees of his effectiveness. In this context the mask plays an essential role: not only does it bring together the stage action and the enunciatee, conse-quently assuring that education takes place, it also makes the education effective by evoking the passions. The role played here by the passions reminds us of the effect attributed to the Gorgon's face; always repre-sented face on, the deformed visage of the terrifying monster works in the same way that masks do, as Jean-Pierre Vernant has shown.[23] Facing its protagonist, the grimacing face looks upon, and at the same time reflects back, the protagonist, but his reflection is totally de-formed. The mirror-face of the Gorgon would thus offer to the on-looker "the Alien," "the Other." But in tragedy, the mask is not a

---

[23] See J.-P. Vernant, "L'autre de l'homme, la face de *Gorgō*," in *Le racisme—Mythes et sciences* (*Hommage à Léon Poliakov*) (Brussels, 1981), 141–55, Vernant 1985, 31ff., and *Figures, idoles, masques* (Paris, 1990), 85ff.

It must be added that, concerning his modalization, the masked enunciator comes under the typology of "scopic" subjects and modalities defined by Landowski 1989, 113ff.

grimacing one; it does not offer a completely deformed face to the spectator; it does not coincide with the face of the Gorgon. In tragedy "the Other" is just a "differentiated" being who inspires horror and terror.

Moreover, since one swallow doesn't make a summer, etymological analysis confirms that the frontal positioning of the Greek mask and its incarnation in the gaze are at the very basis of its character. The word most often used in ancient Greece to signify the mask is identical to the Greek word for the face (*prosōpon*) and to a derivative of the latter (*prosōpeion*); the words of which it consists suggest an etymological meaning that can be rendered in the following ways: "what is in front of [others'] eyes," "that which faces the eyes [of another]" (*pros-ōpon*).[24] The Greek mask, then, as the first meaning here makes clear, is supposed to allow a confrontation.

The frontal angle is made manifest in the gaze, a gaze which in the case of the Gorgon and in that of the drama, inspires terror, a gaze which offers the spectator an image of the different, of that which lies beyond himself. We should remember that Aristotle himself makes the *opsis*, the visual aspect, one of the six distinctive features that define the essence of tragedy.[25] And if we recall that the eye sockets of the Greek mask are empty, thus allowing the eyes of the wearer to appear to the spectator through them, we will understand how the drama's visual aspect refers not only to the enuncive appearance that a mask and costume give to the actors but also to the reality of the enunciator; from the level of the story told and acted on stage, we shift to that of the uttered enunciation. We thus find ourselves returning to the partial character of the shifting-out effected by the mask.

The Mask as Reversal

In comparison with the narrative forms from which the early Greeks learned the myths of their past and its system of values, the drama occupied a unique position in that it completely reversed the conditions of enunciation of this past. If, instead of recounting or singing a myth,

---

[24] The other etymological meaning of *pros-ōp-* is "that which is close to the eyes"; see P. Chantraine, *Dictionnaire étymologique de la langue grecque*, vol. 3 (Paris, 1974), 942, and for a partial interpretation, F. Frontisi-Ducroux, *Le dieu-masque: Une figure de Dionysos à Athènes* (Paris, 1991), 9ff.

[25] See Aristotle, *Poetics* 1449b 33 and 1450b 17ff., Pollux, *Lexicon* 4.115, and the commentary of Lucas [Introd., n. 7], p. 99.

one mounts it on stage, its space-time coordinates and the *he* of its protagonists are made to correspond to the here and now of the play and the *I* of the actors. When the gestures of the myth are situated in the present, the shifting-out that any narrative effects in relation to its enunciation is suppressed. In addition, a visual and somatic dimension is added to the process of communication, as is to be expected in a still largely oral tradition. As a result, the dramatic communication differs from the iconic representation in that the latter's one-dimensional aspect tends to reinstate a kind of shifting-out. The enunciatee of the dramatic narrative is thus set face to face with the protagonists of his legendary past.

It is well known that the actions of the heroes and gods of Greek myth can therefore only take on a paradigmatic value by undergoing a series of reversals:[26] the crimes of Oedipus are simply imaginary negations of the civic order that must be affirmed. So only a cult that lends an institutional and sacred value to reversal can confront the public, without interposing the shifting-out typical of narrative, with the other self represented by the public's legendary forebears. But the Dionysiac cult was doubtless not able to absorb the shock of such an auditory as well as visual confrontation on its own. The mask, essential to the cult of the god, is there precisely for the purpose of re-establishing, at least in part, a shifting-out vis-à-vis the enunciation process; and even in a limited form, this disengagement works on the visual level. We have seen how the tragic mask does not exactly equal the narrative *he/she* but contributes to creating a certain distance for the audience between the *I* of the enunciator and the *I/he* of the protagonist embodied on the stage. The mask not only confronts the audience face on, it also partly recreates a visual—and no longer language-based—action and space-time framework for the myth and for the world of imaginary social possibilities constructed by the myth. So the shifting-out effected by the mask in part restores the narrative distance created by the otherness implied by pronouns and deictics of space and time different from those of the uttered enuncia-

[26] See C. Segal, *Tragedy and Civilization: An Interpretation of Sophocles* (Cambridge, Mass., 1981), 13ff. and 43ff., with the remarks in "Greek Myth as a Semiotic and Structural System and the Problem of Tragedy," *Arethusa* 16 (1983): 173–98, and for comedy, F. Zeitlin, "Travesties of Gender and Genre in Aristophanes *Thesmophoriazousae*," in *Reflections of Women in Antiquity*, ed. H. P. Foley (London, 1982), 119–67. For prudent remarks on the role of the mask in such reversals, see R. Rehm, *Greek Tragic Theatre* (London, 1992), 45ff.

tion. It substitutes a visually veiled presence for the narrative past: even when now present on stage, the protagonist of the myth is kept, through the mask, at a good distance from the enunciator and particularly from the enunciatee.

4. *Mimēsis* at a Distance

It was a problem of this kind that Aeschylus had to solve in 472, when he dramatized the victory of his fellow citizens at Salamis. How could be bring before the public contemporaneous events while observing the rules of shifting-out intrinsic to legendary and mythic narrative? Aeschylus substituted a geographical and actorial distance for the temporal distance of myth by focusing the action of his tragedy not on the Athenians but on the Persians. As it is recounted at the court of Xerxes, the victory is seen through its opposite: the defeat, and the values inspired by this exemplary event, are conveyed, it seems, by their incarnation in the archetypal "Other": the stranger, the enemy, the barbarian—a stranger who nonetheless remains astonishingly close, since he submits the events he relates to a theological interpretation that is utterly Greek. The paradigmatic ethics of the *Persians* is constructed on a reversal that, instead of taking place in time, is realized on the spatial and actorial planes through the eyes of another, one who nonetheless speaks Greek. While serving as a spokesman for Greek values, Aeschylus creates a distancing process in the *Persians* similar to the one the mask brings about for the "instances" of the enunciation.

Like the other forms of poetry, Greek tragedy, as defined by Aristotle, is an imitation seeking to provoke an affective response in the public. But if epic poetry and tragedy are both imitations of an action, the first imitates verbally while the second shows men acting (*prattontas*), in "action" (*energountas*).[27] The first, then, needs a verbal shifting-in/shifting-out procedure, while the second needs just such a

---

[27] Aristotle, *Poetics* 1447a 13ff. and 1448a 19ff.; for the difference between poetry and tragedy, see Plato, *Republic* 394b 8ff. For the thymic aspects of *mimēsis* in historical discourse, see Gentili and Cerri [Chap. 3, n. 24], 13ff.

The Aristotelian theory of tragic action is included in the Greek concept of an action identified with the functional sphere of the agent or, on the contrary, defined as an object attributed to the agent; this concept takes on specific forms in the language itself, as shown by E. Benveniste, *Noms d'agent et noms d'action en indo-européen* (Paris, 1948), 45ff.; see also J.-P. Vernant, *Religions, histoires, raisons* (Paris, 1979), 85ff.

process on the visual plane. Hence the need for the mask. The *mimēsis* in question here is not just a reproduction of reality but the creation of a new reality that is fictional and normative at the same time. The mask serves both to cover up and transpose reality but also to communicate the fiction on stage to its audience.

In the theory developed by Aristotle, it is thanks to the effect of *mimēsis* that the negative passions aroused by the tragic action—fear and pity—can be "purified" and turned into pleasure.[28] What cannot be borne in reality becomes a source of pleasure when it is transposed into the visual and somatic fiction of the dramatic spectacle. The latter's role is to transform reality by way of *mimēsis* and dramatization into something visually bearable. The mask seems to be one of the privileged instruments of this double process of distancing and mirroring, a process carried out through a reversal of the emotional values it engenders. It is therefore, paradoxically, by virtue of the mask's ability to distance and transpose that the "making credible" (*faire-croire*) of the enunciator and the "believing it is true" (*croire-vrai*) of the enunciatee are realized; these two elements together are the basis for the "contract of veridiction" on which the tragic spectacle depends.

Only Dionysus, the god of possession and "otherness," is able to assure this play of deforming mirrors. In the remarks made earlier concerning the face of the Gorgon, we have seen that frontal representation in classical Greek iconography was reserved for those figures who go beyond the limits allowed for human action; Dionysus holds a privileged place at their center.[29] The god of wine is thus the one who guarantees that the epic myth can be staged and presented face to face before the public; he guarantees that in the mask, the enunciator (representing the Self, with his political identity) and the protagonist of the dramatic action (representing the Different, with his "mythological" identity) coexist. Or, to put things somewhat differently, we could say that he assures the recovery of the Other in the Self. He also guarantees, through the process of imitative reversal, the normative, civic values of tragedy.[30]

---

[28] For the transposition of reality brought about by *mimēsis*, see Aristotle, *Poetics* 1448b 6ff., with the commentary by Dupont-Roc and Lallot 1980, 188ff., and especially that of Ricoeur 1983, 82ff.

[29] See Frontisi-Ducroux 1984, 147ff., and Frontisi-Ducroux [n. 24], 177ff. For Dionysus and the gaze, see Otto [n. 20], 97f. For the role of the mask in ancient comedy, I should mention my study "Démasquer par le masque: Effets énonciatifs dans la comédie ancienne," *Rev. Hist. Rel.* 206 (1989): 357–76.

[30] Cf. the remarks of J.-T. Maertens, *Ritologiques*, Vol. 3, *Le masque et le miroir* (Paris, 1978), 89ff. and 107ff., although the psychoanalytic categories and evolutionist struc-

The shifting-out that occurs between enunciator and actor as I have tried to describe it creates distance and lends the mask a "demodalizing" role. But it is this very distance that allows the action to instruct the enunciatee and to acquire an added, deontic modality, instilling the public with a sense of duty. And it is *katharsis* that inspires this process. The public is freed of passion by the mask's instructive capacity. The mask shifts out the action by projecting it onto the plane of appearance and assures, by its emotional effects, the "contract of veridiction" with the audience. Facing the citizens gathered on the steps of the theater (originally the agora, where public and political debates took place),[31] the tragic mask brings into being an identity through the mediation of various images of the strange and the different. Above all, because of the modalities it activates, it is actively involved in the process of manipulation.

---

ture underlying this article often make Maertens's remarks singularly reductive. The theatrical games played by Dionysus, games relying on this god's potential for transvestism and his affinities with the "other," are examined by H. P. Foley, "The Mask of Dionysus," *Trans. Am. Philol. Assoc.* 110 (1980): 107–33, by D. Auger, "Le jeu de Dionysos: Déguisements et métamorphoses dans les *Bacchantes* d'Euripide," *Nouv. Rev. Ethnopsychiatrie* 1 (1983): 57–80, by J.-P. Vernant, "Le Dionysos masqué des *Bacchantes* d'Euripide," *L'homme* 93 (1985): 31–58 (reprinted in Vernant and Vidal-Naquet 1986, 237–70), to be read along with the nuanced remarks on "incarnation" made by P. Vidal-Naquet, "Le dieu de la fiction tragique," *Comédie française* 98 (1981): 23–28 (reprinted in Vernant and Vidal-Naquet 1986, 17–24), and by F. I. Zeitlin, "Playing the Other: Theater, Theatricality, and the Feminine in Greek Drama," *Representations* 11 (1985): 63–94 (reprinted in Winkler and Zeitlin 1990, 63–96).

[31] See F. Kolb, "Polis und Theater," in *Das griechische Drama*, ed. G. A. Seeck (Darmstadt, 1979), 504–45, and H. Kuch, "Gesellschaftliche Voraussetzungen und Sujet der griechischen Tragödie," in *Die griechische Tragödie in ihrer gesellschaftlichen Funktion*, ed. H. Kuch (Berlin, 1983), 11–39.

CHAPTER 5

Vase Paintings: Representation and Enunciation in the Gaze and the Mask

1. Face to Face with the "Other"

An analysis of the way the human form, and particularly the face, is represented in classical vase paintings shows that exceptions to the face in profile are not the result of chance. As others have shown and as I pointed out in the previous chapter, the front view of the face is always connected with specific situations:[1] the cult image of Dionysus, representation of the Gorgon, figuration of death or sleep, iconic marks of superhuman effort during battle or during the throes of death, playing the pipe, and, lastly, drinking wine with eyes staring from the bottom of the cup at the symposiast who has just emptied it. The common denominator among these different facial representations lies in the way they all confront (in the real sense of the word) the person looking at the mask with an affective state outside the norm, such as Dionysiac possession, terror inspired by the Gorgon, sleep or death, effort beyond human endurance, musical performance (pipe), or drunkenness. And as is common in Greece, especially in the expression of love,[2] emotions are communicated through the eyes and the gaze.

But there is one part of the Dionysiac ritual which suggests a quite

[1] See, for example, Frontisi-Ducroux 1984, 147ff.
[2] See the reflections, following several others, offered in "Eros inventore e organizzatore della società greca antica," in *L'amore in Grecia*, ed. C. Calame (Rome, 1983), ix–xl.

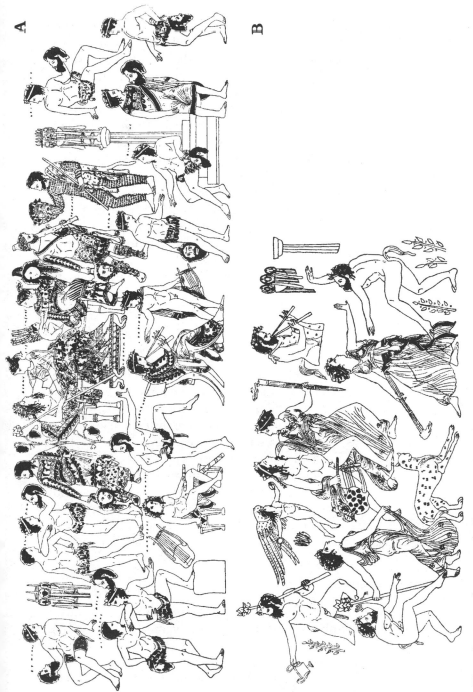

The volute crater known as the Pronomous Vase (note 4, p. 118)

special iconographic treatment, and that is the performance of the classical play: tragedy, satyrical drama, or comedy. In this context, the full-face view is consigned to the mask. We should notice, however, that only as a theatrical prop can the mask represent the full face; as soon as it is worn, the classical painter reverts to representing the profile. A more general look at the function of the tragic mask in the enunciation process of the drama shows how this dual representation is part of the Greek conception of the drama as a whole.[3] From the etymology of the term for drama (*pros-ōpon*, literally, "what is in front of the eyes [of another]") to the Aristotelian concept of a tragic *mimēsis* that, by means of transposition and *katharsis*, creates a new reality, the mask of the classical period seems to be the only possible means for the audience of tragic drama to confront images of "otherness," of a difference and strangeness that are present as much in the myth being staged as in the Dionysiac rituals surrounding it.

Hence the particular interest offered by the illustration of a dramatic scene (or of what at least is traditionally viewed as a dramatic scene) on side A of the famous volute crater said to be "of Pronomos" (see the illustration)[4] and of a "mythological" scene found on side B. The analysis presented here will focus as much on the way in which the painter portrayed the mask as on the faces and gazes of the various protagonists of the action. This will lead us to examine the internal process of the "utterance" of the scene depicted and of its specific Dionysiac traits (the story as told) and to a discussion of the signs of the enunciation process in this scene in relation to the person looking at it, that is, the vase's "public" (a discussion, that is, of how the narrative is communicated). We shall in fact see that it is probably in the gaze that the enuncive and enunciative marks, equivalent to the pronouns and deictics of a text, are concentrated. The scenes on the Pronomos Vase considered in their enunciative aspect will result in a definition of some of the outstanding features in the ritual of Dionysus and also in an interpretation of a contested image.

2. The Interchange of Gazes

Even if we are tempted to think of structural analysis as out of fashion, let us remember its lesson on the problem of value (*valeur*):

[3] See above, Chapter 4, § 3.

[4] Volute crater, Naples MN 3240, *ARV²* 1336, 1; end of the fifth or beginning of the fourth century B.C. Drawing reproduced from M. Bieber, *The History of Greek and Roman Theater* (Princeton/London, ²1961).

the features that define the elements of the object being considered
depend on the relation of each of these elements to the other components of the whole object. When we consider the gaze, the connections
between the protagonists of the two scenes on the Pronomos vase and
how they are defined in relation to each other form a strikingly coherent system.

Side A: Masked Faces

To begin with, leaving aside for the moment the system that defines
the eyes of the masks, if we look at the lower half of the vase's side A,
depicting the dramatic scene referred to above, the gazes of the individuals represented and the directions in which these gazes are pointed
suggest five couples. In the center, facing each other, are the pipe
player, sitting on a *klismos* and dressed in stage clothes similar to those
worn by the actors in the upper half of the vase, and the lyre player—
both are accompanists of the satyr play (for the sake of convenience we
will accept the interpretation of scene A as a play); the lyre player is
looking at the pipe player who has his head bent as if replying to the
other while still concentrating on the tune he is playing. On either side
of this pair, we find two other couples face to face, but asymmetrically.
On the right, the two satyrs, who are members of the chorus, are
looking at each other; one of them is seated. On the left, one chorus
member, the only one among all the characters represented to have his
face covered with a mask, is looking in profile "into the distance";
sitting on a three-legged *trapeza* slightly to the rear of this chorus
member and forming a pair with him is a young man: the roll of
papyrus in his hand and the lyre hanging behind him identify him as
the *khorodidaskalos* and probably the author of the play. His face is seen
in three-quarters view;[5] he seems to be looking at the satyr who is
performing the dance long recognized as the *sikinnis*.[6] But the asymmetry of the looks exchanged by these two couples does not affect the
symmetry of their poses: on the left, the *khorodidaskalos* sits facing the
dancing satyr just as the chorus satyr of the pair on the right is seated.

---

[5] For the function of the choreographer of the chorus, who is usually the author of
the play, see Pickard-Cambridge 1968, 90ff. The identification of the figure of the vase
with a *khorodidaskalos* is the most generally accepted interpretation; see L. Séchan,
Etudes sur la tragédie grecque dans ses rapports avec la céramique (Paris, 1926), 45.

[6] For the distinctive characteristics of the representation of the *sikinnis*, see E. Busch-
or, "Amphora in Neapel: Theater und Thiasos," in *Griechische Vasenmalerei* (*Text*), vol.
3 (Munich, 1932), 141.

On each side of these two couples, there are two more pairs made up of two chorus satyrs looking at each other; they are separated from the three pairs at the center of the lower half of the vase by a block of stone (the *thumelē*) and an architectural object shaped like steps. As for the pair on the extreme right, one of the chorus satyrs is wearing a *khitōn* and a coat instead of the phallic loincloth of his companions.[7]

The same symmetry is found in the upper half of scene A. In the center, above the pair formed by the pipe and lyre players, stands the *klinē* on which Dionysus lies embracing a feminine figure whom dozens of similar representations allows us to identify easily as Ariadne. The heroine's feet rest on a *thrēnus* and she is looking at Dionysus, whose head leans backward in an attitude suggesting bacchic possession.[8] Also on the *klinē*, we find a second feminine figure facing Himeros and looking at Dionysus; her richly embroidered, long-sleeved *khitōn* is exactly the same as the costume worn by tragic actors at the time matching the date of the Pronomos Vase.[9] Two other actors frame the central triad: to the left, an actor as yet unnamed, to the right, Herakles with his club and his lion skin; both of them are looking outward at the chorus satyrs who face them on each side. On the left, two chorus members are looking at the unidentified actor; on the right, they are mirrored by a person wearing the costume of Papposilenos, father of the satyrs, who is himself looking at Herakles; he is surely the leader of the satyr chorus represented on side A.[10] His presence in the context of the two satyrs with whom he forms a

[7] For the probable role of the *khitōn*-clad chorus member, see note 11 below. In the corresponding gloss of the *Etymologicum Magnum* 458 30ff. Gaisford, we are told that the *thumelē* was, at the origin of the tragedy, the table on which the first "actors" stood and sang in the fields.

[8] For the pieces of furniture mentioned in the text, see G. M. A. Richter, *The Furniture of the Greeks, Etruscans, and Romans* (London, 1966), 56ff.

[9] See the prudent remarks of Pickard-Cambridge 1968, 197ff.

[10] For Papposilenos, the father of the satyrs, and for the way he is represented on vases, see T. B. L. Webster, *Greek Theatre Production* (London, 1970), 31ff. The position this character occupies in relation to the two satyrs on the left, as well as the number twelve that is arrived at when he is included, shows that he plays the role of the leader of the satyr chorus. The counterexample of Euripides, *Cyclops* 82ff., cited by Pickard-Cambridge 1968, 236, which makes Papposilenos an autonomous actor, is not pertinent; if in the *Cyclops* Silenus seems indeed to be the third actor facing the leader, on the Pronomos Vase the positions of the three canonic actors are taken over by other characters; Papposilenos is not placed with them, except as a speaker representing the chorus. In other satyr plays, the role of Papposilenos is that of chorus leader: see E. Simon, "Satyr Plays on Vases in the Time of Aeschylus," in *The Eye of Greece: Studies in the Art of Athens*, ed. D. Kurtz and B. Sparkes (Cambridge, 1982), 142f.

threesome strains the mathematical symmetry of the whole—to say nothing of its spatial symmetry; this asymmetry probably results from the difficulty of apportioning the space between a group of three figures (pipe player, lyre player, *khorodidaskalos*) and one of twelve (the twelve chorus members, including the chorus leader). Lastly, at each end of the upper section is a seated chorus satyr, separated from the central scene by a tripod and looking toward the center.

The exchange of gazes between the individuals in scene A is what assures the coherence of the picture. In the upper section, the gazes of Ariadne and the other woman toward the god lend unity to the trio formed by these three figures; because of her costume and the mask she holds in her hand, however, the second woman is also connected to the two actors (Herakles and an adult man) who surround the trio. In their turn, the eyes of these actors, turned toward Papposilenos and the two chorus satyrs who are looking back at them, ensure the connection between actors and chorus. The lower section of the painting, connected to the upper one at the center by virtue of the similar costumes worn by the actors and the pipe player, shows the same kind of symmetry in the two couples facing each other and in the individuals looking at each other two by two. The only exception is the *khorodidaskalos*, whose face is turned three-quarters toward the satyr dancing in front of him; the masked eyes of this satyr are apparently not directed toward any of the individuals in the action represented here.

Let us now consider the masks. If the positions they assume in relation to each other do not form a coherent system, their depiction nonetheless has a certain consistency. The actors' masks, such as that worn by Papposilenos, are painted in light colors (with a slight difference in shade between the masculine and feminine masks) and turned three-quarters toward the viewer; the masks worn by the chorus, in contrast, are shown in profile, full face, or even backward; their base color is red. This iconic distinction seems to coincide with the difference in status between the actors and the chorus members;[11] in the play

[11] About the interventions of the chorus in the recited parts of ancient drama through the mouth of the *koruphaios* alone, see Pickard-Cambridge 1968, 245ff. If one allows a division of the chorus into two groups, it is possible to imagine that the *khoreutai* wearing a short *khitōn* would direct one of them and the other would be led by the chorus member sitting on the extreme left of the upper section; the latter wears a phallic belt made of embroidered material rather than leather. This corresponds at least partially to the hypothesis advanced by Séchan [n. 5], 45ff., and by M. Bieber, *Die Denkmäler zum Theaterwesen im Altertum* (Berlin, 1920), 93, both of whom give the role

it is normal for Papposilenos to wear a mask that groups him with the actors, even though he belongs to the satyr chorus, since as chorus leader, he takes part in the (spoken) dialogue between the protagonists of the play.

Side B: Faces without Masks

Looked at from the point of view of people's gazes and where they are directed, the bacchanalian scene on side B offers the same sort of symmetry that we have found on side A. On the lower half, two couples each consisting of a satyr and a maenad surround a panther, whose head is disposed at a three-quarter angle, while the people are all shown in profile. Framing the two bacchantes, who are looking upward in an attitude of Dionysiac ecstasy, two satyrs are each looking at the maenad they are pursuing.

The couple Dionysus-Ariadne forms the center of the upper section of side B; the heroine gazes at her lover, while Dionysus, lyre in hand and head thrown back, displays a look of ecstasy, as does little Eros, who flits around behind the divine couple, accompanying them on his cymbals. Framing Ariadne and Dionysus are two satyrs; one of them, on the left, is pouring out a libation, while the other, on the right, is playing on his pipe. Their faces are turned to the left and right respectively, away from the scene. At the edges, plant shapes mark the boundaries of the action, also probably suggesting the environment of wild nature in which this Dionysiac scene takes place.

3. The Marks of the Enunciation

Where Greece is concerned, a study of iconographic enunciation seems all the more justified because in the signature conventions of painters, the vase appears to convey a subjective experience in the first person.[12] Let us briefly recall that the problem of the enunciation attempts to grasp the connection between the way in which a text is communicated (here I speak of the "referential," or communication,

---

of chorus leader to the chorus satyr dressed in the short *khitōn* and the role of one of the chorus leader's two *parastatai* to the lyre player; this interpretation means that the Papposilenos figure must be regarded as an actor and the feminine figure sitting on the *klinē* of Dionysus must be attributed a function other than that of actor (cf. n. 19 below).

[12]See M. Burzachechi, "Oggetti parlanti nelle epigrafi greche," *Epigraphica* 34 (1962): 3–54, and the more general study of F. Lissarrague, "Paroles d'images: Remarques sur le fonctionnement de l'écriture dans l'imagerie attique," *Ecritures* 2 (1985): 71–89.

level) and the linguistic expression, in the text, of this communication process (the level of the uttered enunciation, or the "enunciative") as well as the relations between the actants of this process and the protagonists of the story being told (the level of the narration/description, or the "enuncive"). Following Benveniste on this subject, we observe the indices in the narration or in the utterance that denote the level of the uttered enunciation, an expression in the discourse of the extra-discursive communication situation.[13]

But do painted figures offer the same enunciative possibilities as texts? Since the vase itself, in Greek imagery, often says *I*, we are justified, theoretically at least, in looking for iconographic traces of the communication relationship between enunciator (or Sender when it concerns the vase itself) and enunciatee (or Receiver); at the same time we shall examine the connection between the iconic manifestation of the communication relationship and the protagonists of the painted scene, that is, the various *hes* or *shes* of the story being told. As we pass from textual to iconic representation, obviously it will not be in the pronouns (the opposition of the *I/you* and the *he/she*) or the verb tenses or the deictics that we will find the indices of the creation of discourse. The undeniable autonomy of the iconic "language" leads to the hypothesis that it is what is expressed by the gazes and the gestures of the actors in the painted scene, as well as the way space is organized, that will reveal the different processes of shifting-in and shifting-out and thereby distinguish the various levels of the utterance and its enunciation.

Side A: "Ritual"

An enunciative examination of scene A of the Pronomos Crater immediately requires that an extra distinction be made in defining the narration (enuncive) level. Beginning with this enuncive level, according to the way they are grouped in space, the protagonists of scene A seem to exist on the same temporal and spatial plane. The interplay of their gazes, the iconic manifestation of the narrative *he/she*, confirms this impression by referring the figures depicted to one another. This phenomenon is particularly noticeable in the upper section: the eyes of the chorus satyrs are directed toward the two actors on either side of Dionysus and Ariadne; the female figure sitting on the *klinē* and associated with the two actors because of her costume is looking at the

---

[13]See above, Introduction § 1.

divinities, who in turn look at each other. And the symmetry in the lower section of the vase is as regularly imposed on the gazes as in the upper, uniting all the protagonists in the same narrative there and then.

So much for the iconic utterance in which the protagonists of scene A are engaged. But the masks they wear oblige us to distinguish, always on the same enuncive, or narrative, level, a second plane (also enuncive): the plane that defines the eye arrangement of these masks, which do indeed have eyes, contrary to what "realistic" representations of the ancient mask imply. Their position means these masks are "shifted-out" in relation to the narrated action on the vase. Carried in the hand of the actors and the chorus members, they are nevertheless *there*, but their position refers them to a different narrative *then*. There is one exception, however: the satyr dancing the *sikinnis*, facing the *khorodidaskalos*. While wearing the mask hides this individual's face, the absence of a dividing line between the mask and the rest of the body, as well as the dance he is performing, brings together the *then* of the painted scene (narrated action) and the *then* of the dramatic presentation; in this instance, the mask being worn identifies the actor, even if only partially, with the role he plays on the stage.[14] It is doubtless no accident that the chorus satyr, in whom the enuncive meeting (or shifting-in) of the plane of the action on the vase and the plane of the action in the play takes place, forms a pair with the *khorodidaskalos*, the only individual whose face is represented in three-quarter view. By setting the face at an angle, the painter probably wanted to distinguish the two enuncive planes while still having the protagonists look at each other, a disjunction that is also marked by the distance in space that divides them. While the members of the other pairs are on the same plane, facing each other in profile, the dancing satyr is placed explicitly in front of the *khorodidaskalos*, his left foot across the key-pattern border that serves as the ground and marks the limit of the plane. Thus the interplay of gazes between the face and the mask of the pair formed by the *khorodidaskalos* and the satyr dancing the *sikinnis* represents the iconic figurativization, in the semiotic sense of those two words, of the meeting, on the narrative level of the painted scene, of the two enuncive planes we have distinguished.

The subtlety of the painter's representation of faces and gazes invites us to go beyond the enuncive level. Of the pair of chorus satyrs

---

[14]Concerning the very partial nature of the identification of the actor with the characters he seems to portray on stage, see the remarks in Chapter 4, § 3.

forming the counterpart of the pair just described, one wears the only mask shown in the frontal position. One of the essential marks of the enunciative, rather than the enuncive, aspect of the action (even if the enunciative plane, as we have seen, is largely shifted out on the vase) is the possibility of facing the public, the enunciatee of the dramatic spectacle, and confronting it by means of the mask with the (mythological) reality that embodies its own strangeness. But the frontal mask is directed just as much toward the *you* enunciatee of the vase. So this mask recalls not only the enunciative level of the play, to which the iconic representation of the vase refers, but perhaps also the here and now of the communication between the enunciator of the vase and its enunciatee.

The enuncive and enunciative interpretation of the masks of the three actors and Papposilenos is a more delicate matter in that the three-quarter turn of their faces directs their gaze to an undefined exterior. This gaze, which is not empty in spite of what a "realistic" representation of the theater mask would indicate, can establish a relationship either with the enunciatee/receiver of the spectacle, toward whom the mask is directed, or with the "mythological reality" in which the actors are caught up as protagonists as soon as they put on the mask. In the first instance, the gaze would substantiate the enunciative relationship between the action on the stage and the receiver of the communication process of which it is the object; in the second, there would perhaps be a reference to the mythological reality shown on side B of the vase. For the moment, let us leave this question in abeyance.

Side B: "Myth"

The other side of the Pronomos Vase invites us to view the spectacle of the "mythological reality" depicted there. The two sides are explicitly linked, again, by way of the gaze. In scene B, while the faces of the protagonists in profile are all turned upward, signifying orgiastic possession, the left-hand satyr, as previously mentioned, is looking backward at scene A. Actually, only the traditionally separate treatment of the two scenes has managed to conceal the fact of their relatedness. In fact, the disposition of the three chorus members under each of the handles of the crater designates the edges of scene A as "spaces of passage" and leads us to read the two scenes in a continuous way.[15]

[15] See, for example, H. Metzger, *Les représentations dans la céramique attique du IVe siècle* (Paris, 1951), 115 and 118; the expression "spaces of passage" was coined by F. Lissarrague in a seminar held in Paris, EPHE, Vth section, in January 1992.

The narrative space is arranged so that the libation pouring from the cantharus of the satyr on the left in scene B falls exactly above the last chorus satyr in scene A; and the latter's mask is in turn directed toward scene B. Scene B is separated from scene A only by branches of myrtle, which contrast with the architectural or furniture shapes punctuating the space of scene A. Are we dealing with wild nature on one side and civilization on the other? I would say yes if the column and tripod in scene B did not remind us of culture by alluding to a religious event and if, moreover, the painter had not framed both scenes with satyrs, thus doubly connecting the two groups of figures depicted on the vase. Similar comments can be made about the costumes: if the absence of the phallic belt among the satyrs of scene B shows that we have left the level of stage reality, if the nudity of the followers of Dionysus reduces them to a state of wildness, the lyre the god holds in his hand still signals the presence of civilization in the midst of a bacchic revel. Thus, if scene B in general describes the mythological framework in which Dionysus moves, certain signs seem to connect this framework to the cult of which the god was the object.[16] But let us return to the eyes and recall the two other exceptions to the gaze of ecstatic possession in this scene: the pipe-playing satyr, whose posture reproduces that of the lyre player in scene A by conforming to the canonical way of representing pipe players, and the leopard, who gazes out from the scene and seems to stare at the receiver/enunciatee of the precious vase, offering another confrontation, this time of the enunciatee with the real otherness of the wild beast.

4. The Use of Proper Names

The early interpretation of scenes A and B quickly passed into canonical status: scene A shows preparations for the performance of a satyr play; scene B, a mythological scene. Ernst Buschor has been almost alone in objecting to this tradition; he has tried to show that

---

[16] See C. Bérard, "Le corps bestial (les métamorphoses de l'homme idéal au siècle de Périclès)," in *Le corps et ses fictions* (Paris, 1983), 43–54 (also published in *Etudes de Lettres* 6, no. 2 [1983]: 43–54); I do not think that one can go so far as to say that scene B depicts the action prepared in scene A: we are certainly dealing here with "mythology."

Concerning the tripod and the column as signs representing a sanctuary and placing scene B in a sanctuary of Dionysus, see H. Froning, *Dithyrambos und Vasenmalerei in Athen* (Würzburg, 1971), 14.

scene A, at least, depicts the actors of a tetralogy (and not just of a satyr play) being mounted for a Dionysiac festival in a sanctuary consecrated to the wine god.[17] Thus it is less the identity of the characters represented that is a problem than what they are doing. From an enunciative perspective, however, the definition of the one depends on the other.

Let us briefly identify the figures in scene A. Costumes, masks, musical instruments leave no doubt that they are actors: we are dealing with the protagonists in a satyr play. But no enunciative inquiry could pass over their names, especially since the painter carefully inscribed a proper name opposite most of them. The names of the chorus satyrs have been established as common names of Athenian citizens during the classical period: Eunikos, Dorotheos, Euagon, and Kallias appear on the upper section; Nikomakhos, Kharis, Nikoleos, Dion, Philinos, and an unnamed couple are depicted on the lower section. The lyre and pipe players have also been given current names of the era, names known mostly, like the previous ones, from the texts of Greek orators: they are called Pronomos and Kharinos. The name of the *khorodidas-kalos*, Demetrios, could be that of a playwright of the time, just as the name Pronomos was that of a famous lyre player of the end of the fifth century.[18] And as the chorus members are furnished with civic names, the gods have names current in the cult: Dionysus, Himeros, Herakles. No names, by contrast, are provided for either the woman facing Dionysus or the actors of the drama (a man, a woman, and the father of the satyrs).

Here again, the interpretation given at the end of the last century has entered the canon and is practically untouchable. The Phrygian bon-

[17] Buschor [n. 6], 141ff.; Buschor's interpretation was partially discussed by Froning [n. 16], 5ff. P. E. Arias, B. B. Shefton, and M. Hirmer, *A History of Greek Vase Painting* (London, 1962), 377ff., take up Buschor's idea of the tetralogy; there is an exhaustive bibliography in this work of the published studies concerning the Pronomos Vase (379ff.).

[18] Concerning Demetrios, author of comedies at the end of the fifth century, see Diogenes Laertius 5.85, and E. Kaibel, "Demetrios (74)," *Realenc. Alt.-Wiss.* 4 (Stuttgart, 1901): 2805–6; for the pipe player Pronomos, of whom even Alcibiades could have been a student, see Aristophanes, *Ecclesiazousae* 102, *Anthologia Palatina* 16, 28, Pausanias 4.27.7, and 9.12.5, with Buschor's commentary [n. 6], 144, and Pickard-Cambridge [Chap. 4, n. 6], 55.

In the dramatic performances of the Great Dionysia, chorus leader and *khoreutai* are always Athenian citizens; see Demosthenes, *Meidias* 56ff., and scholion to Aristophanes, *Plutus* 954, with the commentaries of P. Ghiron-Bistagne, *Recherches sur les acteurs dans la Grèce antique* (Paris, 1980), 100 n. 74, D. Lanza, "L'attore," in *Oralità scrittura spettacolo*, ed. M. Vegetti (Turin, 1983), 127–39, and Winkler [Chap. 4, n. 22].

nets on the masks of the actor and actress surrounding the divine couple caused them to be thought of as Laomedon and his daughter Hesione, the Trojan princess promised, then refused, to Herakles as the prize for killing the sea monster that was destroying the Troad.[19] But on the Andromeda Vase, for example, a vase dating back to approximately the same period as the Pronomos Vase, the heroine and her father, Kepheus, although both Ethiopian, also wear Phrygian bonnets.[20] Other identifications can be proposed for these nameless figures connected with Herakles: Iole, for instance, beloved of the deified hero, and her father, Eurytos, or her brother, Iphitos; or Deianeira and her father, Oineus—Deianeira being all the more likely to be sitting on Dionysus's bed since certain versions of the myth make her the daughter of the god and his protégée; unless, as has been recently suggested, it is Omphale and her father, Iardanos, king of Lydia, two characters who figured in the satyric plays of Achaeus and of Ion of Chios respectively.[21] The amorous relationships between either of these heroines and Herakles would be designated by the presence and stance of Himeros.

This subtle system of partial identification by proper names—chorus members, *khorodidaskalos*, pipe player, and lyre player named after citizens, actors costumed from head to foot but never named,

[19]This interpretation is taken from H. von Prott, "De Amphora Neapolitana Fabulae Satyricae apparatum scaenicum," in *Schedae philologicae H. Usener oblatae* (Bonn, 1891), 47–59.

Considering that women's roles were played by men on the Greek stage, some have seen in the feminine figure wearing the mask a representation of a Muse (see, e.g., Metzger [n. 15], 118; other references in Buschor [n. 6], 133) or even a maenad (see, e.g., A. D. Trendall and T. B. L. Webster, *Illustrations of Greek Drama* [London, 1971], 29).

In a combination of these two interpretations, the feminine figure sitting on the *klinē* of Dionysus has been thought to be Paideia: see Bieber, *The History of Greek and Roman Theater* (Princeton, 1961), 10, and Froning [n. 16], 10, as well as E. Simon, "Die 'Omphale' des Demetrios: Zur Satyrspielvase in Neapel," *Arch. Anz.* 86 (1971): 205.

[20]Capua Crater, Berlin inv. 3237, *ARV²* 1336, with *Paralip.* 480; see Pickard-Cambridge 1968, 199ff.

[21]For a possible relationship, at least in the iconography, between Iole and Dionysus, see H. von Geisau, "*Iole*," *Kl. Pauly*, vol. 2 (Munich, 1975), 1432–33. For the double paternity of Deianeira, see Apollodorus 1. 8. 1; see also Antoninus Liberalis 2. 7. The vine that separates Dionysus from the actor probably playing Oineus could be an allusion both to the latter's name and more particularly to the god's gift of the vine to the hero: Hyginus, *Fabulae* 129.

The identification with Omphale and Iardanos was suggested by Simon [n. 19], 199–206, though she recognizes that the presence of Dionysus in the Omphale legend is merely hypothetical.

gods designated by their divine functions, except for Herakles and Ariadne—stands in contrast to scene B where no names are used. We shall return to this subject.

5. The Iconic Enunciation of a Ritual Practice

But since we are discussing enunciation, what does the Pronomos Crater tell us? The whole spatial organization of the action represented on the vase brings together in one place, with the help of the gazes exchanged and the interplay of names, a series of planes, distinct as to the actors involved and as to the time period in which the latter exist.

The Planes of the Utterance and Their Enunciation

First let us consider the enuncive level of the narration. Our analysis of the gazes led to a differentiation on side A between the action represented by the painter (narrated action) and the dramatic action in a shifted-out situation. An examination of the proper names given to the protagonists in the scene leads to further distinctions within the first plane, that of the action as recounted by the painter. Each of these distinctions, made according to the naming system in the picture, is confirmed by the way the protagonists are organized in space.

The names of divinities include Dionysus, with Ariadne, and Himeros, in a sequence limited in space by the *klinē*. These three protagonists define what one might call the "divine reality" order.

But the *klinē* also brings into the group the three actors surrounding it: the young woman with the mask, because she is sitting on the end of it and because Himeros is looking at her; the male actor, because he is next to Dionysus; and, above all, Herakles, who is decked out, like Dionysus and Himeros, in his divine trappings. The identity that these three protagonists assume in the dramatic action is, as I have said, shifted out, since they are not wearing their masks; but we have also seen that these actors are not given the civic identity that a citizen's family name would confer on them. The ambiguous position of the actors in the painting's second sequence is made more emphatic by two remarkable facts: first, if the female figure sitting on Dionysus's *klinē* were depicted in her function as an actor, she would have the features of a man; second, the faces of the three figures, as the painter painted them, bear a marked resemblance to the masks they carry in their hands.[22] The spatial arrangement of the three actors in particular can therefore be said to include them in the "divine reality" sequence defined by Dionysus, Ariadne, and Himeros; however, even if their masks are shifted out in relation to the narrated action, their faces and their costumes connect them with the dramatic action.

In relation to the first two sequences that make up the plane of the narrated action, the chorus satyrs form a third sequence; in it they assume a position no less ambiguous but different from that occupied by the triad of actors. As is the case with the latter, an exchange of gazes links the four chorus members of the upper section with those in the lower section beneath the divine couple; so they are also included in the order of reality surrounding the gods. They carry with them, however, not their (partial) stage identities, but the social identities conferred on them by the mention of their respective proper names. But, if carrying their masks in their hands also disengages them in relation to the dramatic action, the phallic belts they wear immediately associate them with their stage identity. Moreover, some of the chorus satyrs carry their masks in such a way as to be face to face with them: here there is a sort of imaging of the meeting of the action narrated by the vase, where the chorus members appear in their social identities, and the dramatic action, in which they assume their stage identities.

Note that Papposilenos, purposely omitted until now, occupies an intermediary position between the chorus satyrs of the painting's third narrative sequence, represented in their social identities, and the three actors of the second sequence, depicted in their stage identities: like the two chorus members who are his symmetrical counterparts Papposilenos seems to be face to face with his mask, but like the actors, he is represented almost entirely in his stage identity. This intermediary situation between chorus and actors corresponds exactly to Papposilenos's role as *koruphaios*, or chorus leader.

The others—the *khorodidaskalos*, the pipe player, and the lyre player—make up a fourth sequence. Their position in the center also links them with "divine reality." Although Demetrios is included in this space and time framework, he serves, with his three-quarter profile, as the point of contact between the narrated action and the dramatic action represented by the satyr dancing the *sikinnis* right in front of

---

[22] In Greek drama, the parts were always played by men; for this reason several interpreters have wanted to see in the feminine figure a representation of the Muse or of Paideia rather than an actor: see n. 19 above. For the facial characteristics of the three actors and their influence on the actors' stage identity, see Shefton [n. 17], 378, and Buschor [n. 6], 133.

him. And once again, it is not by chance that the function of joining the two planes of the enuncive level falls on the one who, as author and choreographer of the chorus, is the principal enunciator of the dramatic action. In addition, if the three protagonists of the fourth sequence appear under their social and civic identities, their physical representation is nevertheless idealized; the stage costume worn by Pronomos and the nudity of the two other place them, pipe player, *khorodidaskalos*, and lyre player alike, in the sphere of "divine reality."

But the position of Demetrios and the *sikinnis* dancer is not the only point of contact between narrated action and shifted-out dramatic action. Some interpreters of the vase have pointed out correctly that Dionysus wears not only a costume that associates him with the stage identity of the actors but also the same buskins as the latter. Thus, while the interplay of gazes connects Dionysus with the actors on the level of the narrated action, his costume connects him with them on that of the dramatic action. And the actors who make up the second sequence are not the only ones involved; in the same way, the phallic belts worn by the actors and the costume worn by Pronomos link the protagonists of the third and fourth sequences with the god, again on the plane of the dramatic action.

To sum up, the organization of space, the interchange of gazes, and the fact that the protagonists are named on side A of the Pronomos Vase mark out a double plane where the enuncive level is concerned. The plane of the narrated action and that of the dramatic action are both dominated by the painting's divine figures; but whereas the latter is (partially) shifted out in comparison with the former, the protagonists of the scene, according to the individual characteristics conferred on them, determine different modalities among the possibilities for exchange and overlapping which exist between the two levels in spite of everything. The circular route by which the costume of the lyre player Pronomos brings us back to the deity (with its double engagement in the action narrated by the vase and in the dramatic action evoked) seems to find its parallel in the circularity of the scene itself: the spatial arrangement of its protagonists probably denotes less the two linear bands placed one above the other that we referred to for descriptive convenience than a circular organization, perhaps recalling that of the Dionysiac *thiasos*.

As regards the enunciative level, we must acknowledge that its organization is much more difficult to discern but no less complex. We have seen how the frontal representation of the mask found more or less in the center of scene A could refer to both the enunciation process of the dramatic action (confrontation with the public of the satyr play) and the enunciation of the vase itself in its relation to its enunciatee, be the latter its receiver in the classical period or we ourselves. This same enunciation process is perhaps also evident in the three-quarter-profile masks carried by the actors, unless they relate to the scene painted on side B!

It is therefore essentially in the masks that the enunciative level is actualized, particularly in the mask worn by the chorus satyr at the center on side A. And it is by virtue of the dramatic action that this mask links the narrated action in scene A with the communication situation in which the receiver of the image is positioned. At the moment when the vase was crafted, this here and now of the communication corresponded to the same social reality as that in which the chorus satyrs were included by virtue of the proper names they bear.

As a result, scene A contains two utterances (the narrated action and the dramatic action) within which the enunciative marks (facial direction and proper names) refer back to a double "referential" communication situation: one communicates to the receiver of the vase the narrated action in which the chorus satyrs appear with their civic identities (resulting in the here and now of the communication coinciding with the there and then of the narration); the other connects the same receiver—the potential theater audience—with the dramatic action, the protagonists of which are shown partially disengaged. We should not, of course, forget that when the historical distance is placed in abeyance, it is we ourselves who are the receivers.

Ritual and Myth?

How, then, should we define the narrative plane where the gods are, which, enunciatively speaking, is linked to the social identity of some of its protagonists? The ivy wreath worn by most of the chorus members and their "trainers," as well as their individual association with the two divinities according to their positions and costumes, seems to suggest that the action depicted on side A of the vase represents a cult and therefore falls under the modern category of ritual.[23] It is not impossible that the ritual took place in the theater itself, as is

---

[23] For the iconic description of the ivy wreath and the role it plays in the Dionysiac cult, see M. Blech, *Studien zum Kranz bei den Griechen* (Berlin, 1982), 54ff., 192, and 206ff.

perhaps suggested by the block of stone on the left, which might be taken for the *thumelē* (or the *bēma*) in the center of the orchestra, and by the steps on the right, which might suggest the stairway leading to the *proskēnion*.[24] The tripods hung with garlands framing the scene could represent the celebration of victory at the end of the tragic *agōn* of the Great Festival of Dionysus, as could the pouring or consumption of wine suggested by the cantharus worn by the satyr linking scene A to scene B: alas, we know very little about this ritual celebration.[25] But the absence of any allusion to a particular ritual and the relaxed attitude of most of the protagonists suggest that the rite in question here incorporates the actors and the chorus members into the divine sphere in a general and symbolic manner.

Scene B, closely linked to scene A, as we have noted by virtue of the organization of its space and utterance, allows the plane of the so-called myth to include the gods present in the ritual (narrated action), their servants arrayed in the same circle and, most probably (by way of the *sikinnis* dancer's gaze "into the distance" or the mask worn by the chorus member on the far right of scene A), the dramatic action that brought about the victory. In addition, if scene B seems to be organized in the same circular fashion as scene A, with Dionysus and Ariadne occupying a central position, there is a general movement of the whole to the right, toward the sanctuary suggested by the column and the tripod at the edge of the picture. Everything takes place, therefore, as if the actors in the mythological scene carried with them, in a movement both circular yet directed, the actors of the ritual scene toward the reality of the Dionysiac sphere.

[24] The *thumelē* in the center of the orchestra could be, according to Pollux, *Lexicon* 4, 123 (see also *Etymologicum Magnum* 458, 30ff. Gaisford), either a podium (*bēma*, for the actor speaking with the chorus?) or an altar: see W. Dörpfeld and E. Reisch, *Das Griechische Theater* (Athens, 1896), 33ff. and 177ff.; concerning the steps between the orchestra and the *proskēnion*, see Pollux, *Lexicon* 4, 127, with the commentary of P. Arnott, *Greek Scenic Conventions in the Fifth Century b.c.* (Oxford, 1962), 15ff. and 25; Arnott refers particularly to the *Ichneutai*, a satyr play by Sophocles.

Another possibility is a place near the theater, somewhere on the Tripods Way: see Travlos 1971, 537ff. and 567ff.

[25] See Pickard-Cambridge 1968, 77ff. (for the celebration of the victory won in the same festival but in the dithyramb competition), and H. Blume, *Einführung in das antike Theaterwesen* (Darmstadt, 1978), 17ff.; Blume (97 n. 308) proposes again on his own account the interpretation of scene A as a rehearsal of a satyr play!

Blech [n. 23], 311, regards the wreaths that crown those in scene A as cult wreaths. For Froning (n. 16], 13, the place in which the action takes place corresponds to the sanctuary of Dionysus Eleuthereus, whence led the road bordered with tripods dedicated after the various victories in the dithyramb competitions.

This reference in the ritual utterance to the mythological utterance conforms very well to the Greek idea of a ritual with respect to which the story of the myth represents the manipulation phase, if not the sanction phase (to borrow some of the concepts of semiolinguistics):[26] it is not enough that the gods are present in the action of the ritual; the action of the (mythological) story in which they are involved is narratively integrated into that of the ritual (which is therefore not a simple repetition by *mimēsis* of the myth). And that is not all: the Pronomos Vase shows how the Dionysiac framework not only turns a ritual action, in which the protagonists have their identities as citizens, into a divine action (the norm in Greek culture) but also represents the action of the gods (on the stage); it then connects this action, by means of the ritual following the dramatic performance, to the reality of the cult and of the divinity to which it belongs.

Hence the ambiguous position of the protagonists in the picture: they are represented as much by their function as actors and by the mythological characters of their stage roles as by their social identities and their roles as performers of a ritual in honor of Dionysus; this is why the god is present twice, once on side A, as recipient of the honors about to be conferred on him by his servants (represented in their double identities), and once on side B, in his mythological and cult context. It is thus that the god, or more precisely the divine couple, becomes the focal point of the narrated (ritual) action and of the dramatic action represented on scene A (as well as of the "mythic" scene represented on side B. This superimposing of actions and actorial roles in the same fresco can only be understood in its complexity and subtlety, as some interpreters have sensed, by an enunciative analysis.[27]

It is obviously the mask, by contrast, that causes the reversal of the mythological action so that it passes as dramatic action in the presence of a public ensconced in its social context before being reintegrated by the practice of the ritual into the "divine reality" to which it belongs. We know that this privilege of reversal and reintegration is reserved for

[26] Concerning the manipulation and sanction phases in semiolinguistics, see Greimas and Courtés 1979, 220ff., 244ff., and 320; for a preliminary approach to the problem of the relation between "myth" and "ritual" in this sense, see the remarks in Chapter 8, §§ 1 and 6, and in Calame 1990, 165ff.

[27] The dramatic and ritualistic (therefore divine) reference in scene A has been approached by Buschor [n. 6], 141ff., Simon [n. 19], 200ff., and F. Brommer, "Zur Deutung der Pronomosvase," *Arch. Anz.* 79 (1964): 109–14.

the god of "otherness" and of the exterior [28] From an iconic point of view, this reversal followed by reestablishment can only work when the masks are used as intermediaries between the plane of "mythic" or divine action, that of dramatic action, that of ritual action, and the receiver (or the enunciatee) of the vase with its painted figures.

But what this vase also shows us is some of the features that constitute the special character of iconic language as opposed to natural language. Recognizing these features should preserve the analysis of the image from the hegemony of the model offered by the written text, without denying the value of the linguistic tool. The painter can incorporate the levels of ritual and myth, distinct in both time and quality, on the same spatial plane by virtue of the coincidences I have tried to describe. We thus arrive at a representation that brings together the various narrative levels and planes which, in the text, have a tendency to be reduced to a simple dichotomy: dispersed in the picture on several planes at once distinct and superimposed, the categories of myth and ritual risk exposure to questions regarding their relevance. Yet, in substituting facial direction for a system of pronouns, the relationships between the different *he/she*s of the story's protagonists become apparent in all the subtlety implied by the various enuncive planes on which the protagonists perform; in addition, by means of the gaze, the enunciation process becomes a direct confrontation with the receiver/enunciatee of the image.

But in a study intended to be enunciatory, little has been said of the iconic equivalent of the *I*, an *I* that must be recognized in the full-face mask present on side A and if not in the three-quarter masks of the actors that seem to refer to side B, at least in the eyes of the leopard at the center of scene B. This *I* would correspond, I repeat, to the vase itself, a vase that expresses itself in the first person when endowed with a signature, in a first person which naturally subsumes its maker and the person who dedicates it. So the Pronomos Vase addresses itself to its receiver by way of a Dionysiac exterior embodied in the full-face stare of the satyr's mask and the leopard. But the *you* replying to this *I* does not belong only to the enunciatees of the vase, the citizens of

[28] Cf. F. Frontisi-Ducroux and J.-P. Vernant, "Figures du masque en Grèce ancienne," *Journ. de Psych. Norm. et Pathol.* 80 (1983): 53–69 (reprinted in Vernant and Vidal-Naquet 1986, 25–43), and Chapter 4 of this volume.

fifth-century Athens and ourselves, thanks to the fact that the object has survived for us; he addresses himself also to the god Dionysus, who is probably the one to whom the vase was dedicated. In this way, if the three-quarter faces of the masks worn by the actors of scene A seem turned toward the Dionysus of scene B on the narrative (enuncive) plane, the full-view faces would be addressed to him on the enunciative plane in the reality created by the cult and the dedicatory practices of classical Athens. In this enunciative complexity, the scenes represented form the content of the communication that the vase sets up between artist, dedicator of the vase, receiving god, Athenian audience, and finally ourselves. The iconic representation allows the narrative *then* and the *now* of the consecration ritual to coincide. Probably dedicated to Dionysus on the occasion of a victory at the Great Festival of Dionysus, the Pronomos Crater would itself finally be transformed into a ritual object.[29]

With these concluding remarks, we should realize that we enter the realm of conjecture. The analysis requires us to take three directions. To begin with, we should be aware of the various inconsistencies in the picture, such as the absence of a name or a crown for two of the chorus satyrs; is this mere accident? We should fill out the enunciative analysis by studying other iconic systems of deictics, such as gestures. Only a comparative analysis would allow us to see the hypothetical character of the ideas advanced here concerning the enunciation process of the Pronomos Vase. For the moment, we shall simply acknowledge the fecundity of the enunciative approach in analyzing the narrative complexity of the crater, while understanding that the conceptual tool used to study textual evidence, one that has undergone modification during the course of the analysis, must be still further refined. When Dionysus enunciates himself, does he not, in so doing, refer us back to ourselves?

[29] The Naples vase as a probable ritual object dedicated to Dionysus (by Pronomos?) has been addressed especially by H. Bulle, "Weihbild eines tragischen Dichters," in *Corolla Ludwig Curtius* (Stuttgart, 1937), 151–60; see also von Prott [n. 19] and Brommer [n. 27], 114.

REPRESENTATIONS

CHAPTER 6

Myth and Tale: The Legend of the Cyclops and Its Narrative Transformations

1. From Homer to European Folklore

One of the basic problems in an analysis of folklore narrative is the many variants popular stories tend to have. A story may undergo so many transformations that it will change into a completely different story; it could become what common lore calls a myth or, alternatively, a tale.

With this in mind, the analysis that follows has four goals: The first is a comparative examination of narrative in seven European and non-European stories that, on first reading, sound very much like the Homeric story of the adventures of Odysseus with Polyphemus, or the Cyclops; this analysis will give us a definition of the distinctive features that make these stories similar or dissimilar on the narrative plane. A model of the narrative structure common to the whole group will then be constructed. Such a model will allow us to define, beyond individual variations, a provisional narrative category to be called the *Cyclops story.*

In addition to this common structure, my study will attempt to uncover the mechanisms that allow the story to "vary" and perhaps even to move from one narrative category to another.

Probably because the semiotics of narrative is comparatively new, its theories have not always been subject to experimental verification. Therefore, any attempt at using one of these theories without a good look at its value as a tool would be vain. The third aim of this study, then, is to test the usefulness of the model of narrative analysis borrowed from Greimas.

The fourth objective is to compare the stories under analysis with the Homeric story already studied in two previous articles[1] and to see whether my borrowed theoretical model, which in principle explains the syntax of the story, will be sufficient to define the specificity of the tales in question. My goal is thus to determine in what way the syntax and the semantics of the narrative are connected with each other.

2. Historical Perspectives

To say that the Polyphemus story as told in the *Odyssey* is related to various European and non-European tales is to say nothing new or original. As early as 1857, Wilhelm Grimm thought he had found in one of these stories, in which the sequence of events closely follows that of the Cyclops episode, "die ursprüngliche Auffassung," the original of the Homeric story.[2] In spite of a very modern awareness of how a story varies according to its cultural context, Grimm conformed to the analytic theory in vogue at the time, which declared that to explain the reality being analyzed, it was necessary to return to its primitive state, that is, to its simplest state; we are here at the height of "Indo-European historicism."

Fifty years later, Oskar Hackman, who had the merit of putting together a body of 221 variants of the Polyphemus episode, was concerned with the very same things. To the historicist perspective he adds a geographical approach: to compare the different versions of the Polyphemus story, versions raised to the status of variants, is not only to reconstruct the "Grundform" of the original story but also to trace the stages of its successive transformations.[3]

In spite of these assumptions, Hackman's analysis is not lacking in interest for us. Whatever the objective, a comparative approach forces the analyst to define a limited number of narrative categories in order

[1] C. Calame, "Mythe grec et structures narratives: Le mythe des Cyclopes dans l'*Odyssée*," in *Il mito greco, Atti del convegno internazionale* (*Urbino 7–12 maggio 1973*), ed. B. Gentili and G. Paioni (Rome, 1977), 369–92, and "L'univers cyclopéen de l'*Odyssée* entre le carré et l'hexagone logiques," *Živa Antika* 27 (1977): 315–22.

[2] W. Grimm, "Die Sage von Polyphem," *Abhdl. kgl. Akad. zu Berlin, Phil.-Hist. Klasse* (1857): 24ff., reprinted in *Kleinere Schriften*, vol. 4 (Gütersloh, 1887), 428–62.

[3] O. Hackman, *Die Polyphemsage in der Volksüberlieferung* (Helsingfors, 1904), 6; Hackman, 2ff., summarizes the theses of the scholars who studied the same subject before him. Note, in addition, that the Homeric story has been examined with specific regard to its "original" form: see, e.g., D. Muelder, "Das Kyklopengedicht der Odyssee," *Hermes* 38 (1903): 414–55, which reconstructs, by omitting "superfluous" pas-

to reduce the differences in the stories to entities that can be compared with one another.[4] Hackman points out that the stories in his corpus pit a rough and brutal giant, usually cannibalistic, against a weaker but more intelligent human being; and when he states that these "characters" can take on various forms according to the story in which they appear (dragon, devil, or werewolf for the giant; warrior, traveler, or shepherd for the hero), he is not so far from Greimas's idea of the actor, a narrative entity at the crossroads of the tale's actantial structure and its figurative and semantic realization.[5]

In conjunction with the dichotomy established between categories of "characters," Hackman distinguishes an action and divides it into various "episodes," of which there are three: (1) the blinding of the giant; (2) the flight of the hero under the belly of a ram; (3) the episode of the ring. These episodes can also take different forms. Episode 1 can take place without the giant's consent when the hero offers to improve the giant's eyesight but deceives him. The second episode has two variations: the hero hides under a ram to escape the giant or covers himself in a sheepskin for the same purpose. In addition to these three basic events, there is sometimes a fourth corresponding to the episode in the *Odyssey* of the false name the hero gives the giant in order to deceive him.

So, even if this utterance of the action "episodes" calls on elements foreign to a syntax, Hackman's analysis contains the preliminary steps toward a vocabulary and grammar of the Polyphemus narrative. And Hackman's formulation is certainly more acceptable than that of his critic Arnold Van Gennep, who merges the different elements into a single list of eight "themes" taken from the *Odyssey*:

1. the Cyclops
2. the cannibal monster
3. getting drunk
4. the false name
5. the stratagem (ram)
6. the Cyclops's speech to the ram

sages, the "ancient poem" of the Polyphemus episode. For the variants added to Hackman's corpus by other scholars, see the bibliographical reference given by K. Meuli, *Odyssee und Argonautika: Untersuchungen zur griechischen Sagengeschichte und zum Epos* (Berlin, 1921), 66 n. 3, and by W. Burkert, *Structure and History in Greek Mythology and Ritual* (Berkeley, 1979), 156 n. 13.

[4] Hackman [n. 3], 157ff.

[5] A. J. Greimas, "Les actants, les acteurs, et les figures," in *Sémiotique narrative et textuelle*, ed. C. Chabrol (Paris, 1973), 161–76, reprinted in Greimas 1983, 49–66 (citations following this work).

7. the hurling of boulders
8. the Cyclops's curses[6]

Not only does Van Gennep take the Homeric version of the Cyclops episode as the version of reference, but he also introduces the worst possible confusion between elements arising from the action and from its syntagmatic development, and elements referring to the qualities of the actors.

In spite of the nuances introduced by Hackman into his four-episodes formula, with options for two of the episodes and the possibility of the fourth not existing, we nonetheless have to acknowledge that not all the stories of the corpus fit into the structure. Using the historical and geographic approach, the analyst finds more and more opportunities for speculation as he searches for the "volkstümliche Grundform," the "popular primitive form" of a tale that has undergone various metamorphoses owing to the tradition of adding and subtracting. In Hackman's scheme of things, the story of the *Odyssey* is reduced to a supposedly original form that included only the first two episodes (the blinding of the giant without his consent and the flight of the hero under the belly of a ram), with the addition of the episode of the false name; the magic ring episode, in which the blinded Cyclops gives a ring to the hero to try and trick him into staying and in which the hero must cut off his ring finger in order to get free, could also be part of the primitive form, but is supposedly skipped in the Homeric version.[7] According to Hackman, the tale underwent the different changes to which its many versions are witness in a journey in time and space that brought it to northern Europe via Asia Minor or Greece.[8] We should note that Hackman's conclusions are based on either statistical criteria or criteria evincing a very vague notion of

[6] A. Van Gennep, "La légende de Polyphème," in *Religions, moeurs, et légendes: Essais d'ethnographie et de linguistique, 1re série* (Paris, 1908): 155–64. G. Germain, in *Genèse de l'Odyssée: Le fantastique et le sacré* (Paris, 1954), 77, also divides the story into several sections, which he calls "elements of the theme"; they are (1) the place, (2) the arrival of the victims, (3) the ogre's meal, (4) the blinded eye, (5) the escape. His study of the Cyclops legend, which Van Gennep reduces to a ritual (a cult of the ram!), still takes a historical and geographic approach: the Polyphemus episode, which he enriches with four Berber tales (5ff.), supposedly originated in Egypt and North Africa. The analysis of the legend in twenty-four parts by J. Glenn, "The Polyphemus Folktale and Homer's *Kyklopeia*," *Trans. Am. Philol. Assoc.* 102 (1971): 133–81, is certainly more subtle but just as heterogeneous.

[7] Hackman [n. 3], 220ff.

[8] For other speculations regarding the transmission of the Cyclops legend, see Van Gennep [n. 6], 162ff., and Germain [n. 6], 121f.

narrative probability,[9] while historical considerations springing from the dating of the versions involved—a very difficult task, to be sure—play a paradoxically minor role in Hackman's analysis.

The difficulties that Hackman encountered in defining the "original version" of the Cyclops story no doubt derive primarily from the total lack of explanation for the criteria used to limit what went into the corpus. The 221 variants seem to have been selected on the basis of a general and imprecise test of similarity with the Homeric tale. In dividing the corpus into three groups, Hackman realized that his group B contained fifty variants that had nothing in common with the other variants except for the false name episode (generally *Myself* rather than *Nobody*). After isolating this group, it was easy to conclude that the *Odyssey* took the episode of the false name from the primitive form of these stories, stories that otherwise have no connection to the Cyclops legend.[10] If we also say, however, that the same episode is combined with episodes specific to the Cyclops story in forty-seven variants coming from Finland and neighboring areas, why should the contrary not be true?[11] Why would it not be the variants of group B that had borrowed this episode from the versions of the Cyclops story in which it is used?

Without being able to cite dates of versions that, for the most part, go back to an oral tradition, the question of the influence of one type of story on another, and the direction of this influence, is really irrelevant.

3. Neither Myth nor Legend nor Tale

It is vain to seek to reconstitute the original story of the Polyphemus episode, which in any case dates from the eighth century B.C., by basing it on stories that date back no further than the twelfth century A.D.[12] It seems judicious, however, to compare some of the more

---

[9] Hackman [n. 3], 203, explains the passage from variant "alpha" of the second episode to variant "beta" by evoking the fact that the ram used by the hero to escape the giant shrinks in size: when the ram is not big enough for the hero to cling to with any degree of probability, the version of the hero disguised as a sheep is invented!

[10] Hackman [n. 3], 203.

[11] The possibility of the false name episode being borrowed by the stories in group B from one of the versions relating to the Polyphemus legend could be resoundingly confirmed owing to the fact that Hackman [n. 3], 199f., acknowledges the existence of several tales related to group B that do not include the false name episode.

[12] The oldest version in Hackman's corpus, taken from the *Dolopathos sive de Rege et Septem Sapientibus*, was written down at the Abbaye de Haute-Seille in Lorraine shortly

characteristic variants of the Cyclops story with one another in order to define the specific traits of the Cyclops episode and thus achieve what this study set out to do.

We shall deliberately ignore the problems associated with limiting the corpus to those stories that could be possible variants of the Cyclops "legend." Not only would a new analysis of a corpus similar to Hackman's take more than a chapter, but some of the stories gathered by Hackman are so different from one another that any attempt to put a limit on the corpus would be sure to fail. As Lévi-Strauss has made clear, oral stories can cross the traditional boundaries between tale, legend, and myth and change into one another in accordance with certain rules of transformation affecting syntax as well as semantics; every story refers to other stories and ideally to the whole collection of possible narratives.[13] That is why I have chosen to use here the more neutral concept of the Cyclops story.

Seven texts from Hackman's collection will be analyzed. Their choice was determined by their wide range both geographically (from Italy to Lapland by way of Arabia and the Caucasus) and temporally (from the thirteenth century to the end of the nineteenth). I have also chosen stories in the more modest collection of about thirty versions of the Cyclops story offered by James Frazer, who often quotes Hackman's stories only in a brief summary.[14] My study will be strictly synchronic, although I am aware that the changes the story undergoes occur on a diachronic axis. But my approach denies any particular orientation in this sequence of variations.

4. Problems of Method

Narrative Syntax

In my effort to define the respective characteristics of the stories chosen by means of a contrastive and therefore comparative study, I

---

after 1184 (see Hackman [n. 3], 26). It would be meaningless to try to criticize the comparative analysis of the Odyssean episode proposed by D. Page, *The Homeric Odyssey* (Oxford, 1955), v ff., by replying that this episode could not be anything but the result of an entirely Greek tradition, as does J. N. O'Sullivan, "Observations on the Kyklōpeia," *Symb. Osl.* 62 (1987): 5–24.

[13] See, for example, C. Lévi-Strauss, *Mythologiques*, vol. 4, *L'homme nu* (Paris, 1971), 603f., and *Anthropologie structurale*, vol. 2 (Paris, 1973), 152ff. and 301ff., with the remarks of D. Sperber, "Le structuralisme en anthropologie," in O. Ducrot et al., *Qu'est-ce que le structuralisme?* (Paris, 1968), 203ff.

[14] J. G. Frazer, *Apollodorus*, vol. 2 (London, 1921), 404ff.; I will cite each story by its number in Frazer (F), followed by Hackman's number (H).

have recurred to a tool of analysis almost identical with the one I used to examine the story of Odysseus in the essay cited in note 1. In that study, devoted to the Homeric episode of Polyphemus, it was basically a matter of showing the processes in a specific story whereby a taxonomic structure of semantic values turns into narrative; it was thus a question of descending from the discursive and linguistic levels to the deep structures of the semantic microuniverse underlying the story. In the present case, a similar type of analysis should show which syntactical factors or, conversely, figurative elements of the story constitute, on the intermediary semionarrative levels, the distinctive features of the variants chosen.

To this end I will operate on the intermediary level of the "semionarrative grammar"; I will use the syntactical rules of circulation/ communication in the narrative of objects of value defined by Greimas, as I did in my earlier analysis of the Homeric story, and I will extend them to cover the statements of the narrative model established by the same author some years previously.[15] Thus I am obliged to burden my reader with a few technical remarks.

In the formal description of narrative syntax that I will be using, a *modal statement of will*, or MS(w) (*énoncé modal du vouloir*) will be transcribed not by the formula 'MS(w) = F: will / S; O /', but by 'MS(w) = S n P: will (S > (S n P))'. This sequence of symbols indicates the conjunction of a narrative Subject with a Predicate corresponding to the will of the Subject that links the Subject with a new Predicate. In this formula, not only is the notion of a narrative Predicate substituted for that of an Object, as I proposed in this volume's introduction, but the modality (in this case, the will) is marked by a preliminary conjunction of a Subject with a Predicate. Within the "canonical scheme of narration" articulated by Greimas and others, the modal statement above corresponds to the constitution of the *manipulation* phase and to that of the *competence* of the semionarrative Subject. There follows a series of narrative statements called the *ordeal* and the *counterordeal*: they correspond to the confrontation between the two actantial Subjects of the narrative (S_1, the Subject, and S_2, the Antisubject), and this phase coincides with the narrative *performance*. Finally, the attributive statement (which entails the attribution of a Predicate, coinciding with an object of value, to the Subject of the narrative) represents the

[15] See A. J. Greimas, "Eléments d'une grammaire narrative," *L'homme* 9, no. 3 (1969): 71–92, reprinted in Greimas 1970, 157–83 (I quote from this work), and "Un problème de sémiotique narrative: Les objets de valeur," *Langages* 31 (1973): 13–35, reprinted in Greimas 1983, 19–48 (subsequent quotations from this work).

conclusive moment of the narrative, which is canonically understood as the phase of the *sanction*. It should be clear that, at the level of semionarrative grammar, the positions distinguished here by capital letters are *actants*; thus they have to be considered as syntactical narrative positions that can assume various values on the semantic level, as do the different phases of the scheme of the narration. So the position of the actantial Subject can be occupied in the narration by different actors.[16]

The breakdown of the seven Cyclops stories into narrative utterances can be found in Table 1.

The Semantics of the Narrative

Before performing comparative syntactical analysis of the seven Cyclops stories, we must first examine the qualities invested in each of their actants.

Beginning with S_1, we note that this designation generally corresponds to several actors: a Florentine traveler, a priest, and an artisan in the Pisan story (8F), four hunters in the Lappish story (12F), a young Christian helped by his sister and mother in the story from Gascony (21F), and so on. These actors take on different actantial roles in the course of the story; but, as in the *Odyssey*, the qualities they embody are hierarchically subordinate to those of the principal protagonist, the hero, who takes on most of the actions that fall to S_1 (Subject). In terms of semantics, the hero and his aides always come from the social world in which the story is produced; they are therefore usually the bearers of the same cultural values as those subscribed to by the receivers of the story. It is quite different for S_2, the Antisubject. The qualities invested in this actant are generally those of large size, brutality, physical abnormality (a single eye), and savagery (living in a cave). But S_2 sometimes also has attributes desired by S_1, even though they are supernatural: a large quantity of gold and silver (12F), the golden horns of the giant's rams (21F), a beautiful palace (30F). The aides of S_2 only play a minor part and have qualities similar to those of the principal character.

In the attribution of semantic qualities to S_2, the description of the milieu within which he acts is included; it is always a region at a

[16] For the definition of the terms *actant* and *actor*, see Greimas 1983, 49f.; as far as the substitution of the notion of Predicate for that of Object is concerned, see the references quoted above, Introduction, n. 23. For the canonical scheme of the narration, see Greimas and Courtés 1979, 244ff., as well as Adam 1985, 76ff., and 1991, 65ff.

distance from the civilized world, a place deep in the forest (8F) or lost among the mountains or on a distant island (12F, 21F, and 33F). Like the giant who inhabits it, this region can be given a positive value and may resemble a land of milk and honey (as in the river of honey in the Caucasian tale [33F]). It is the story from Gascony (21F) that goes furthest in linking narrative settings to the characters of their inhabitants; the black and savage region surrounded by huge mountains, with neither church nor priest, inhabited by the Cyclops, is diametrically opposed to the world of the hero, which is poor but civilized and Christian.

Into this homogeneous semantic picture, a note of discord enters with the Estonian tale (11F): S_2 is here not a one-eyed giant but the devil, and the confrontation of the hero (a farmhand) with the devil happens not in the devil's land but in the socialized world of the hero. I shall return to this semantic and topological difference after having examined the syntactical structure of the story.

Comparative Analysis of the Syntax: The Nuclear Structure

A syntactical investigation leads us to modify to a large extent the analogies that our preliminary semantic examination has appeared to establish, with one exception, between the seven stories.

What could be called the syntactical heart of the Cyclops story, the basic structure of the transfer of Predicates coinciding with objects of value between S_1 and S_2 in the *performance*, is practically identical in all seven stories. S_2 deprives S_1 of one of his companions by eating him, and in response to this act of cannibalism, S_1 deprives S_2 of one of his possessions: sight. Since the Subject of the narrative action (*faire*) is the same as the Subject conjoined with the transferred object of value, the transfer operates (using Greimas's terms) in the appropriation/dispossession mode; it follows the narrative program of the ordeal.[17] The ordeal of S_1 corresponds symmetrically to that of S_2; there is no reciprocal gift but, rather, a reciprocal ordeal (or an ordeal and a counterordeal); S_2's initial appropriation provokes the virtualization of S_1 and, consequently, a situation of "lack," as described by Vladimir J. Propp.[18] To this situation S_1 responds by another appropriation, one that virtualizes S_2; the virtualization of S_2 as the Subject of the narrative action indicates that the story is not yet at an end.

[17] Cf. Greimas 1983, 36ff.
[18] V. J. Propp, *Morphologie du conte* (Paris, 1970; original edition: Leningrad, 1928), 59f. and 157ff.

Table 1. Narrative utterances of the Cyclops stories

	8F = 12H: Pisa	11F = 218H: Estonia
(Manipulation/ competence) MS(w)	S_1: $\begin{cases} \text{priest} \\ \text{Florentine n P: will} \\ \text{artisan} \end{cases}$ $(S_1 \rightarrow (S_1 \text{ n P: } \begin{cases} \text{adventure} \\ \text{riches} \\ \text{work} \end{cases}))$	S_1: *farmhand* $\rightarrow$ *(S_1 n P: knowledge n S_2: devil)* S_2 n P: will $(S_1 \rightarrow (S_1 \text{ u P: new eyes n } S_2))$
(Performance) FIRST ordeal	S_2: *giant* $\rightarrow$ *(S_1*: $\begin{cases} \text{priest} \\ \text{artisan} \end{cases}$ *P: work u S_2)*	
SECOND ordeal	$S_2 \rightarrow (S_1: \begin{cases} \text{priest} \\ \text{artisan} \end{cases}$ u P: life n S_2) S_1: *Florentine n P: will* *(S_1 → (S_1 u P: sight n S_2))*	$S_1 \rightarrow$ *(S_1 n P: knowledge (false name) n S_2)*
FIRST counterordeal	$S_1 \rightarrow (S_1 \text{ n P: sight u } S_2)$	$S_1 \rightarrow (S_1 \text{ n P: sight u } S_2)$ $S_1 \rightarrow (S_1 \text{ n P: devil's helpers u } S_2)$
SECOND counterordeal	$S_2 \rightarrow$ *(S_1 n P: ring u S_2)* S_2 *(S_1 u P: S_1 n S_2)* S_1 *(S_1 u P: finger S_1 n S_2)* $S_1 \rightarrow (S_1 \text{ n P: } S_1 \text{ u } S_2)$ $S_1 \rightarrow (S_1 \text{ u P: desire for adventure})$	$S_1 \rightarrow (S_1 \text{ n P: life u } S_2)$
(Sanction) Final attributive statement		

Note: Italics = seeming mode utterance; n = conjunction; u = disjunction.

The reciprocal structure we have noted is generally doubled and framed by a second, similar structure, one organized in a slightly different way. In stories 21F, 30F, 33F, and 36F, the monster (or his aide, in 30F) carries off the hero and his companions into his cave before roasting and eating one of them. From the point of view of the grammar of the narrative, the hero occupies two distinct actantial positions in the statement that expresses his abduction by the Cyclops: he is both the Subject separated from the Predicate and also the separated Predicate. Everything occurs, with regard to the abduction, as if the hero were being deprived of the ability to dispose of himself: the hero is the "object" circulating between S_1 and S_2. In order to assure

12F = 30H: Lapland	21F = 17H: Gascony	30F = 123H: 1001 Nights
S_1: 4 Lapps n P: will ($S_1 \rightarrow (S_1$ n P: food))	S_1: poor young man n P: will ($S_1 \rightarrow (S_1$ n P: gold horns u S_2: Cyclops))	S_1: Sinbad seamen n P: will ($S_1 \rightarrow (S_1$ n P: wealth in a palace adventures))
	S_1: mother $\rightarrow (S_1$ u P: crucifix n S_2: youth's sister)	
$S_1 \rightarrow (S_1$ n P: ox u S_2)	S_1: youth $\rightarrow (S_1$ n P: gold horns [u S_2])	
	S_2: Cyclops $\rightarrow (S_1$ u P: S_1 n S_2)	S_2: dwarfs, giant's helper $\rightarrow (S_1$ u P: S_1 n S_2: giant)
S_2: giant $\rightarrow (S_1$ u P: a Lapp n S_2)	$S_2 \rightarrow (S_1$ n P: knowledge (stories) n S_2)	
S_2 n P: will ($S_2 \rightarrow (S_1$: a Lapp u P: life n S_2))	$S_2 \rightarrow (S_1$: youth's sister u P: life n S_2)	$S_2 \rightarrow (S_1$: a sailor u P: life n S_2) 3 x
S_1: a Lapp n P: will ($S_1 \rightarrow (S_1$ u P: sight n S_2))		
$S_2 \rightarrow (S_1$ n P: 15 quiet days u S_2) *$S_1 \rightarrow (S_1$ n P: knowledge (false name) n S_2)*		$S_1 \rightarrow (S_1$ n P: rafts)
$S_1 \rightarrow (S_1$ n P: sight u S_2)	$S_1 \rightarrow (S_1$ n P: sight u S_2)	$S_1 \rightarrow (S_1$ n P: sight u S_2)
$S_1 \rightarrow (S_1$ n P: giant's helpers u S_2)	$S_1 \rightarrow (S_1$ n P: Cyclops's helpers u S_2)	
$S_1 \rightarrow (S_1$ n P: S_1 u S_2) sheep	$S_1 \rightarrow (S_1$ n P: S_1 u S_2) sheep	$S_1 \rightarrow (S_1$ n P: S_1 u S_2) rafts
$S_1 \rightarrow (S_1$ n P: riches of S_2 u S_2)	$S_1 \rightarrow (S_1$ n P: riches of S_2 u S_2)	
$S_1 \rightarrow (S_1$ n P: life u S_2)	$S_1 \rightarrow (S_1$ n P: youth's sister u S_2)	$S_2 \rightarrow (S_1$: some sailors u P: life n S_2)
$S_1 \rightarrow (S_1$ n P: riches)	$S_1 \rightarrow (S_1$ n P: riches)	

his victory over the giant, S_1 has to regain his liberty, by way of a statement symmetrical with the first, and can then again dispose of his person. The same thing happens at the end of the story when the hero and his surviving companions manage to escape from the blinded giant by taking advantage of the Cyclops's sheep, which fill the helper's role. This counterordeal, which corresponds to the abduction ordeal, is found in stories 12F, 21F, 30F (the helpers in this case are represented by rafts), 33F, and 36F. In the sequence made up of the first ordeal and the second counterordeal, the Predicate transferred is semantically the same, by contrast to the central sequence, in which the

	33F = 110H: Caucasus	36F = 118H: Oghuz (Turkmenistan)
(Manipulation competence) MS(w)	S_2: fish $\rightarrow$ (S_2 n P: S_1 u S_1: 7 fishers) $S_1 \rightarrow$ (S_1 n P: honey)	S_2: Cyclops $\rightarrow$ (S_2 n P: Oghuz youth u S_1: Oghuz people) S_1: Bissat n P: will ($S_1 \rightarrow$ (S_1 n P: life u S_2)) $S_1 \rightarrow$ (S_1 n P: life u S_2) but *without effect*
(Performance) FIRST ordeal	S_2: Cyclops $\rightarrow$ (S_1 u P: S_1 n S_2)	$S_2 \rightarrow$ (S_1 u P: S_1 n S_2)
SECOND ordeal	$S_2 \rightarrow$ (S_1: sailor u P: life n S_2) 5 x	S_2 n P: will ($S_2 \rightarrow$ (S_1 u P: life n S_2)) S_2: Bissat's helper $\rightarrow$ (S_1 n P: knowledge (Bissat's quality) n S_2)
FIRST counterordeal	$S_1 \rightarrow$ (S_1 n P: sight u S_2)	$S_1 \rightarrow$ (S_1 n P: sight u S_2)
SECOND counterordeal	$S_1 \rightarrow$ (S_1 n P: S_1 u S_2) sheep $S_1 \rightarrow$ (S_1 n P: sheep of S_2 u S_2) $S_2 \rightarrow$ (S_1 u P: life n S_2) but *without effect*	$S_1 \rightarrow$ (S_1 n P: S_1 u S_2) sheep $S_2 \rightarrow$ (*S_1 n P: ring u S_2*) $S_1 \rightarrow$ (S_1 u P: ring n S_2) $S_1 \rightarrow$ (S_1 n P: life u S_2)
(Sanction) Final attributive statement		$S_1 \rightarrow$ (S_1 n P: life of S_2)

hero appropriates the giant's sight in exchange for the life of the hero's companion taken by the cannibal giant.

But not all the stories analyzed conform to the double structure of ordeal and counterordeal, which I shall call the nuclear structure of the Cyclops story.

In the tale from Lapland (12F), for example, the four hunters, heroes of the tale, enter the giant's cave spontaneously, without being abducted. But when the giant falls asleep, they save their companion from the cauldron in which the giant intends to cook him before eating him. Neither the first nor the second test depending on the actions of S_2 (abduction and cannibalism) happens in this story. It is only after having noticed the disappearance of his supper that the giant closes the cave with an enormous stone, thus accomplishing after the fact the narrative utterance corresponding to the abduction: the heroes can no longer dispose of themselves. If it is typical to find in the story the counterordeal of the sheep in which the hero manages to free himself by a ruse, the counterordeal of the blinding loses its syntactical motivation; we shall see how the story justifies it anyhow.

We also find that the second counterordeal (cannibalism) does not occur in the Oghuz tale (Turkmenistan [36F]); I shall return to the reasons for this.

The Pisan story (8F) varies from the norm in more than one regard. Not only does the giant kill but not eat the hero's companions, which actually has no effect on the syntax of the story, but he goes through the first ordeal, the abduction, by means of a trick. With this ordeal, the story moves from the level of being to the level of seeming: pretending to give the story's traveler from Florence and his companions the work they seek, the giant makes an attribution that marks the beginning of a contract and seems to involve the protagonists in a structure of gift and countergift, in what might even be seen as a structure of exchange.[19] But this false gift gives rise to the second ordeal of the nuclear structure: the hero's helpers end up being killed by the monster as in the other stories. The substitution of a simulated gift for the first ordeal has an important impact on the corresponding counterordeal: the story has no counterordeal involving sheep. Again, I shall return to this question.

The Structure of the Framework

If, as we saw at the beginning of this section, the first ordeal in the confrontation of S_1 and S_2 introduces a situation of lack that starts the story off, we have not yet provided the reasons for this confrontation. In order for the story to begin, one of the actors in the actantial positions S_1 or S_2 must be possessed of the desire to have or appropriate a Predicate, an object of value. This desire is present in all the stories studied in the form of a preliminary modal utterance of the will

[19] Note that even if one disregards this first passage on the plane of simulation, since the attribution of a task is not the real aim of the giant's will (*vouloir*), the act of making an attribution of this task is itself only simulation. By providing work for the hero, the giant in the Pisan story only usurps his hireling's capacity for work in order to appropriate it for himself. In order for the rules of a true exchange structure to be respected, the giant should give the hero a salary equivalent to the strain of the work offered. The attributing utterance of the Pisan tale is thus formulated from the perspective of a protagonist endowed with superior power, of an employer who, because of his position, can argue that in dispossessing his employee of his strength for work, he gives him an object of value! In this case, the employee has no pretensions as regards his salary. . . .

(*vouloir*) of which S_1 is the Subject. The object desired as Predicate, however, varies from story to story.

A quest for adventure is the origin of the Pisan and Arabian stories (8F and 30F). In the versions collected by Hackman, the search for adventure is by far the most common motivation, and then narrative *manipulation*, for the confrontation between S_1 and S_2. I include in this category all the tales with fearless heroes on the lookout for an adventure that can make them experience this feeling (see, for example, 46H, 66H, and 108H). One would have to add the many stories in which the motivation is a quest for misery or misfortune (see 46H, 50H, 53H, 54H, 63H, 64H, 68H, 71H, 73H, 75H, etc.). In all these tales the object of the hero's desire is adventure, in other words, all of the narrated events, and this object is introduced only indirectly during the development of the story; if I may be permitted the analogy, everything happens as if the hero wanted to live the very adventure the receiver of the story wishes to hear.

But the initial MS(w) can also be evoked by a situation or lack, either because the hero, lost, is looking for food and lodging (12F) or because he finds himself in very modest circumstances and wants to get the gold the Cyclops cares nothing about (21F). In Hackman's collection there are several stories the motivation for which falls into the first of the two categories (search for food/lodging; see, e.g., 9H, 10H, 58H, 34F = 113H, etc.). Very similar are the even more numerous variants in which the search for food disappears and only the initial situation of losing the way remains; the encounter between S_1 and S_2 is then mere chance (see 4H, 8H, 12H, 19H, 39H, 52H, etc.: S_1 and S_2 confront each other after S_1 loses the way in a forest or on a mountain; 43H, 45H, 49H, etc.: S_1 and S_2 confront each other after the shipwreck). In this case the initial MS(w) of the hero tends toward zero. It is possible to fit into this category the Caucasian story (33F; see also 38F), in which seven fishermen are drawn to a river of honey by a fish that has taken their bait. The tale then develops in a manner similar to that of the story from Gascony (21F): the fishermen could load their boat with honey and go off with it, just as in the other story the heroes manage to appropriate the golden horns of the Cyclops's cattle; the story would end there if they had not by chance met the one-eyed giant, who carries them off to make a meal of them. In the tales in which the accidental meeting of S_1 and S_2 has no motivation, it is the first ordeal, the abduction, which provokes an implied MS(w); the hero, naturally, wants to free himself from the monster's clutches!

The Oghuz story (36F) is an interesting exception. The dispossession/appropriation of which S_2 is the Subject and S_1 the Predicate, an act that usually follows the initial MS(w) of S_1, in this story precedes the hero's first desire. It is because the "Cyclops," Dépé Ghoz, has already received and consumed more than once the tribute of twelve men exacted from the neighboring town and, among his other victims, has eaten the hero's brother, that Bissat intends to free his fellow citizens of this scourge; and it is because Bissat tries to kill him that Dépé Ghoz carries the hero off with every intention of eating him too. The second ordeal forming part of the core of the syntax (the act of cannibalism) is thus disconnected from the two counterordeals (the blinding of the giant and the flight under the sheep); it is offered as the cause of the hero's MS(w), and from now on its contents change; its object is no longer adventure or the search for safe lodgings but the life/death of the giant himself. The quest for fear or the chance meeting with the giant has given way to a desire for vengeance. The basic impact that this modification has on narrative causality in this particular tale and, consequently, on its meaning will have to be described.

Just as the story must be set in motion by an MS(w) that puts into circulation a Predicate/object of value of which the hero is the virtual Subject, so it must end with the attribution of this object to the hero. Since S_1's object of desire is not initially defined in relation to an S_2 who turns out to be the owner and from whom the object is eventually taken, it is normal for this object to be attributed to S_1 without there being a counterpart to it for S_2. Moreover, in the nuclear narrative structure of the Cyclops story, the final utterance, that of the second counterordeal, carries with it a "virtualization" of S_2: S_1 gets away from S_2, he himself "dispossesses" himself, but S_2 can still assail S_1, and that is what happens in the two cases I am going to analyze. Conversely, in the attributive statement that ends the story, the Predicate/object of value can be united with S_1 without, in return, being separated from S_2: the latter is definitively out of the action and narratively neutralized.

From now on, I shall call the narrative structure made up of the MS(w) that begins the story (*manipulation*) and the utterance of attribution that ends it (*sanction*) the framing structure; it frames the nuclear structure previously defined.[20]

[20] Since I wrote these lines, the concepts of nuclear structure and framing structure developed here have been formulated more rigorously in Greimas's theory. To the modal statement of will (*vouloir*) initiating the story corresponds the *manipulation* phase establishing the *competence* of the Subject of the action (*performance*); the attribution of

The final statement of attribution naturally takes different forms according to the story. In the Oghuz tale (36F), S_2 is out of the picture since he is killed by S_1, an act that conforms to the initial MS(w), which expressed the desire of S_1 to take S_2's life. In the story from Gascony (21F), the neutralization of S_2 is brought about by the flight of S_1, who escapes after acquiring the object of his search (riches). In the Lappish tale (12F), there is an initial search for shelter corresponding to the final attribution of the gold and money belonging to the giant who would not give the shelter requested; the neutralization of S_2, the only one capable of fulfilling the attribution, is accomplished by the death of the giant. The Pisan story (8F), where S_2 is also neutralized by the departure of S_1, is an exception insofar as the final utterance consists of a separation rather than a union: the risks the hero undergoes in the monster's house take all his desire for adventure away from him. The tale ends not with the acquisition of the initial object of desire but with a negation of the desire, which is another way of creating narrative balance. In the Caucasian story (33F), if the neutralization of S_2 comes about simply by the flight of S_1, the lack of an initial MS(w) (it is a matter of seafarers faced by chance with the Cyclops) leads to the absence of a final attributive utterance. There remains the adventure of Sinbad (30F), which does not end with a final attribution because the hero and his companions manage to escape the giant on their rafts, taking nothing but themselves away. But would one find a concluding utterance in a tale that is an episode in a much larger story? The desire for adventure and riches that constitutes the initial MS(w) of this episode in fact extends beyond the limits of this tale to motivate the whole series of Sinbad's adventures during his third voyage. The final attributive statement will thus appear at the end of the last story of the sequence.

It is clear that the *sanction* imposed in the final attributive utterance is essential for understanding the "meaning" of the story, for grasping, in other words, the semantic organization that develops during the narration. That organization of meaning can also work in reverse, as it does in a story from eastern Finland (106H) in which the struggle against the giant and the money thus obtained cause the hero, who at the beginning was only a poor, simpleminded creature, to be honored by the whole community and become marriageable.

---

the object/Predicate to this Subject corresponds to the *sanction* phase, which puts a limit on the *performance*, and consequently to the story. The nuclear structure with its framework has thus become the "canonic narrative schema": see Groupe d'Entrevernes, *Analyse sémiotique des textes* (Lyon, 1979), 13ff. and n. 16 above.

Internal Accretions

The two large structures so far revealed by our narrative analysis (the twofold ordeal and counterordeal and the framing structure) are common to the stories we have examined, with the slight differences mentioned. Some of the utterances that make up these common structures appear twice in order to enlarge the narration from within. Such an enlargement can come about in various ways.

For example, in the Oghuz story (36F), when the hero, Bissat, has escaped the clutches of the giant, Dépé Ghoz, the latter gives him a magic ring. This gift seems to set the narration in motion again just as the second counterordeal is concluding; the narrative does not resume in the mode of the ordeal, however, but in that of attribution/renunciation. This new narrative direction is made possible because, in the last statement of the counterordeal, S_2 is still present as the virtual Subject. But the shift to gift mode is short-lived, since the ring is no sooner given than the giant tries to attack Bissat; the latter finally gives him back the attributed object without there being any exchange, either virtual or actual.

This microstory, which starts the narration going again at the moment it is nearing its end, is found in several of the stories in Hackman's collection (see 5, 6, 10ff., 60ff., 72H, etc.).[21] The ring given by the giant only represents a gift in these stories according to the *seeming mode*; no sooner has the hero put it on than it signals his position to the blind monster. The hero then has to nullify the attribution, which is really an appropriation on the part of the giant, by cutting off his finger and thus relinquishing the poisoned gift.

In the Pisan story (8F), the microstory of the ring is a substitute for the second counterordeal (the flight under the sheep). As soon as the monster is blinded, in order to prevent the hero from escaping the monster proposes giving him a ring as a keepsake. And, as in the stories mentioned, the hero gets rid of this magic ring by cutting off the finger he had put it on. If the giant's gift can be expressed in the *seeming mode* (*mode du paraître*) as an attribution/renunciation utterance, in the *being mode* (*mode de l'être*) it corresponds to a dispossession/appropriation utterance (S_2 appropriating S_1 by dispossessing him of himself); and by the same token, if the statement of attribution/renunciation is expressed on the plane of seeming, the act of cutting off the finger corresponds on the plane of being to a disposses-

[21] Hackman [n. 3], 174ff.

sion/appropriation utterance: S_1 removes himself from S_2's clutches. This final utterance is identical with that of the second counterordeal which generally closes the nuclear structure of the story. This substitution at the level of syntax heralds the first transformation of the tale.

The Arabian and Caucasian tales (30F and 33F) each show a similar reanimation of the narrative at the very moment when the story seems about to end with an attribution in favor of the hero. In the first of these tales, the giant and his assistants throw huge stones down onto the rafts of the hero and his companions as they are escaping, and he has almost succeeded in his act of dispossessing/appropriating the hero's life when most of Sinbad's companions are drowned beneath the hail of rocks. In the second, when the hero escaping in his boat reveals his identity to the Cyclops, the latter throws his club and almost scuttles the hero's boat. In each case the story seems to want to continue with another ordeal, one that actually aborts as soon as it begins. The virtualization of S_2 in the statement of the second ordeal of the nuclear structure makes such a new ordeal perfectly possible and realizable.

A final variation on the nuclear structure is offered by the tales from Pisa and Lapland (8F and 12F). Here, a new narrative statement is inserted between the second ordeal (the first for 12F, where, as we saw, the second did not take place) and the first counterordeal of the nuclear structure. When the hero blinds the giant by means of a trick and not by force, the ordeal of the blinding is preceded by a narrative statement in the seeming mode; during this utterance, the hero pretends that he wishes to improve the monster's sight, while in reality he intends to take it away. The dispossession/appropriation utterance in the *being mode* (the blinding) is thus represented in the *seeming mode* as an statement of attribution/renunciation. The gift seems to take the place of the ordeal, but it is only a trick.

In the tale from Lapland (12F), the apparent gift given by S_1 to S_2 is echoed by a gift also given on the plane of *seeming* by S_2 when the giant promises the hero, in exchange for improved eyesight, to allow him two weeks' respite before eating him. To this seeming counteroffer, S_1 responds with a second gift of the same sort: the hero tells the giant that his name is *Nobody*. This second trick, transmitting false knowledge, causes an utterance to be added to the first counterordeal: not only is the giant weakened by his loss of sight, but his kith and kin, deceived by the hero's false name, refuse to help him.

Outside the Norm

S_1's apparent attribution to S_2 of better eyesight and S_1's deception of S_2 by way of giving a false name lead us to the seventh story (11F). The syntactical structure of this tale from Estonia, like the first semantic structure articulated above, is an exception to the rules previously formed.

The confrontation between S_1 and S_2 in the Estonian story is exceptional in that it begins immediately with an attribution statement made by S_1 to S_2. But the Predicate attributed to S_2 by S_1, consisting of knowledge, is only semblance: the hero, if one can use the term in this case, is fashioning not eyes, but buttons, as he assures his questioner, the devil. The story continues on the *seeming* plane, since the first utterance initiates the MS(w) engagement of the rest of the story: not noticing the hero's trick, the devil says he would like to have new eyes. No sooner said than done. Now the performance moves onto the plane of *being* and instead of giving the devil better sight, the hero pours boiling lead into his eye sockets and blinds him. Thus we pass directly from the initial MS(w), the Subject of which is S_2 and not S_1, to the sequence corresponding to the first counterordeal, as we have seen in the stories just analyzed.

In the Estonian tale there is no second ordeal, since the devil goes to the hero and not the other way around. The potential helpers of the devil are neutralized, however, as in the Lappish story (12F), by a second trick, the trick of the false name. This second gift, again performed on the *seeming* plane, once more has the effect of a dispossession/appropriation statement with S_1 as its Subject.

The story does not end with an actual attribution but with what might be called an executed dispossession. The storyteller recounts that the devil, deprived of all assistance, dies of his wounds. By dispossessing S_2 of his sight and his helpers, S_1 has also dispossessed him of his life. In this way S_1 neutralizes S_2, but he himself has received nothing concrete in return. The narrative structure of the Estonian story is composed simply of a double unilateral ordeal in the modes of seeming and being. The ordeal with S_1 as the Subject corresponds to none of the ordeals initiated by S_2, and no doubt it is because of this that S_1, who has done nothing but appropriate the qualities of a passive S_2, gains nothing in so doing. We would therefore be loath to grant him the status of hero.

5. Narrative Transformations

The Avatars of the Structure

Our analysis, based on Greimas's model, of the narrative structures in seven stories from Hackman's and Frazer's collections yields the following results in summary:

—First, we have defined a nuclear syntactic construction made up of four statements: a double ordeal with S_2 as Subject and a symmetrical double counterordeal with S_1 as Subject.

—Second, we have identified a framework structure consisting of two statements: an initial modal statement of will with S_1 generally as Subject and a final attributive statement with S_1 as Subject again.

—Lastly, we have discerned a structure of complementary utterances that either doubles the ordeal and counterordeal statements or provokes a final jolt to the narration before its end or brings into play utterances of ordeal and counterordeal alternatively on the planes of being and seeming.

All these narrative statements together define the syntactical limits within which the Cyclops myth stories examined here function.

The syntactical structures are not rigid, and the basic modifications to which they are subject have been touched on. Their flexibility in combining the utterances that their narrative structures allow can lead to important changes in the meaning of the story; it is from the variations of these combinations of narrative utterance that transformations in the story spring.

Simply inverting the order of statements in the Cyclops story makes the Oghuz story (36F), for example, more like the legend of the Minotaur. Since the cannibalistic act precedes the encounter of the hero with the giant and is the motive for the meeting, and since the act is repeated in the form of a regular tribute demanded by the monster from the surrounding populace, the counterordeal (the blinding of the giant) of which the hero is the Subject is no longer a means of freeing himself from a dangerous situation but a way of wreaking vengeance on behalf of a whole community. This syntactical reversal, combined with elements that our formula does not, it is true, allow us to read and which will be dealt with later, organizes the statements that make up the Cyclops story in such a way that it becomes a different story in spite of appearances. What is more alien to the Cyclops tale than an attempt to kill the giant by conventional means (arrows) before blinding him? Such modifications with respect to the events and, finally, the meaning of the traditional story also reveal its distance from the legend in general. In the Oghuz story, and in no other, the single eye appears to be the only vulnerable part of the monster, and this information is communicated to the hero by the giant's servants, who consequently betray their master. Here again we see how a modification can affect the story's relationship to the norm: the hero wants to kill the monster; he does not just want to escape from the giant after meeting him by chance.

Simply displacing the order of the narrative statements, thereby giving each of them a distinct position and thus a different function in relation to the others, transforms the logic of the story. That is why in following the structuralist method, the utterances of the story must be understood in their mutual interrelations and why an examination of the functions they perform in relation to one another must be substituted for an analysis in isolation.

The outer structure of the story, for its part, is linked to the autonomy of the tale; its narrative function consists in motivating the action. When the Cyclops tale, as in the Arabian version (30F), is integrated into a series of stories and is thus reduced to an episode in a larger entity, the utterances of the narrative structure surround the larger story rather than the Cyclops story per se. The transfer of the structure surrounding the narrative unit to a series of stories does not generally affect the events of the unit itself. This can be seen in the Russian stories (numbered 60H and 61H) which follow the narrative structure of the Cyclops tale but are included in the larger context of stories recalling the exploits of Theseus and the Argonauts respectively.

It is, rather, in the possible amplifications of the nuclear structure that the potential for transforming the story resides. These changes can range from the simple substitution of narrative statements, without any impact on the sequence of events, to the complete reorganization of these statements, resulting in a reversal of the logic of the action.

I have already mentioned the example of substitution represented by the Pisan story (8F). In this tale the second counterordeal (the flight under the sheep) is replaced by the microstory of the ring. This substitution is probably motivated by the absence of the first ordeal (abduction), which corresponds to the second counterordeal in the nuclear structure of the Cyclops story. In the Pisan tale, the heroes enter the palace of the Cyclops of their own free will, attracted as they are by the giant's (apparent) offer to provide them the work they are seeking. The first ordeal is here replaced by an ordeal in the *seeming mode*, and it is to this ordeal that the counterordeal of the ring, also in the *seeming mode*, corresponds. Thus by substituting for a statement of the nuclear syntax a series of statements that normally represent one of the possible extensions of this nuclear structure, the narrator can move his story between the planes of being and seeming. If the narrative result of the new statement is the same as that of the first, the logic of the story is not affected.

The extension of the first counterordeal (the blinding of the giant) onto the plane of seeming, as found in the Pisan and Lappish stories (8F and 12F), by contrast, can have far more radical consequences for the development of the story. Such an extension can also be found in the Estonian tale (11F), of which I have described the "abnormal" elements compared with the other stories analyzed. If in the Pisan and Lappish tales expressing the first counterordeal of a statement in the seeming mode does not affect the logic of the nuclear structure of the stories, in the Estonian tale the same double utterance takes the place of the two ordeals in the evolution of the story's syntax and completely modifies the meaning of the narrative. This substitution brings into focus the MS(w) that constitutes the narrative extension in question here (the devil wants the hero to give him new eyes), and this MS(w) becomes the utterance that "engages" the story. Moreover, it provokes an inversion for the actors in the actantial positions of the statements making up the extension: the hero, and no longer the monster, is the subject of the ordeal, and the monster is now the subject of the MS(w) instead of the hero.[22] In the Estonian tale, the blinding is not a road to liberation, a counterordeal allowing the hero to contest the giant's power by way of a ruse, but an unprovoked attack; the right of self-defense then reverts to the monster!

We can see that the new narrative structure in which the counter-ordeal takes the place of the ordeal and the giant asks the hero to give him better vision can be included in a structure comprising the first ordeal of the Cyclops story (abduction), the corresponding second counterordeal (the flight under the sheep), and the MS(w) common to all these stories (the search for food after being lost). This modification

[22] The MS(w) whose Subject is the giant is implicitly present as well in stories 8F and 12F since it is with the giant's assent that the hero pours lead into the cavity of his eye, but the role is minor in the initial MS(w); moreover, in these two stories, it is the hero who proposes giving the giant better sight, whereas in story 11F the Cyclops asks the hero for it.

of the single center of the nuclear structure of the Cyclops story is found in the Finnish tale numbered 175H. Like the Pisan and Lappish tales, this story is a good example of how a Cyclops narrative can turn into a story like the Estonian one (11F). The different combinations of narrative statements and the actantial modifications resulting from them can transform a story into something quite different.

The distinctive characteristic of the Cyclops story does not, of course, depend on the syntactical transformations that result in a narrative scheme such as that of the Estonian story. So all the stories Hackman includes in his group C (175H–221H), except the borderline story 175H, are characterized by having nothing to do with the Cyclops story; they should therefore be excised from the corpus.[23] Hackman is partially aware of this when he says that in all these tales the monster approaches the hero in friendship and the hero is not put in the position of having to defend himself.[24]

This discussion of the distinctive features of the tales in the Cyclops-story category brings us to a comparison of the results of our analysis with Hackman's traditional division into episodes.

The Dangers of Creating Sequences

What is remarkable in the way Hackman divides up the Cyclops stories is that he completely neglects the two ordeals (abduction and cannibalism) for which the "blinding" and the "flight of the hero" are merely the symmetric counterordeals. This omission leads him to include among the Cyclops story all those that have a scene in which a blinding occurs, without being aware of the motivation for the scene (in the Cyclops story, the act of cannibalism). If one agrees that cannibalism and blinding complement each other and that this is the distinctive feature of the Cyclops story, then all the stories in Hackman's group C (175H–221H), along with numbers 30H, 31H, 32H, 40H, 71H, 72H, and so forth, should be removed from the list.

We have seen, however, that several narrative elements common to these tales represent in reality only extensions, or amplifications, of the tales' basic structure. Hackman passes by some of those elements in silence (for example, the attempt of S_2 to kill S_1 by throwing stones at him)[25] in order to raise others to the rank of "episode"; such is the case

[23] Hackman [n. 3], 134ff. and 206ff.
[24] Hackman [n. 3], 211.
[25] See, however, Hackman [n. 3], 180f.

for the "episode of the ring." I have shown that this narrative element plays a minor role as regards the second counterordeal of the nuclear structure (the flight under the sheep).

Though Hackman considers the "ring episode" to be an integral part of the "original form" of the story, he confers an optional character on the "false name episode." The rare occurrences of this element in the stories with the nuclear structure of the Cyclops story lead Hackman himself to have doubts about its narrative necessity; and he naturally enough resolves the problem historically by presuming that the episode was borrowed by Homer from the stories Hackman brings together in group B (125H–174H) and that the stories stemming from the Cyclops story and containing this event (30H = 12F, 175H) in turn bear the mark of the direct influence of the Homeric tale. No lengthy analysis is required to show that group B does not belong in the framework of the Cyclops story; and Hackman realizes this.[26]

As I have already said, the syntactical elements of the story are like semantic units: taken out of context or treated in isolation, they make no sense, and it is only by analyzing their syntagmatic dimension and defining their role in the logic of the narration that sense is made of them. Each element examined, either syntactical or semantic, should always be linked to a hierarchically superior element;[27] a traditional division of the story into episodes or sequences is dangerous because the elements that emerge from such an analysis are rarely studied in the context of their relationships with one another or in terms of their syntagmatic linkages.

The "false name episode" actually looks like a very common narrative "trick" by means of which a hero can neutralize his enemy's helper. It can be found in the Lappish story (12F) as well as in the Estonian tale (11F, a story in Hackman's group C) or in the tales of Hackman's group B. The roles played by the hero and the monster respectively can just as easily be reversed by the false name ruse, as happens in story 129H. But it must be pointed out that with regard to the action, the series of statements corresponding to the false name stratagem play a role in the nuclear structure of the stories in group C (see the Estonian tale), while in the stories based on the model of the Cyclops story, they do no more than contribute to enlarging one of the

---

[26] Hackman [n. 3], 179ff. and 189ff.

[27] See, from a pragmatic point of view, the remarks of S. J. Schmidt, *Texttheorie: Probleme einer Linguistik der sprachlichen Kommunikation* (Munich, 1973), 151ff.

counterordeals and to making it operate on the planes of seeming and being.

The same can be said of the monster's desire to get new eyes from the hero. In the group C tales, the statements that turn this desire into narrative are the core of the narration, while in the Cyclops stories they represent an extension of the utterance of the first counterordeal (the blinding). The fact that this extension is not present in all the stories examined and that it has no impact, whatever the reversal of syntax, on the unfolding of the story proves its contingency.[28]

As we have seen, an analysis of narrative that goes beyond the surface structures and tries to take into account the rules governing the way semionarrative grammar functions in the story avoids the pitfalls of a description that merely divides the events of a story into often heterogeneous units. It also takes into account the transformations that are constantly occurring in any literature composed and handed down orally.

6. The Homeric Tale

If we leave aside the evaluation of the superficial type of narrative analysis and begin comparing the seven Cyclops tales with the episode from the *Odyssey* that serves as pretext for the analysis presented here, we shall see how similar their respective syntactical structures are.[29]

The story in the *Odyssey* follows the nuclear syntax of the Cyclops story exactly. It reproduces the successive symmetrical ordeals and counterordeals, which are at the heart of the story's nuclear structure. The outer structure we have found in the Cyclops tales is also present with statements identical in their syntax but slightly different in their

[28] Note that for Hackman [n. 3], 161, this enlargement of the story is an alternative to the utterance of the counterordeal, while in reality it is optionally complementary to it: the giant's desire to see better is never substituted for the blinding itself.

[29] If one compares the narrative schema common to the seven stories studied here with the result of my analysis of the Homeric Cyclops story undertaken some years ago [n. 1], it is easy to see the differences. There are two reasons for these differences: first, the use in my earlier study of a model of narrative analysis notably different from the one used here (though it, too, had been created by Greimas) in that the transformation of the narrative statements into statements of value-object transfer was merely interpolated as a suggestion; second, given that the Homeric story is more developed than the stories examined here and was studied more for semantic reasons, my earlier analysis developed on a different level.

content from that of the stories examined. If the situation in which Odysseus and his companions find themselves from the moment they set foot in Polyphemus's land is indeed a situation of need, as in many of the stories collected by Hackman, the MS(w) that initiates the story, of which the hero is the Subject, has as its Predicate not a need for food but a desire for knowledge; Odysseus wants to know if the Cyclopes are savages or civilized. And the attributive statement that ends Homer's story corresponds semantically to the MS(w) that opens it: civilized values are attributed to the hero, whereas the giant is classed among the savages. But the framing structure here is itself part of a larger structure covering the whole of Odysseus's adventures, as in the Sinbad tale (30F). This larger structure probably influenced the modification of the MS(w) that opens the story of Odysseus; it is also certainly at the origin of the curse the giant puts on the hero at the end of the tale, the narrative function of which is to reintegrate the story into the sequence of Odysseus's adventures.[30]

Where Homer's story clearly differs from the seven tales I have analyzed, and those that Hackman collected, is in its length. In the *Odyssey*, the narration is not only fleshed out in ways that I have mentioned (the Cyclops's granting of a respite to the hero, the episode of the false name, the hurling of the rocks, the repetition of the giant's cannibalism), it creates new events.

Among these, some simply replace amplifications that are already included in the narrative possibilities of the Cyclops story but do not appear in Homer's account. The wine of Maron, for instance, an attribution made in the seeming mode by S_1 in order to appropriate S_2's sight more easily, is substituted for the simulated gift of better eyesight that we find in the Pisan and Lappish tales (8F and 12F). In the logic of the story, these two narrative statements, semantically different, have the same function: to neutralize by trickery the monster's power and, consequently, to set the stage for the first counterordeal (the blinding).

In the *Odyssey* other extensions are added to the preexisting utterances in the narrative scheme underlying the Cyclops story. Before blinding Polyphemus, the hero convinces the monster, for example, that his boat has been destroyed and that he is therefore at the giant's mercy; this apparent attribution of information sets the stage for

---

[30]For the giant's curse and its narrative function, see Van Gennep [n. 6], 157, and S. L. Schein, "Odysseus and Polyphemus in the *Odyssey*," *Greek Rom. Byz. Stud.* 11 (1970): 73–83.

the second counterordeal, in which the hero escapes from the giant and leaves his land. Along the same lines, the narrative extension of the deceptive gift of a false name should be noted. I have described the narrative role this gift plays in preparing the neutralization of the helpers and its function in doubling the first counterordeal. In the *Odyssey* the false name utterance occurs in the seeming mode and is accompanied by an utterance not present in the other versions examined; before leaving the land of the Cyclopes, Odysseus reveals his real identity to Polyphemus, so the attribution of the deceptive information represented by the false name is followed by the attribution of real knowledge. This utterance occasions a microstory during which Polyphemus tries in vain to convince the hero to make an exchange, not in the mode of the ordeal but, rather, in the mode of the gift.[31]

Scholarly comparisons of the *Odyssey* story with folklore variants have pointed, however, to the absence of the "ring episode" in the former. But to wonder whether this so-called episode belongs to the original, popular form of the story is as pointless as to state that it "would be out of harmony with the tone of this realistic narrative."[32] If we admit, as has thus far been the case, that all known variations of the Cyclops story are potentially present from the very first known appearance of the story, I can do no more than state the following: Homer's narrative behaves in the same way as the other versions examined, it is only one variant among several, and the absence at its

---

[31] The uncovering of Odysseus's real identity is one of the corollaries of the deceptive gift of the false name and not an act of hubris brought about by Polyphemus's curse on the hero as C. S. Brown imagines in "Odysseus and Polyphemus: The Name and the Curse," *Comparative Literature* 18 (1966): 193–202; I have already pointed out that Polyphemus's curse serves to reintegrate the general motivation of the story and that it sets up the rest of the hero's adventures; it is, however, not a substitute for the microstory of the ring.

It is correct to say, however, that the false name episode serves as the author's pretext for a sequence of puns on the words *mē tis* ("nobody") and *mētis* ("cunning intelligence") which brings into focus the semantic values of the debate about civilization in which Odysseus and Polyphemus are anthropomorphic figures: see A. L. T. Bergren, "Odyssean Temporality: Many (Re)Turns," in *Approaches to Homer*, ed. C. A. Rubino and C. W. Shelmerdine (Austin, 1983), 45ff., and J. Strauss Clay, *The Wrath of Athena: Gods and Men in the "Odyssey"* (Princeton, 1983), 113ff., P. Pucci, "L'io e l'altro nel racconto di Odisseo sui Ciclopi," *Stud. It. Filol. Class.* 3, no. 11 (1993): 26–46, and below, Chapter 7, n. 8.

[32] See Hackman [n. 3], 177ff. (Van Gennep, [n. 6], 161f., comes to diametrically opposed conclusions), and Page [n. 12], 9; see also Glenn [n. 6], 178ff. On the whole problem of the development (and interpretation) of the Cyclops story into a more comprehensive narrative in the *Odyssey*, see L. Edmunds, *Myth in Homer: A Handbook* (Highland Park, N.J., 1992), 27ff.

core of the microstory of the ring proves this. The fact that the rhapsode who sang the version of the *Odyssey* of which we have the transcript did not include this element certainly does not mean that it did not appear in other recitations of the adventures of Odysseus with Polyphemus.

Does Homer's story differ from the seven tales examined and from those in Hackman's collection only because of the narrative amplifications it contains? And, on a higher level of abstraction, does the Homeric narrative differ from other series of tales with parallel syntactical structures? In other words, can the model borrowed from Greimas to analyze narrative account for the distinctive character of a story or a category of stories without help?

7. The Logic of the Narrative

Greimas's Model

With regard to the formula proposed by Greimas for the transfer of objects of value, I have said in a previous study that I would prefer not to use utterances that bring together subjects and objects. These utterances, by assuming such forms as '$S_1 \rightarrow (O_1 \text{ u } S_1 \text{ n } O_2)$', intersect with the categories of simple utterances. This formulation breaks down into '$S_1 \rightarrow (P_1 \text{ u } S_1)$' = renunciation and '$S_1 \rightarrow (S_1 \text{ n } P_2)$' = appropriation, although it is the utterances of renunciation and attribution, or appropriation and dispossession, that are interdependent: the ordeal would thus be confused with the gift.[33] To avoid this ambiguity, I prefer to write the gift/countergift as '$S_1 \rightarrow (S_1 \text{ u } P_1 \text{ n } S_2)/S_2 \rightarrow (S_1 \text{ n } P_2 \text{ u } S_2)$' = double renunciation/attribution and the ordeal/counterordeal as '$S_1 \rightarrow (S_1 \text{ n } P_2 \text{ u } S_2)/S_2 \rightarrow (S_1 \text{ u } P_1 \text{ n } S_2)$' = double dispossession/appropriation.

Notice that the ordeal/counterordeal, an example of which we find in the Cyclops story, is given no designation by Greimas but is treated as a gift/countergift (or an exchange). But the reciprocal transfer of objects of value can take place in the mode of the ordeal as well as in the mode of the gift and merits a place in the terminology. In order to designate the twofold ordeal/counterordeal, I therefore propose using the term *confrontation* (*affrontement*).

[33]C. Calame, "Discours mythique et discours historique dans trois textes de Pausanias," *Degrés* 17 (1979): 1–30; see also Greimas 1983, 40ff.

Elements of Narrative Logic

Having discussed the form of our analytical model, let us now return to the question that opened the discussion: does applying this model of narrative analysis fully define the distinctive features of the stories we are examining?

The syntagmatic series of narrative utterances that constitute the story does not of course encompass the Cyclops story if the semantic features vested in the syntactical positions of these utterances are not taken into account. But the distinction made by Greimas between actants and actors makes it easy to integrate the semantic dimension into the syntax of the story. The double confrontation at the core of the Cyclops story's syntax is distinctive of this type of story only if one knows that the narrative Subject (S_1) represents a fearless and cunning hero, that the Antisubject (S_2) is a cannibalistic giant usually with only one eye and superhuman strength, and that the objects transferred in the story are successively the hero himself, his helper, the giant's sight and, once again, the hero. Consequently, Greimas's model does a certain degree of justice to the figurative richness of the tale. But is it sufficient when it comes to the syntax?

The narrative structure of the transfer of objects of value entails only three syntactical operations: joining (n), disjoining (u), and transformation ($\rightarrow$), a result of either joining or disjoining.[34] The extreme simplicity of the syntactical operations in this model has forced me to analyze the transient as well as the reflexive actions of the story as narrative statements of the transfer of Predicates and values. So "to blind" has become "to appropriate the sight of," and "to escape" has become "to attribute oneself to oneself." One wonders whether the expression of the content of the action as an object of value is justified; what about an act like "to kill," for instance, for which the formula 'S_1 n P: life u S_2' (= appropriation of someone else's life) does not express the disappearance of S_2 as the potential Subject of the narrative action (always acknowledging that S_1 is the Subject of the action that leads to this state of affairs)?

One of the possible solutions to this difficulty would be to draw up a classified list of all the actions present in any given story and an inventory of all the syntagms in which these actions can be linked together. I am thinking here of a narrative model inspired by Propp's

---

[34] Greimas 1983, 27ff.

research. This analysis of the action would naturally take place on a much more concrete plane, much closer to the story than the level of analysis engaged in by Claude Bremond and Pierre Larivaille when they define the three-part or five-part structure of narrative action.[35] The phases in these models are made up of the before and after of the action, especially when the unfolding of the whole story is concerned, and arise from what I have called the surrounding structure of the story.

Such an analysis of the concrete action would naturally take into account the possible modalities of the action: modalities of will (definition of the intention, the desire of the actant Subject), of power (in the sense of "being able to," definition of the competence of the actant Subject), of seeming (definition of the way the actant Subject may organize his action), of the lack of effect (action completed without an effect), and so forth. In this hypothetical formulation, the analysis of a story such as the Estonian tale (11F) would immediately be seen as being different from the other stories studied; as I have said, in this tale the hero is the first to say to the devil who is visiting him that he is engaged in fashioning eyes, whereas in reality he is making buttons, and it is because of this false information that the devil asks the hero for new eyes; according to the hypothesis I have advanced, the giant would appear as the Subject of a will motivated by the transmission of information in the seeming mode on the part of the hero. Because of the wealth of syntactical positions it reveals, a concrete analysis would help avoid having to "compress" linguistic statements to fit them into the narrative mold of three positions linked only by a joining or a disjoining; and it would lead to the development of an analysis of singularity.[36]

Greimas's model does, however, provide a formula for the transfer of values regularly seen in stories and thus accounts for an essential element of the narration. We have seen that it is possible to integrate the modalities of action into this model.[37] If we consider that Greimas's

[35] C. Bremond, *Logique du récit* (Paris, 1973), 32 and 65, and P. Larivaille, "L'analyse (morpho)logique du récit," *Poétique* 19 (1974): 368–88; see also Adam 1985, 57ff., and 1991, 86ff. For another attempt at framing a logic for the actions from a cognitive point of view, see the suggestions of J.-P. Desclés, "Représentation des connaissances: Archétypes cognitifs, schèmes conceptuels et schémas grammaticaux," *Actes sémiotiques: Bulletin* 36 (1985): 9–32.

[36] C. Calame, "L'analyse sémiotique en mythologie," *Rev. Théol. Philos.* 109 (1976): 95.

[37] Since I wrote these lines, the modalization of being (*être*) and doing (*faire*) has been more or less integrated into the concept of surface syntax; see, in particular, Greimas and Courtés 1979, 230ff., and 1983, 67ff. and 93ff., and Coquet 1989, 87ff.

formalization of the gift and the ordeal is sufficiently fertile to organize the story into its essential narrative elements, we could try to define semantically the syntactical operations it represents by formalizing either the ways in which joining and disjoining are achieved or the semantic content invested in those operations.[38] The narrative propositions 'the hero blinds the giant with the help of a stake heated in the fire' and 'the hero escapes from the giant with the help of his sheep' could be rewritten in the following manner: 'S_1: hero n: stake P: sight u S_2: giant', and 'S_1: hero n: sheep P: hero u S_2: giant' (where the position of S_1 at the beginning of the statement indicates that S_1 is the Subject of the action leading to this state).

8. The Semantic Dimension

Before beginning the syntactical analysis of the Cyclops tale, I listed the different qualities of the actors who play actantial roles and said that the description of the context from which they have come enriches a semantic definition of those actors.[39] Where the unfolding of the narration is concerned, such a definition has several basic functions: first, it defines the competence of the actors, thus modifying the action and its modalities (the hero resorts to a ruse or to a stratagem according to what he knows, to physical force and to violence according to his power, etc.); second, in the repetition of analogous semantic elements through the narrative, it determines the *isotopies* that will establish the semantic coherence of the story;[40] third, in general, it describes the ideological background from which the narration emerges. The semantic microuniverse underlying the story receives its necessary elements from a semantic definition.

In this context, the smallest figurative elements play an important role. It is useful, for example, to point out that though the giant is generally blinded by means of a stake in the versions examined, in the

[38] Some suggestions have recently been put forward in this direction; see n. 20 above.

[39] One would have to integrate the spatial structure of the story, which L. Marin calls the "topographical code," with the logic of the narrative; see his "Essai d'analyse structurale d'*Actes* 10, 7–11, 18," *Recherches de science religieuse* 58 (1970): 39–61, reprinted in *Etudes sémiotiques* (Paris, 1971), 263–84.

[40] For a definition of *isotopy*, see F. Rastier, "Systématique des isotopies," in *Essais de sémiotique poétique*, ed. A. J. Greimas (Paris, 1972), 80–106, and *Sémantique interprétative* (Paris, 1987), 87ff. and 109ff.; see also M. Mathieu, "Les acteurs du récit," *Poétique* 19 (1974): 357–67, who shows that the actorial system in the story has a cohesive function, and J.-M. Adam, *Pour lire le poème* (Brussels, 1985), 119ff.

Odyssey the blinding is done with a hunting spear heated in the fire. One does not have to look far to find the reason for this variation: the giants in the seven analyzed tales impale their victims on a stake in order to roast them before eating them, while in the *Odyssey* Polyphemus, who eats Odysseus's companions raw, does not have such an instrument. Though this is a minimal modification to the way in which the second ordeal comes about, it is essential to understanding the values of the society described by the story. In the *Odyssey* the opposition between civilization and savagery organizes the semantic world expressed in the syntagmatic unfolding of the story. The eating of raw flesh underscores the savagery of the monster who, in the Homeric version, does not own any iron instrument, in accordance with the norms of ancient Greek culture.[41]

In Greece, moreover, civilized conduct was governed by a complex system of norms that regulated in particular how a stranger should be treated. In analyzing the various narrative amplifications in Homer's tale, it is clear that the syntactical structure of the utterances making up these amplifications is marked by this very important social code. So, after having given his identity as a warrior, Odysseus asks Polyphemus for hospitality; in Greece this request for a countergift in response to the transfer of information about one's own identity has its place in the system of rules governing contact with a stranger; we have here, therefore, a positive feature of civilized behavior. Similarly, a little further on in the story, Polyphemus promises (in the seeming mode, it is true) to give Odysseus a gift of hospitality. This promise also corresponds to one of the rules of exchange that constitute a civilized attitude. So it is not just the qualities attributed to the actors that define the isotopies of the story; the qualities of the objects exchanged, the qualities of the actions created by the narration, and the

---

[41] I reject the opposite view of Page [n. 12], 9ff.; Page says quite correctly, however, that the Cyclops's victims as portrayed by Euripides (*Cyclops* 243ff. and 397ff.) are roasted or boiled before being eaten. The profound influence on the story of social problems of the time has been recognized by Meuli [n. 3], 79ff.; however, without denying the tale's folk origin, Meuli emphasizes this influence to the point of eliminating the specific qualities that distinguish the tale from Homer's verses (see also 69ff.).

W. Burkert's attempt [n. 3], 31ff., by contrast, to see in the Homeric episode traces of a primal search for food and a primordial sacrifice going back to Paleolithic days is doomed from the start. Only within the legend as told by Homer is it possible to conceive of the spear heated in the fire not as a primordial weapon, but as an instrument of savagery. See, for instance, G. S. Kirk, *Myth: Its Meaning and Function in Ancient and Other Cultures* (Cambridge, 1970), 162ff., despite the criticisms of J. N. O'Sullivan, "Nature and Culture in *Odyssey* 9?," *Symb. Osl.* 65 (1990): 7–17.

transfers determined by these actions contribute equally to strengthening the semantic coherence of the narration.

I could give several more examples. In one of the Berber versions of the Cyclops story added by Gabriel Germain to Hackman's corpus,[42] it is Allah who whispers to the hero the stratagem of the sheepskin to escape from the Cyclops, and the whole story is basically an excuse for a confrontation between Allah, who inspires and supports the hero, and the giant, also described as an "enemy of God." The version from Gascony (21F), by contrast, is full of Christian ideology: it is the hero's sister's prayers to God and the Virgin that provoke the act of cannibalism, and it is owing to her silver cross that the girl finally emerges alive from the giant's belly. In the Lappish story (12F), it is just as likely that the fact that the Cyclops's victims are boiled and not roasted has some very precise cultural motivation.[43] This variation cannot be understood in relation to the other versions unless its ethnographic context is taken into account. Indeed, the way cultural context gives meaning to and systematizes narrative values should be examined individually for every story in the collection.

In any event, cannibalism in these contexts is not a mere figure of speech; it is not a figurative element chosen from among others in order to establish the hero by way of contrast, as has been suggested.[44] In the stories analyzed, it is an integral part of the ideological system underlying the tale.

Thus the figurative elements vested in the actors as well as in the relations linking them to one another can only be explained with the help of a "syntax and semantics" of narrative. But these elements, the organization of which is revealed by the grammar of the narrative, in turn make sense only if placed within the ideological context and cultural system from which the story emerged.

9. Unresolved Problems

Let us recall, in conclusion, some of the problems which have not been tackled owing to the limits of this study but which could be included in an exhaustive narrative analysis.

[42] Germain [n. 6], 58ff.

[43] The human flesh eaten by the Cyclops is also boiled in a version from Brittany (19F = 19H) and in a German version (26H).

[44] J. Geninasca, "Conte populaire et identité du cannibalisme," *Nouv. Rev. Psychanal.* 6 (1972): 215–30.

First, to be defined as a distinctive feature of the Cyclops story, the syntactical narrative structure articulated here should be compared to the narrative structures of other stories in which a hero confronts a giant. An encounter with the stories in Hackman's groups B and C, even though this model furnished one of the terms of the comparison, is not sufficient to affirm whether the model fits the Cyclops story.

Moreover, a comparison within the Cyclops corpus of several versions having the same cultural heritage would have allowed us to determine the operating rules of narrative variation. In Greece, for example, comparing and contrasting Odysseus's story with the *Cyclops* of Euripides or with the legendary tradition which makes the Cyclopes into Titan blacksmiths would have shown not only that the Homeric tale is merely one version among several but that the narrative program of the *Odyssey* eliminates at the same time it actualizes a whole series of narrative possibilities contained in the "competence" of the legend.[45]

Finally, if the question of the meaning of the story has often been posed in this study, the problem of its function, that is to say, the role it plays within a textual and cultural entity hierarchically superior to it, has not been addressed. Yet it is clear that some of the tales in Hackman's group C are different from the tales related to the Cyclops story not only because of their narrative structure but also because of their function. In stories 193H, 195H, and 199H, for example, the devil's complete or partial blindness is said to be the result of molten lead that was poured into one or both of his eyes. Thus these tales take on the aetiological function of explaining, of establishing a belief, which is not the case with the versions related to the Cyclops story. In two previous studies, moreover, I went so far as to call the Homeric narrative of the adventures of Odysseus with Polyphemus a myth, with no intention of questioning its traditional classification as epic: this latter category, in Greece at any rate, refers to a certain textual form (hexameters recited to the accompaniment of the lyre, the use of formulaic language, the mixture of dialects, etc.) rather than to a genre characterized by a specific content. Any attempt at defining tale and myth, to say nothing of legend, by means of contrasting the terms would be doomed, as this study shows. I will simply say this: without

[45] Euripides, *Cyclops* 23ff., Hesiod, *Theogony* 139ff., Apollodorus 1.2.1, etc.; cf. R. Mondi, "The Homeric Cyclops: Folktale, Tradition, and Theme," *Trans. Am. Philol. Assoc.* 113 (1983): 17–38, and my "Les figures grecques du gigantesque," *Communications* 42 (1985): 147–72, esp. 157ff.

mentioning the commonsense criteria for integrating any story into one of the categories mentioned, the study of a large number of tales would probably show that if there are distinctions in their respective narrative structures, the differences have more to do with figurative elements and the ideological universe the story expresses than with the syntagmatic unfolding of the action. The distinction between tale and myth seems to be most apparent in the qualities possessed by a story's actors and in the isotopies those qualities define by means of the values vested in the narrative action. But this distinction would probably seem minimal if one did not take into account the role played by the enunciation of these forms within the society from which they spring. A narration that explains and prepares the performance of a ritual will never be classed as a tale, and a tale told to children at bedtime, whatever its value as an example, will never be called a myth—a narrative category, for that matter, which is completely ethnocentric and Western.[46] What should we say of a story like the one in the *Odyssey*?

The difficulty suggested by this question and the misunderstanding of scholars on this point show how urgent is the need for an entirely new definition of narrative categories.

[46] Cf. Detienne 1981, 123ff., and my brief remarks in "Evanescence du mythe et réalité des formes narratives," in *Métamorphoses du mythe en Grèce antique*, ed. C. Calame (Geneva, 1988), 7–14, with the studies cited below, Chapter 8, n. 3.

CHAPTER 7

Narrative and Names: Laconian Women's Names as Figures of Speech

> If we think of a poem as a work of art, it is immaterial whether the name "Odysseus" has a referent or not.
>
> —G. Frege

1. The Name as "Rigid Designator" and Classifier

Justifiably perhaps, proper names have always been an embarrassment to linguists and anthropologists alike. The practitioners of language analysis have been intrigued by the very specific process that lends signification to an anthroponym, the particular form of the proper name examined here. Since the beginning of time, the unambiguous function of the anthroponym (a function the Ancients were well aware of) has been to designate the identity of an individual in a univocal manner. This unique referential capability induced Jakobson to take the proper name as the prime example of a coded system that refers, in the final analysis, back to its own code.[1] Beyond the study of the pragmatic functions of the name when used as a form of address or as a baptismal appellation, we now have at our disposal the notion of the name as "rigid designator" developed by S. A. Kripke; this term means that, in contrast to other types of "designators," the proper name always points to the same unique object, in any possible world.[2]

---

[1] Jakobson 1963, 117f. For the proper name in general and the linguistic analyses of it, see J. Lyons, *Semantics* (Cambridge, 1977), 1:215ff., and, in particular, J. Molino, "Le nom propre dans la langue," *Langages* 66 (1982): 5–20.

[2] S. A. Kripke, *Naming and Necessity* (Cambridge, Mass., 1980), 8ff., 48ff., and 57ff.; cf. the remarks of L. Doležel, "Proper Names, Definite Descriptions, and the Semantic Structure of Kafka's 'The Trial,' " Working Papers, *Centro internazionale di semiotica e di linguistica di Urbino* 115 (1982): 2ff., and R. Martin, *Langage et croyance: Les "univers de croyance" dans la théorie sémantique* (Brussels, 1987), 137ff.

In anthropology, by contrast, more importance was of course placed on the social dimension of the name as a means of classifying an individual within a hierarchy based on social function, family structure, or some other taxonomy.[3] Thus the name becomes a way of assigning to each individual a determinate place in a social and world order; it also becomes a way of recognizing, at any given moment, the status of which it is the mark.

An excellent marker of the individual's identity in either a fictional world or a social organization, when it does not assign a particular classified status, the proper name, by its very definition, seems to escape the use of rhetoric. How can one play on the meaning of a "rigid designator"? How can divergence occur (if we associate figures of speech with such a phenomenon) in what is preeminently divergent? According to the semantics I will shortly describe, ancient Greek literature breaks through the limitations of the current definitions of the proper name and uses it as a true figure of speech, as a rhetorical figure.

2. From Morphology to Semiotic Narrative Structures

The Greek system of naming heroes and other figures has two signal characteristics. On the one hand, Greek names are often formed of compound words, and the two lexemes making up the combination generally refer to a precise signified. On the other hand, literary texts, beginning with Homeric poetry, show that the Greeks were aware of the possibilities of meaning which reside in a name; they continually play with the etymologies of names, a game that can go as far as the speculations in Plato's *Cratylus*. Thus, aside from the linguistic and/or nonlinguistic reference to an individual, Greek names are indeed signifiers.

As regards the first distinctive characteristic of the Greek naming system, different types of formations can be distinguished. In taking over the classification of the Indian grammarian Pāṇini of the fourth century B.C.,[4] the German practitioners of Greek grammar excelled in

---

[3] See C. Lévi-Strauss, *La pensée sauvage* (Paris, 1962) 226ff. and 253ff., as well as C. Bromberger, "Pour une analyse anthropologique des noms de personnes," *Langages* 66 (1982): 103–24.

[4] See Pāṇini 2.2.23 and 2.1.22.

determining morphological categories. The principal ones are the following:

- "possessive" compounds (of the type *bahuvrīhi* 'one who has much rice'), which describe a quality possessed by the subject thus named; the typical example is *Eteoklēs* 'one who possesses true fame';
- "determinative" compounds (of the type *tatpuruṣa* 'his servant'), in which the second element is determined by the first; the paradigm would be *Theodōros* 'a gift of god' or *Dēmokleitos* 'renowned among the people';
- compound names with a verb element, in which the first part modifies the second; the example can be cited of *Agēsilaos* or *Agelaos* 'one who leads the people'.

Cases where the determining lexeme and the determined lexeme, or governing element and governed element, are reversed are numerous: we find *Hippostratos* and *Stratippos* 'one who has an army of horsemen' and *Lokhagos* and *Agelokhos* 'one who commands a company'.

In addition to these compounds, one often finds proper names in the form of patronymics (*Pēleidēs* 'son of Peleus') or, less frequently, matronymics (*Lētoidēs* 'son of Leto'). There is also a whole series of forms made up of a single lexeme, generally a noun or an adjective, with a suffix (*Polemōn* 'the warrior', *Agathōn* 'the good', *Philōn* 'the loved one', etc.). In this latter group, we find names of women taken from plants or animals (*Melissa* 'the bee', *Khelidōn* 'the swallow', *Daphnis* 'the laurel branch', *Murrhinē* 'myrrh', etc.).

If we move from morphology to semantics—and with names formed on the basis of adjectives or taken from plants and animals, we have already moved there—we notice that in compound names reference is generally made to aristocratic qualities or to the qualities of heroes of an earlier time: strength or courage, aptitude in fighting and commanding, glory, reputation, piety, and so forth. And women's names are no exception: being based as they often are on men's names, their signifiers consequently refer to similar signifieds.[5] This type of compound proper name is not unique to ancient Greece, it is also found in several ancient Indo-European languages, such as Iranian,

---

[5] For all these morphological and semantic remarks, see the primary article by Ernst Fraenkel, "Namenwesen," *Realenc. Alt.-Wiss.* 14, no. 2 (Stuttgart, 1935): 1611ff. and 1644ff., and the chapter about names in early Greece by E. Schwyzer, *Griechische Grammatik*, vol. 1 (Munich, 1939), 427ff., 452ff., and 634ff.

Celtic, or Germanic.[6] Semiotically, the names belonging to this category of compounds are particularly interesting in that nearly all of
them are not only utterances but also condensed microstories made up
of an utterance either of state or of action according to their form.

3. Playing with Names in Homer and Hesiod

It has been said that the Greeks had a particular penchant for playing
with the etymologies of names, one dating at least from the time when
their use of a written alphabet allows us to observe it. In Homeric
poetry, it is mainly a matter of attributing to the hero the qualities
evoked by either the signifier or the signified of the lexemes into which
his name can be broken down. Besides being called *Skamandrios*,
Hector's son is also called *Astuanax* 'he who rules the city' because, as
Homer says, his father 'protects the city'. Though the play on words
here involves the signifieds of the lexemes of the son's name, more
often it concerns the signifier, as is the case with the name of Scylla,
Skulla, which is clearly associated with the lexeme *skulax* 'little dog'.[7]
Moreover, the etymological play on words allows the signified
attributed to the name to be integrated with the action in progress.
Odysseus's complaint to Calypso allows the nymph to associate the
name *Odusseus* with the verb *oduresthai* 'to mourn'. Thus at the level of
syntactical surface structure, the procedure is to articulate the signified
given to the name as a microstory involving one of the narrative
utterances of which the bearer of the name is the subject. As regards
the semantic surface of the semiotic narrative structures, the procedure
in question here affixes to the name the qualities that the action attributes to the actor.

It is interesting to note with respect to the name Odysseus that the
play on *Odusseus* has no basis in etymology, since the origins of this

---

[6] For compound names in other cultures see G. R. Cardona, *Introduzione all'etno-
linguistica* (Bologna, 1980), 139, and M. Durante, *Sulla preistoria della tradizione poetica
greca*, vol. 2 (Rome, 1976), 102ff.

[7] Homer, *Iliad* 6.402f., and *Odyssey* 12.85f.; these examples and the following ones
are taken from the excellent analysis by E. Risch, "Namensdeutungen und Wörter-
klärungen bei den ältesten griechischen Dichtern," *Eumusia: Festgabe für E. Howald
zum. 60. Geburtstag* (Erlenbach, 1947), 72–91 (reprinted in *Kleine Schriften* [Berlin,
1988], 294–313); see also H. Mühlestein, "Redende Personennamen bei Homer," *Stud.
Mic. Egeo-anatol.* 9 (1969): 67–94, and the many examples given by Nagy 1979, passim;
see further Svenbro [Chap. 1, n. 25], 74ff.

name seem not to have been Indo-European. In other passages, the same name is aligned with the verb *odussasthai* 'to be angry with', as well as *oduresthai*. The narrative context of this association is of course different, since it concerns Poseidon's anger toward the hero; Odysseus becomes the one who polarizes the anger, he "who is hated" (by the god).[8] In the *Odyssey* the narrative pleasure that the poet derives from playing on the meaning of the anthroponyms culminates in the confrontation of Odysseus with Polyphemus. In the famous series of etymologizing echoes with *outis* and *mētis*, the resonances on the name become an essential element of the plot itself. The play on the proper name is to some extent "narrativized." The historical and philological truth contained in the etymology is of little importance since some of the compounds in Greek names make no sense; what is important is the syntactical and semantic associations made by the enunciator of the name. In the Greek epic, etymological play on a name is dependent on narrative verisimilitude. The person manipulating the name is unconcerned with the objective meaning of the etymology he proposes, nor does he wonder about its external reference: it is enough for him that this etymology fits into the logic, the syntax, and particularly the semantics of the narrative fiction where the name and its wearer are inserted.

Hesiod indulges in the same game for speculative purposes. When tracing the genealogies of gods in the *Theogony*, the Boeotian poet follows the lead of epic poetry and starts with the signifiers of the divinities' names to lend some shape to their histories: Aphrodite thus becomes *aphrogenēs* 'born of the foam'. But Hesiod sometimes also gives the impression of forming names from a narrative statement or, at any rate, of creating a new "mythic" statement based on what the name says. This is what happens in the case of the Nereids *Kumodokē* and *Kumatolēgē*, who, with Amphitrite, are the calmers of the waves; the name of the first one indicates that she "receives the waves"; the

---

[8] Homer, *Odyssey* 5.160 and 339f.; the two approaches to the etymological pun on the name *Odusseus* are both found in 1.55ff. For modern speculations on these "etymologies," see G. E. Dimock, Jr., "The Name of Odysseus," *Hudson Review* 9 (1956): 52–70 (reprinted in *Essays on the Odyssey*, ed. C. H. Taylor, Jr. [Bloomington, Ind., 1963], 54–72), and N. Austin, "Name Magic in the *Odyssey*," *Calif. Stud. Class. Ant.* 5 (1972): 1–19. Odysseus's name takes on other forms in other texts: see H. von Hamptz, *Homerische Personennamen* (Göttingen, 1982), 355ff., and J. Peradotto, *Man in the Middle Voice: Name and Narrative in the* Odyssey (Princeton, 1991), v ff. For the story of the Cyclops, see *Odyssey* 9.355ff., 405ff., and 502ff., with the commentary of Goldhill, 1991, 31ff., and the references given above, Chap. 6, n. 31.

second "calms them."[9] Doubtless this way of "making narrative" out of names from a catalogue of mythological figures tends, in a poetry that is still oral, to help fix them in people's memory and to contribute to their figurativization. Once again, we have to realize that the word-play involving Aphrodite's name is not based on any etymological reality. The association suggested by Hesiod in his speculations in the *Theogony* does not stop Euripides, through the mouth of a Hecuba sorely afflicted by the same Aphrodite, from going in a quite different direction and associating her name with *aphrosunē* 'madness'.[10] Plato in the *Cratylus*, of course, has stretched to the limit such speculations on the form and meaning of names in general.

In Greek epic poetry, therefore, to utter a name is not merely to identify a (fictional) individual but also sometimes to express what one thinks that person is; it sometimes means breaking the link of pure denotation, of rigid designation (to return to Kripke's concept); it means making the proper name into a metaphor of sorts for the narrative actor so named, by attributing to him the signifieds of the lexemes that form his name.

4. Names of Young Women in Alcman

Besides the epic texts attributed to Homer and Hesiod, Greek lyric poetry, with its pragmatic character, allows us to dispense with the narrow framework of the fictional text and extend our criticism of Kripke's concept of "rigid designation."

Successive Significations

Two fragments of poems by Alcman, the poet of ancient Sparta at the end of the seventh century B.C., offer a list of young women's

[9] Hesiod, *Theogony* 195ff. and 252ff.

[10] Euripides, *Troades* 990. Other examples are related to epic poetry and to tragedy by A. Moreau, "Etymologie et mythe originel: Adraste, Andromaque, Déjanire," in *Sens et pouvoir de la nomination dans les cultures hellénique et romaine*, ed. S. Gély (Montpellier, 1988): 105–24, and N. Loraux, "*Poluneikēs epōnumos*: Les noms des fils d'Œdipe, entre épopée et tragédie," in Calame [Chap. 6, n. 46], 151–66. For the development by the sophists and the philosophers of the etymological wordplay in question here, see M. Salvadore, *Il nome, la persona: Saggio sull' etimologia antica* (Genoa, 1987), 53ff. That wordplay leads the first pre-Socratic philosophers to question the conventional character of nouns and names: see M. Kraus, *Name und Sache: Ein Problem im frühgriechischen Denken* (Amsterdam, 1987), 147ff.

names that seem to imply a signified which goes beyond the simple identification of an individual. These were poems sung during a ritual, compositions referring to protagonists who had real social existences. Composed for choruses of adolescents, these verses were recited by young women in various rites that marked the successive phases of tribal initiation for girls becoming women. In Alcman's verses the group of young Spartan women express their affectionate admiration for the chorus leader, the *khorēgos*; she is a girl possessing outstanding beauty and general excellence and has most probably completed the initiation cycle; therefore, as a recent initiate, she plays a pedagogical role vis-à-vis the adolescents in the chorus. In ancient Sparta a girl's transition to adulthood entailed an education in the civic values that defined the role girls were destined to play as the future wives of citizens, as well as in beauty and sexuality.[11]

After evoking a myth from the legendary history of Sparta and praising the qualities of the *khorēgos*, the young women who sing our first poem name themselves. Neither Nanno with her flowing hair nor godlike Areta nor even Thylakis or Kleēsithēra can rival the *khorēgos*; none of them will go to Ainēsimbrota to beg that Astaphis might be hers, that Philylla might look upon her or Demareta or the charming Vianthemis. We will briefly examine the morphology of these different names and find their corresponding signifieds, although this is not a game in which Alcman indulges. *Areta*, with no suffix, means "excellence"; *Nannō* 'the little doll' and *Philulla* 'the beloved child' are diminutives; the names *Sulakis*, *Astaphis*, and *Vianthemis*, by way of their various suffixes, derive from the plant world: "poppy heart," "raisin," and "violet," *Damareta*, a determinative compound name, excels in the heart of the *dēmos*, while *Kleēsithēra*, a compound name with a verbal element, is "famous in hunting."[12] *Ainēsimbrota*, another verbal compound, ought to be "praised among mortals"; her place in the catalogue of chorus members gives her a special status outside the chorus. Ainesimbrota, who perhaps possesses magic powers, probably led a different group of young women from the one singing Alcman's verses.

[11] The poems of Alcman analyzed here are fragments 1 and 3 Page = 3 and 26 Calame. On Alcman's position as narrator in the poems performed by the choruses of young women, see above, Introduction, § 7.

[12] The verb *kleein* can also have the active meaning of "celebrating" as well as the passive meaning of "being celebrated." On the similarly formed names of *Patroklos* and *Kleopatra*, see Nagy 1979, 102ff. and 318f.

With its references to merit and reputation in the eyes of the people, its appeal to feelings of affection evoked by diminutives, and its metaphors inspired by the plant world, the system of signifiers of the names of the adolescents taking part in the Spartan choruses seems to conform to the Greek norm.

There remain Agido and Hagesichora, the two girls whose praises the chorus members sing, displaying their rivalry in affection.

The name *Agidō* not only assigns to this friend of the *khorēgos* the function of "directing" (by association with the verb *hēgeisthai*) but also designates her possibly as a descendant of Agis, founder of the Agiades dynasty, one of the two royal families that held power in Sparta. The name *Hagēsikhora* describes the function this figure performs vis-à-vis the young women who announce her role and sing her virtues: Hagesichora "leads the chorus," she is the *khorēgos*.[13]

Proofs of Veridiction

With the young women in Alcman's poems, we move away from the heroes and heroines of myth in the epics and the *Theogony* to the real participants in a ritual set in time and space, in the Sparta of the seventh century B.C. It is appropriate to ask whether the qualities suggested by the names of these adolescents refer to a social existence beyond the linguistic and textual context.

There is no evidence to suggest that name giving was any different in Sparta than in the rest of Greece. In Laconia, as in Attica, the name was conferred about a week after birth, probably on the occasion of the presentation of the newborn boy to the old men, as described by Plutarch.[14] If this custom was also observed for baby girls, the names of Alcman's chorus members are not initiation names describing the qualities of the initiates at the moment of their rite of passage to adulthood. Insofar as they are spoken with meaningful intention, these names, given shortly after birth, project the values they denote onto

[13]Cf. Calame 1977, 1:92ff., 2:46, and 2:140f.

[14]For the giving of names in Greece, see Fraenkel [n. 5], 1615f.; for the Spartan ceremony presenting the newborn to the *leskhē*, made up of the oldest members of the tribe, see Plutarch, *Lycurgus* 16.1ff., and the commentary by W. Den Boer, *Laconian Studies* (Amsterdam, 1954), 234ff. This presentation rite has been compared, with good reason, to the Athenian rite of the Amphidromia by J.-P. Vernant, *Mythe et pensée chez les Grecs* (Paris, ²1966), 134ff. See also A. Paradiso, "L'agrégation du nouveau-né au foyer familial: Les Amphidromies," *Dial. Hist. Arch.* 14 (1988): 203–18.

the child's future; it is essentially a question of enunciating an infant's potential. When growth has been completed and has established the distinctive features of a nearly adult person, there is nothing to prevent the enunciator (taking on the role of the textual narrator/speaker in the case we are considering) from comparing a posteriori the qualities implied by the name and the values that have developed over time in the bearer of the name. If one looks at this process from a semiotic point of view, the enunciator (depending on the narrator in a text), as it were, takes on the actantial role of Sender, subject of an act of confirmation concerning the values given to the bearer of the name. The syntactical and semantic interplay based on the morphology of the name offers the bearer the pretext for a real (semionarrative) *sanction* phase.[15] As a result, this interplay is no longer the prerogative of the literary text, it becomes a possibility open to general linguistic use. The enunciator of the play on names is not necessarily a narrator and the *sanction* that his name–play represents as regards the qualities of the person named can also exist outside the logic of the narrative. Verisimilitude and confirmation are at stake, but a verisimilitude that informs a social reality, or at least its representation, and not solely a fictional world.

It is in fact to this double interplay of confirmation on the plane of literary fiction and on the plane of social representation that Alcman devotes himself in the second poem we will consider, one also composed to be sung by a chorus of young women. The nearly adult woman who attracts the attention of the chorus members and who probably leads the group is called *Astumeloisa* 'object of solicitude for the citizens'. First, she is evoked as running across the ceremonial ground "like a star crossing the sparkling sky, a golden branch or a light feather," then the poet takes apart her name (a compound of the determinative type), attributing to her the signified indicated by its elements: Astymelousa is now "the object of everyone's affection" (*melēma damōi*). We can thus infer that in the first poem, Alcman, and through him the chorus, used the pretext of the signified discernible in the name of the *khorēgos*, *Hagēsikhora*, to emphasize that figure's qualities as leader of the chorus. This development in the meaning of

---

[15] On the semiotic and narrative concepts of enunciator/narrator, receiver, sanction, and veridiction, see above, Introduction, § 1, and Chapter 6, § 4, as well as Greimas and Courtés 1979, 125, 320, and 417f.

proper names is of particular relevance to poems composed to be performed as part of a ritual. The name exerts a ritual impact on the construction of the new status and social identity for which the young girls singing the song are destined. It probably allows as well the ritual reperformance of this highly pragmatic poetry.

The works of the iambic poet Archilochus, Alcman's contemporary, and those of the comic author Aristophanes in the fifth and fourth centuries generally confirm the veridictory use of the Greek naming system in the area of both semiotic and social representation.[16] Though the tone changes when satire is the medium, the process is the same: it is a question of playing on the syntax and semantics suggested by the particular morphology of the Greek name in such a way as to double one or the other of the narrative statements of which the person named is the subject, and particularly in the case of comedy, to refer to the (alleged) faults of the character who bears the incriminating name. In literary texts linked to a specific event and social situation, what should be pure naming becomes the occasion for a metaphorical narrative, one that is both intra- and extrareferential.

5. Rhetorical Play on "Speaking Names"

The potential meanings that reside in the Greek name turn it into a microstory. At the moment of the "baptismal" ritual, the utterance is only self-referential; later on, its enunciator can give it an extralinguistic and extradiscursive reference by associating certain of its potential meanings with the qualities of the name bearer, now an adult; in compositions for special occasions such as those of Alcman and Archilochus, this process of extralinguistic reference is combined with the internal reference implied by the etymological play, a combination brought about by way of integrating the name into the narrative development of the text. In the special case of Alcman's ritual poetry and in the satirical compositions of an Archilochus or an Aristophanes, we move from the narrative verisimilitude of the epic to the (social) truth value of the name. If, in this etymological play, we turn back to

---

[16] See M. G. Bonanno, "Nomi e soprannomi archilochei," *Mus. Helv.* 37 (1980): 65–88, who describes the names as being semantically "recharged" by Archilochus and Aristophanes; see also A. Aloni, *Le Muse di Archiloco: Ricerche sullo stile archilocheo* (Copenhagen, 1981), 123ff.

the denotative function of the proper name, we see, without excluding the name's identifying function, that it refers only to certain qualities of the individual named. And the sanction imposed by the one who speaks the name and plays with its meaning affects the internal (intra-discursive) reference (*référentialisation*) as much as the external (extra-discursive) reference (*référenciation*) of the micronarrative.[17]

As a category, Greek anthroponyms assume, in addition to their role in identifying individuals, the classification function that anthropologists attribute to them, with good reason. Because of the qualities they designate, they often confirm the social status that family origin automatically confers on the newborn; thus we frequently find reference to aristocratic values in the semantic elements of the Greek anthroponyms. But added to the classifying function widely recognized in anthropology is the very original possibility of attributing a posteriori to the now adult individual the qualities suggested by the meaning of the lexemes composing his name. In this way the Greek name gives its enunciator/narrator the occasion for an act of veridiction as regards the attributions of the social or narrative actor named. The men of letters in the Classical period certainly knew how to play on the "ontological" character ascribed to the nature of the name by members of the Tartu School; because of the imitative value assigned to them by Plato in *Cratylus*, "to know names is also to know things"; that, at any rate, is what the philosopher himself affirms.[18] Therein lies, at least in poetry of a ritual and occasional character, the source of the dialectical relationship we have observed between the internal and external references produced by etymological play on the meaning of Greek anthroponyms. When this knowledge about names is incorporated into literary discourse, it contributes to the figurativization and metaphorization of the text and also to the process of (extradiscursive) *référenciation*.

We have come a long way from the idea of the rigid designator developed by Kripke and from the idea of self-reference proposed by Gottlob Frege. In the case discussed here, the identity denoted by the name can vary according to the world of which the name is part. In its

[17] For *référenciation* as opposed to *référentialisation* within the text, see above, Introduction, § 3 with n. 15.

[18] See J. M. Lotman and B. A. Uspenskij, "Mito—nome—cultura," in *Tipologia della cultura*, ed. J. M. Lotman and B. A. Uspenskij (Milan, 1975) (orig. ed.: Tartu, 1973), 83–109. See also Plato, *Cratylus* 422d ff. and 435d; cf. T. M. S. Baxter, *The Cratylus: Plato's Critique of Naming* (Leiden, 1992), 90ff.

literary usage the Greek proper name becomes the equivalent of a rhetorical figure: in addition to its designating role, it performs an indisputable figurative and descriptive function, one deriving from the play on etymology. The name is a metaphor for the identity of its bearer.

CHAPTER 8

Myth and Rite: Theseus and the Double Utterance of a Space

1. The "Action" as "Spoken"

The problem of how myth and ritual relate to each other has become a topos of anthropological research and discourse. It originated in the study of Greek religion. Using Greek examples, Jane Harrison, at the end of the last century, based her theory of myth on ritual: myth is the "spoken" aspect, the *legomenon*, of ritual, which itself is conceived as being "acted," *drōmenon*.[1] The story of the myth becomes the plot of the ritual. At the end of the nineteenth century, ritual was viewed as an act of consecration, connected with the rhythm of the vegetal world; the latter, in turn, was supposed to have inspired both ancient religious feeling and its ritual expression. Independently of the growth processes of vegetation, Harrison's theory continued to thrive among the various directions taken by anthropology.

Though the problem of the relation between myth and ritual can no longer be described in terms of the primacy of one over the other, the use in France of linguistics and semiotics in anthropological discourse has helped to reinforce and confirm the criterion for distinguishing them, as defined at the end of the nineteenth century. If we follow the more recent—and repeated—statements of Claude Lévi-Strauss regarding the linguistic nature of myth as language in contrast to that of ritual as action, we arrive at the reflections that close his book *L'homme*

[1] See especially J. Harrison, *Themis: A Study of the Social Origins of Greek Religion* (Cambridge, 1927), 42ff. and 328ff.

nu: ritual gestures, condensed substitutes for mythological speech, are an attempt to fill the gaps in continuity arising from the conceptual process of mythic production.[2] When the perspective is reversed, ritual is seen as a response to the effect created by mythological activity.

The nature of the categories myth and ritual would no doubt have to be clearly articulated before any relationship between them could be established—particularly in light of Marcel Detienne's 1981 discussion of the concept of myth.[3] Without entering into the details of ongoing work on this subject, we should first realize that any series of Greek texts regularly connects actions that take place within a cult with stories featuring gods and heroes; the sequence of codified acts of which ritual consists then appears as the logical consequence of the actions forming the legendary narrative. It follows that according to the theory of narrative put together by Greimas's group, the action narrated in a given myth serves as the manipulation phase for the ritual acts that are repeated whenever the corresponding ritual is performed.[4]

Moreover, the semiotic objects that we perceive as "myths" and "rituals"—categories developed in Western anthropological thinking—seem to depend on the same process of conceptualization, the functioning of which can crudely be termed "symbolic." Myths and rituals share with such other means of expression as iconic representation or spatial organization the status of products of symbolic thinking, the principle of which consists in combining and reorganizing on different levels the particulars of the natural and cultural worlds; very briefly, and certainly simplistically, we can say that myths and rituals depend on a semiosis (the operation that installs a relation between the signifier and the signified) of the second degree.

2. The Construction of Space

With these theoretical perspectives in mind, space will be considered as a constructed object, one which constructs itself and which is

[2] Lévi-Strauss 1958, 257ff., and Lévi-Strauss, *L'homme nu* [Chap. 6, n. 13], 600ff.

[3] See the reflections of Detienne 1981, 87ff., reflections I tried to extend in "Illusions de la mythologie," *Nouveaux actes sémiotiques* 12 (1990): 5–35, and " 'Mythe' et 'rite' en Grèce, des catégories indigénes?" *Kernos* 4 (1991): 179–204; for a tentative definition of myth in the modern acceptance of the term, see Calame, "Le discours mythique," in *Sémiotique: L'école de Paris*, ed. J.-C. Coquet (Paris, 1982), 85–102. For the rite, see, for example, Burkert [Chap. 6, n. 3], 35ff.

[4] For a definition of the *manipulation* phase, see Greimas and Courtés 1979, 244ff. I developed the suggestions of these authors in Calame 1990, 162ff.

endowed with different qualities depending on the subjects who perceive it as they move through it and organize its distinctive features into a syntagmatic order.[5] The construction of space thus corresponds to a progression of a narrative nature during which space is gradually defined not only by its geometrical limits but also by its semantic qualities. This is all the more true in the present instance, since Greek myths and rituals are, of course, only available in written texts. The mode in which information is transmitted strongly influences the process used to construct space. In a text, the actor who constructs the space of a myth or a ritual as the action progresses can be the same as the one who is the enunciator of the space; the space is thus grounded in the *he/she* (simulated) of the different actors who move through it. Built only in part from previously defined places, it is made up of the actions of these actors and their qualifying characteristics.

The assimilation of the construction of space with its enunciation has two consequences. First, a careful distinction must be made between the process of enunciation of mythological discourse or of the text in which the ritual is described—a process that brings to the fore the author of the source as enunciator and the reader as enunciatee—and the enunciation of the space in the interior of the discourse with its narrative aspect, a process that has just been highlighted. In the second case, the enunciator, internal to the text and the story, corresponds to the actor who constructs the space. Since we are here at the level of the story with its pronominal indices referring to a third person and its space-time framework corresponding to a "mythic" or "ritual" past, it is clear that the level of the uttered enunciation is bracketed. In the enunciation process within the text, by contrast, the construction of space again appears to be linked to the linearity of narrative development; it can thus be seen as a path that follows the direction of the stages of the narrative.[6]

One more remark concerning ritual is in order. The protagonists of a ritual that is either "acted out" directly or described in a text are generally the users and "consumers" of cult sites which themselves consist of spaces constructed prior to their use. The problem then arises as to the relationship between the enunciation process in which these spaces are constructed by their enunciator (the architect) and the

---

[5] Cf. the remarks of Greimas and Courtés 1979, 132ff.

[6] On the possible use of this idea of a narrative "path" (*parcours*) in architecture, see J.-M. Floch, "Sur l'usage du terme 'parcours' dans le discours sémiotique," *Bulletin G. R. S. L.* 18 (1981): 9–15.

subsequent enunciation when the spaces become the object of their consumers during any celebration of the cult. The enunciatees of the space constructed by the architect-enunciator become its enunciators the moment they occupy and "use" it. In the texts examined here, this relationship is difficult to grasp and will not be discussed. The problem of the dual process of constructing space, however, is worth scrutiny.

3. The Diachronic Perspective

Conforming to the Greek schema previously mentioned, Plutarch, in his *Life of Theseus*, describes the celebration of a series of Athenian rituals as the logical consequence of the legendary return of the hero to the city after his success in conquering the Minotaur.[7] If some of these festivals—for instance, the Cybernesia or the Theseia—are organically linked to the return of Theseus, others seem to have little to do with the myth—from a narrative point of view, at any rate—such as the Oschophoria and the Pyanopsia. In the latter festival, which we shall return to later, eating a vegetable stew and carrying an olive branch hung with the first fruits of various edibles are the only things attached narratively to similar acts carried out by Theseus; and the author of *Parallel Lives* states that these same ritual acts are linked to the very old myth of welcome that the Athenians reserved for the Herakleidai. One can hazard a guess that the Cretan episode of the Theseus story did not always refer to the ritual it is linked with through the narrative logic of an aetiological play.

The use of writing, as well as the Greek taste for representing the figures of myth, put the historian of Greek religion in a situation that anthropologists know only rarely: it affords us the opportunity to study the development and the evolution of a myth in different versions. Without wanting to evoke a historicism that might risk drowning the question of the relation between myth and ritual in a bog of chronology problems, we have to admit that the story of Theseus, and particularly the episode of the Cretan Labyrinth, did not always enjoy the same popularity, especially in Athens. It was only under Peisistratos in the middle of the sixth century that Theseus was gradually

[7] See Plutarch, *Theseus* 22f., with the useful commentary of C. Ampolo and M. Manfredini, *Plutarco: Le vite di Teseo e di Romolo* (Milan, 1988), 230ff.

substituted for Herakles and became the supreme Athenian national hero. The Homeric epic certainly knew of the expedition of Theseus to Crete and the abduction of Ariadne, but we must wait until the end of the sixth century before an epic tradition appears in Athens entirely dedicated to the myth of Theseus. These chronological facts are fully confirmed by the extraordinary diffusion in Athens of vase paintings showing the different episodes of the Theseus myth and by the inscription of those episodes circa 500 B.C. on the metopes of the Athenian Treasury at Delphi, parallel to the labors of Herakles.[8] Even if the promotion of this myth was backed by the aristocratic family of the Alkmaionidai at Delphi, there is no doubt that as early as the tyrants, and certainly by the end of the Persian Wars, Theseus had become the model of the Greek citizen.

The historians of Greek religion agree that the Pyanopsia and the Oschophoria are festivals that predate by a good deal the period when the Theseus story was current in Athens. The intrusion of the Cretan episode as a myth of founding (*aition*) is therefore secondary to the ritual celebration. If the historical argument is not convincing, one can cite rituals similar to those celebrated at Athens, particularly on the Island of Samos, which have nothing to do with any episode of the Theseus myth.[9] The ritual is therefore not an offspring of the myth; the myth developed independently and did not emerge from the ritual. The privileged cases of the Pyanopsia and the Oschophoria, by showing the almost casual relationship of two preexisting rituals with an independent legend, raises the question as to what similarities between these two different orders of cultural manifestation paved the way for their alliance; the immediate motivation is found in the need for political propaganda and arises from external circumstances. In ex-

[8] *Odyssey* 11.322ff.; on the dating of the first *Theseid* mentioned by Plutarch, *Theseus* 28.1, see H. Herter, "Theseus," *Realenc. Alt.-Wiss. Suppl.* 13 (Munich, 1973): 1046 and 1233f.; according to F. Jacoby, *Atthis* (Oxford, 1949), 219f. and 394f., the Athenian poem about Theseus would have come from the circles of those opposed to the tyrants, those circles that would have favored the reforms of Cleisthenes at the end of the sixth century: cf. Calame 1990, 398ff. For the development of the iconography of figures, see K. Schefold, *Götter- und Heldensagen der Griechen in der spätarchaischen Kunst* (Munich, 1978), 150ff., and F. Brommer, *Theseus: Die Taten des griechischen Helden in der Antiken Kunst und Literatur* (Darmstadt, 1982), 73f. and 149f.

[9] See Deubner 1932, 142 and 198; the case for the Oschophoria is particularly convincing since an inscription proves that it was at the origin of a cult belonging to one of the great Athenian families; see Parke 1977, 79f. For the festival of Samos, see especially Pseudo-Herodotus, *Vita Homeri*, 462ff. (V, p. 213f. Allen), and M. P. Nilsson, *Griechische Feste von religiöser Bedeutung* (Leipzig, 1906), 116ff.

ploring this question, I shall stay within the narrow bounds of the problem posed by the construction of mythical and ritual space.

4. The "Space" of the "Myth"

The sources of the Theseus story are numerous, and many are the versions based on it. I shall therefore follow, with one exception, the most explicit and complete text, that of Plutarch in the *Life* that he dedicates to the Athenian hero.[10] The very narrowness of the framework for this study makes it easier to keep it simple.

A Space Created in the Narration

The following is a summary of the movements of Theseus that serve to construct space. First, we find the city of Athens, where Theseus voluntarily puts himself at the head of the third tribute of seven young men and seven young women to be sent each year to Minos in compensation for the murder of his son Androgeos. Theseus then receives two pilots from the Island of Salamis to help him; on his return he will consecrate a monument in their honor at the port of Phaleron and institute the feast of Cybernesia. Then Theseus starts out on an itinerary of propitiation with multiple stops. From the Prytaneion where he takes charge of the adolescents destined for the Minotaur, Theseus goes to the Delphinion, one of Apollo's sanctuaries near the temple of Olympian Zeus at the foot of the Acropolis.[11] There he places the suppliant's branch, a sacred olive branch wrapped in wool. Plutarch links this act of supplication with the procession at the beginning of the month of Mounychion that brought the young Athenians to the Delphinion. From there, Theseus goes down to the sea where he sacrifices a goat to Aphrodite.

Plutarch totally omits the detail of a storm that descends on Theseus during the crossing and the hero's dive into the watery domain of his divine father, Poseidon; the latter ordeal, which implies the presence of Minos on the ship taking the hero to Crete, is essential, however, to the ideological use the Athenians made of the myth. It can be consid-

[10] See Plutarch, *Theseus* 15ff., to be read with the commentary quoted in n. 7 above; see also Bacchylides 17.

[11] The remains of the temple came to light in 1962; see Travlos 1971, 83ff.

ered an integral part of the story, all the more so since it was already known to Bacchylides and illustrates the dual origin—human and divine—of the hero. Theseus then lands in Crete. Ariadne falls in love with the young man and gives him the ball of thread that will save him in the Labyrinth. There follows the fight with the Minotaur and the hero's victory over the monster, half man, half bull. Free of the Labyrinth, Theseus takes away Ariadne and the adolescents he has saved, and they sail home. After another tempest, he arrives at Naxos and, voluntarily or against his will, depending on the version, abandons the young Cretan woman who falls under the sway of Aphrodite and Dionysus; there follows the assumption into heaven of the heroine and the celebration of her cult by the people of Naxos. Theseus then arrives at Delos, where he sacrifices to Apollo; following that, with the young men and women saved from the Labyrinth, he dances the dance of the crane, which will be incorporated into the feast of Aphrodisia.

The hero then sails to Athens; he forgets to change the sails of his ship, thus prompting the suicide of his father, Aegeus. Theseus lands at Phaleron, the old port of Athens, and makes sacrifices and libations to unnamed gods. He is informed of his father's death, and the procession that accompanies him on the seashore is full of lamentation. Arriving in the city, Theseus buries his father and then, as the text says, "he fulfills the vow he made to Apollo" in recognition of the role played by the god in his safe return; everything points to the fulfillment of this vow taking place at the Delphinion where it had originally been made. It is also probably in this sanctuary that Theseus and his companions, in a ritual feast, eat the soup made of the remains of the expedition's food. This communal meal is the origin, according to Plutarch, of the Pyanopsia festival. Theseus then proceeds to the consecration of his ship, probably in connection with the feast of Cybernesia and the dedication at Phaleron of the monuments to the pilots, the hero's assistants.

Plutarch then describes the actions of Theseus in connection with the ritual practices of the Oschophoria: a procession with the fourteen adolescents brought back from Crete, with two of the young men dressed as girls, and with branches (ōskhoi) carried in honor of Dionysus and Ariadne; add to that the meal prepared by the mothers of the young people on their departure and the repetition of the stories they told to give them courage. As the study of the space of the Oschophoria will confirm, these practices are certain to have taken place on the road from Phaleron to the city; they thus precede those connected with the Pyanopsia and should be linked to the libations mentioned in connection with the hero's landing. The ritual of the consecration of the ship, the origin of the Cybernesia, also originates in the arrival at Phaleron.

Finally, the *sanction* phase at the conclusion of the story synchronizes perfectly with the mode of the *manipulation* phase: at the beginning of the tale, the hero is his own Sender, and at the end he sanctions himself. It is Theseus himself who orders the families of the adolescents he saved to contribute to the sacrifice celebrated in his honor in the space reserved for him. This space most probably corresponds to the sanctuary where the bones of the heroes brought back from Skyros in the first half of the fifth century were buried: it was near the Agora and beside the Prytanikon.[12]

Isotopies of Narrated Space

The space through which Theseus moves is made up of a series of places defined by their geographical positions: Athens, Phaleron (by the sea), the sea, Crete, the sea, Naxos, Delos, the sea, Phaleron (by the sea), Athens. But these places themselves serve as socially constructed spaces meant for political or religious functions; some predated Theseus's presence: the Prytaneion and Delphinion in Athens, the Palace of Knossos and the Labyrinth on the island of Crete, the sanctuary of Apollo at Delos, and so forth; others come into being because of the hero's actions: the probable place of the cult of Aphrodite Epitragia, the sanctuary of Ariadne at Naxos, the sanctuary around the statue of Aphrodite consecrated at Delos, the monuments to the pilots at Phaleron, the Athenian sanctuary of the hero himself. In addition, because of his actions, in each of these places Theseus enters into communication with an actor who in turn determines the semantics of the place; Theseus's movement through space can thus be charted (see Figure 5).

Each place visited is defined paradigmatically by its geographical position, by its sociological function, and by the qualities of the actor with whom the hero comes in contact there. But the process of constructing space operates because of Theseus's journey, in other words on the syntagmatic axis. The space of the "mythical" narrative,

[12] See Plutarch, *Theseus* 36.4, and Parke 1977, 81. On the position of the sanctuary of Theseus, see Travlos 1971, 234 and 578; see also the complementary bibliography in Calame 1990, 180 n. 32. The Prytanikon should by no means be confused with the Prytaneion.

Geographical setting	ATHENS		PHALERON (seashore)	
Sociological setting	*Prytaneion*	*Delphinion*	*Salamis*	*Sacrificial site*
Actor	Theseus	Apollo	Assistants (pilots)	Aphrodite

SEA		CRETE		SEA
storm	*Amphitrite*	*Knossos*	*Labyrinth*	storm
	Poseidon	Ariadne/Minos	Minotaur	

NAXOS	DELOS		SEA/CITY
Site of Ariadne's cult	*Sanctuary*	*Cult site*	*Phaleron/ Acropolis*
Dionysus	Apollo	Aphrodite	Aegeus

PHALERON		ATHENS	
Cult site?	*Monuments*	*Delphinion*	*Sanctuary*
Ariadne, Dionysus	Pilots	Apollo	Theseus

Figure 5. Theseus's movement through space

a space with a semantic complexion based on two figurative iso-topies,[13] one geographical, the other "actorial," is constructed by the unfolding of the action; when enunciated, it becomes one of the Predicates for the *he*-Subject of the story.

The geographical isotopy can be defined thematically on the axis of civilization/noncivilization, Athens representing the civilized pole and the sea with its storms encountered on the outward and inward jour-

---

[13]Regarding isotopy as a repetition of analogous semantic elements throughout the narrative, see above, Chapter 6, n. 40.

neys representing the opposite pole. Between these two poles there are intermediate positions defined by the seashore (the place where civilization and noncivilization meet) and the islands such as Crete and Delos (very near civilization) or Naxos (close to the opposite pole). On this scale, two sites occupy a special position: the house of Amphitrite, to which entry is gained from the sea (noncivilization) but which permits the hero to make contact with the domain of the divine (beyond civilization), and the Labyrinth of Crete, which contains the noncivilized in the civilized. From a syntagmatic point of view, the space occupied by the hero's journey on this isotopy is a circle: leaving civilization, he returns to civilization after having been confronted with different values (situated on the axiological scale), culminating in the absence of civilization, a category that must be defined more precisely.

It is also on the semantic axis of civilization/noncivilization that the "actorial" isotopy turns, doubling the figurative path defined by the geographic isotopy. In their respective areas of intervention, the gods with whom Theseus communicates relate to civilization in different ways: Aphrodite as the patron of sexual instinct and by virtue of her irresistibility, Poseidon as the master of unrestrained physical forces (tempests, earthquakes), Ariadne as the earthly representative of Aphrodite, Dionysus in his function as master of the uncontrollable urges lurking within humans; Apollo, master of the arts of the Muses and deliverer from the scourges of nature, is on the side of civilization and serves as its protector. Syntagmatically, the path of Theseus along this isotopy again takes the form of a circle leading from civilization back to civilization, passing through different modes and degrees of noncivilization. At the center is the ordeal of the Labyrinth, site of the noncivilized in the civilized, and the battle against a being that is half animal, half man. And the path along the actorial isotopy is framed by the double conjunction of the hero and his own person, that is, his role as representative of civilization and of civility, a role consecrated at the cult site he founds for himself near the Prytanikon in the civic center of the city of Athens. And Aegeus should not be forgotten; the human equivalent of Theseus's divine father, Poseidon, Aegeus follows a path opposite to that of his son: abandoning the civilized world and the territory of the city, he drowns himself in the sea. The death of Aegeus allows his son, Theseus, to succeed him on the throne of Athens.

Having opened the way for the sons and daughters of the citizens of Athens to return, the death of Aegeus also allows the value of the civilization/noncivilization opposition on which the Cretan episode, semantically speaking, is based to be defined more accurately. Within this opposition, the roles played by Apollo Delphinios in administering the *dikē*, by Minos as the first political enemy of Athens, and by both Aegeus in Athens and Poseidon in Trozen as *basileus* emphasize a civic element relative to the administration of power in the city. Aphrodite, Ariadne, and Dionysus define a second semantic trait that corresponds to sexuality, and more precisely, to adult sexuality. If Theseus leaves, then returns to, civilization, the circle is complete only when the hero has acquired the values that will prepare him to use his civic power and to experience adult love.

Many historians have interpreted Theseus's expedition to Crete as a rite of passage, one characterized by the three typical phases of a break with the old order (adolescence of Theseus), a plunge into chaos (his dive into the sea, the battle with the Minotaur), and a return to the new order of adulthood (Theseus as king of Athens).[14] But if it is true that Theseus's journey leads eventually to his ascension to the throne of Athens, its circular aspect defines it as the confirmation of the values already attributed to the hero rather than a transition from a previous state to a new one. By successfully exploring a space of which the various stations correspond semantically to the different values defined by the axiological gradation from the absence of civilization to a civilized state, Theseus sharpens his image as civilizing hero in the realms of sexuality and civic administration. He thus takes the place of Herakles and shows himself to be superior to his model. By constructing the space in which he evolves, he creates and confirms his own identity.

5. "Ritual" Space

Lack of space, as it were, compels me to choose among the rituals linked with the return of Theseus to Athens and to consider only those festivals in which the actors are adolescents, namely, Oschophoria and Pyanopsia in the month of Pyanepsion (end of October), to which should be added the procession of young women on the sixth of the month of Mounychion (end of April). I shall also have to draw a

---

[14]See, for example, H. Jeanmaire, *Couroi et Courètes* (Lille, 1939), 312ff.; other references are found in Calame 1990, 461 nn. 77 and 78.

curtain over the philological problems raised by the often ambiguous and incomplete texts that describe the way these three festivals were celebrated.

Little more is known about the festival of the sixth of Mounychion than has been noted already. Probably the young women carried suppliant branches, like the one Theseus had previously carried, to Apollo Delphinios and perhaps to Artemis. The spatial function of this ritual can only be seen in relation to the other Athenian rituals performed under the aegis of the Theseus myth.

The Oschophoria festival is somewhat better known. Spatially, the central action of this feast consists of a procession from the temple of Dionysus to the sanctuary of Athena Skiras at Phaleron. The temple of Dionysus probably corresponds to the sanctuary of Dionysus *en Limnais*, situated at the southeast of the Acropolis not far from the Delphinion.[15] The procession consisted of adolescents chosen from families living within sight of the city; two of the boys were dressed as girls. They carried vine branches with grapes attached (*ōskhoi*), and sang "Oschophorian" hymns. The celebration also contained a footrace in which young men competed on behalf of their tribes. There followed a banquet featuring dishes prepared by *deipnophoroi* representing the mothers in the myth who gave their children food as they left for Crete. The festival naturally ended with libations accompanied by ritual shouts; the composite character of this ritual recalls, according to Plutarch, both the victory over the Minotaur and the stupor brought on by the news of the death of Aegeus.[16]

The Pyanopsia took place on the seventh of the month of Pyanepsion, perhaps on the same day as the Oschophorian celebration. Singing a ritual song, adolescents went around to houses and hung on their doors olive branches wrapped in wool and decorated with figs, small loaves of bread, a pot of honey, a flask of oil, and a wine goblet. A young man whose mother and father were still living carried the same kind of branch, called an *eiresiōnē*, a suppliant's branch, to Apollo's temple; this temple can almost certainly be identified as the Delphinion. The gift of the *eiresiōnē* was supposed to mark the end of

[15] On the position of the temple of Dionysus "in the marshes," see Travlos 1971, 169, 274, and 332. On the temple of Athena Skiras in Phaleron, see T. Kock, "*Skiras*" (2), *Realenc. Alt.-Wiss.* 3, no. 1 (Stuttgart, 1927): 534–35, as well as Ampolo and Manfredini [n. 7], 231.

[16] Texts on the Oschophoria can be found in Deubner 1932, 142ff.; see also Parke 1977, 77ff., and Calame 1990, 143ff.

sterility in the opinion of the Ancients. On the same occasion, a soup made of vegetables was eaten in honor of Apollo and to ward off famine. Hence the name of the festival, the Pyanopsia, or feast of the bean soup.[17]

In spite of gaps in documentation, the gestures and objects used in these rituals are rich in symbolic value and cry out to be decoded. I shall limit myself here to a space constructed henceforth not by the *he* of the hero but by the *they* of the adolescents celebrating the three rituals. The syntagmatic development of the geographical isotopy is also circular: we shall make our way from the Delphinion (for the ritual of the sixth of Mounychion) to the Dionyseion to the Sanctuary of Athena Skiras at Phaleron (for the Oschophoria) and back to the Delphinion (for the Pyanopsia). Beginning with the civic values (justice, citizenship) of the cult of Apollo Delphinios, this itinerary will take us to the margins of civilization:[18] the Dionyseion is near Ilissos, "in the marshes," at the edge of the urban space circumscribed by the walls of Athens in the classical period; the temple of Athena Skiras stands at the end of the *khōra*, at the point of passage to noncivilization represented by the open sea. Moreover, as in myth, the qualities and fields of action of the gods with whom the actors of the rituals come in contact define an "actorial" isotopy. There is no need to repeat the values attributed to Apollo and Dionysus. It is much more surprising to find Athena, guardian of the city, on the margins of civilization; but the added name Skiras refers to places at the limits, and explains the inclusion of the goddess in this particular cult.

The age of the participants, the cross-dressing, the expression of mingled sorrow and joy, the *eiresiōnē* marking the end of a period of "sterility," all these elements seem to classify the rituals in question here, especially the Oschophoria, as cult practices associated with tribal initiation rituals. Scholars have already confirmed this observation for the story on which these festivals are based.[19] But spatial exploration here, even more than in the mythological narrative, is limited to the margins of civilization without any incursion into the

[17] Cf. Parke 1977, 198ff., 75f., and Calame 1990, 150ff.
[18] For the cult of Apollo Delphinios, see F. Graf, "Apollon Delphinios," *Mus. Helv.* 36 (1979): 1–22.
[19] See, in particular, the excellent remarks of P. Vidal-Naquet, "Le chasseur noir et l'origine de l'éphébie athénienne," *Annales E. S. C.* 23 (1968): 947–64, reprinted in *Le chasseur noir* (Paris, [2]1983), 151–76.

realm of pure savagery. In addition, the path taken by those practicing
the ritual, in its circularity, does not seem to indicate a transition: at the
end of the circle, in the Pyanopsia, the actors are still adolescents.

6. Specific Features of "Myth" and "Ritual"

I shall not belabor the common elements linking the space defined
in the Theseus myth to the space through which the actors in our
rituals move, namely, the probable design of the "parcours," the
semantic and thematic character of the isotopies which turn that route
into an exploration of values existing on the edge of civilization, and
the age of the enunciators of the space, corresponding for Theseus as
for the protagonists of the ritual to adolescence. These similarities
certainly make it possible, in a given historical situation, to bring
together the myth and the preexisting Athenian rituals. But the differences stand out as much as the similarities; there is no ritual equivalent
to the Labyrinth ordeal, no return from Phaleron to Athens, no contact with the adult sexuality represented in the myth by the union with
Ariadne and Aphrodite, a temporal displacement with regard to the
intervention of the *deipnophoroi*, and so on. It is evident that the
somatic and spatial contingencies governing the ritual action do not
permit the metaphorical journeys that the imagination is able to construct in the story.

In the case considered here, however, there is more; to cite only the
example of Theseus, the journey enunciated by this figure from the
Prytanikon to the sanctuary consecrated to Theseus near the Agora by
way of Crete, Naxos, and Delos forms, as we have seen, a civic and
political isotopy that does not exist in the corresponding rituals. The
latter, for their part, give rise to an isotopy of the vegetal world that is
more or less absent from the Cretan episode of the myth. At the end of
last century, this observation would have led to a historical argument
regarding the chronological precedence of the rituals linked to the cult
of the forces of nature and vegetation. The fact that the vegetation
isotopy represents only one of the levels of expression of the rituals in
question here would have been forgotten. Likewise omitted would
have been the fact that the vegetable products presented and consumed
in these ritual celebrations are cooked meals, prepared for consumption by civilized man. "Myth" and "ritual" can develop independently,
saying in their own semiotic ways only very partially the same things.

When a certain sameness of theme (here the semantic axis of civilization/noncivilization) makes it possible, however, the relating of ritual actions to mythological actions, where the former become the logical consequence of the latter, adds to the ritual a syntactical as well as a semantic dimension. Because the ritual sequence is recorded in the mythic narrative, Theseus becomes the Sender of the *they*, subject of the actions in the Pyanopsia and the Oschophoria. Thus the action of the myth assumes the function of the *manipulation* phase, and social practice takes on that of the *sanction* phase with respect to the action performed in the ritual: the story superimposes an indispensable cognitive dimension on the pragmatic dimension of the ritual to which it is linked; and in the particular case studied here, this cognitive dimension exists on the political plane, if not on the plane of sexuality.

In conclusion, let us consider again the specific character of myth, or more simply, of myth's narrated story, as it relates to ritual action. However clearly the two are connected, myth cannot be viewed as a commentary on ritual or as the paradigm ritual mimics or even as the (verbal) language of ritual. If myth in Greece seems to be the "foundation" for ritual, it is only to the extent that it allows the cognitive dimension to come into being and inserts ritual action in a true narrative sequence. By using the term "cognitive dimension," I am borrowing a concept that belongs to the semiotics of narrative and I should define its meaning. The expression does not mean that myth is an explanation of ritual but that myth includes ritual as it unfolds in a program which not only confers authority on its actors but at the same time sanctions the action once it is accepted in social practice.[20]

Theseus, hero of the myth of which he is the Subject, becomes the one who guarantees the validity of the performance of the corresponding ritual. His action is more than a model of behavior for young participants in the Pyanopsia and the Oschophoria. Because of the qualities invested in the hero's image and the space created during his journey, we can articulate the categories brought into play in the ritual and enrich their semantic value. Bearing branches of vine or olive, cooking vegetarian food as opposed to meat, lamentations contrasting

[20] These reflections have appeared in expanded form as "Mythique (discours, niveau)" and "Rite/rituel" in Greimas and Courtés 1986, 148f. and 189f. As for the visions to which the Theseus myth was subjected, see, in particular, L. Bertelli and G. F. Gianotti, "Teseo tra mito e storia politica: Un' Atene immaginaria," *Aufidus* 1 (1987): 35–58.

with expressions of joy, and so forth, all take on a civic sense the moment Theseus becomes the Sender. If the ritual in question expresses the progression of its protagonists to the boundaries of the uncivilized according to an essentially vegetal isotopy, the myth describes the same progression in the episode of the struggle against the Minotaur with all its political and sexual implications. The myth has recourse to political and sexual images in order to confer narrative consistency on the theme (the exploration of the margins of civilization) that is realized by the ritual with images from the growing of vegetables and from the production of civilized alimentation.

The Theseus legend does not merely organize rituals that were probably originally independent into a coherent sequence; it also allows the relationships between Aphrodite, Dionysus, Poseidon, Athena, and Apollo to be rethought by connecting them to the history of the city; and above all, it makes the action involving the performers of ritual the same as the action involving its own protagonists. Ritual and myth are finally both *drōmena*; but in the case dealt with here, the action of the second completes that of the first in the sense of a "resemanticization." The ritual is deflected in the direction of the civic and the political. The myth allows us to reconsider the intellectual and operative development that the ritual represents;[21] it reinforces the ideology played out in the ritual. The adolescents taking part in the Pyanopsia and the Oschophoria, while acting on the plane of the fertility of the vegetal world and of the cultivation of its products, acquire through ritual action and social practice those values that Theseus affirms during the stages of his Cretan journey.

Because the thematic and figurative similarities between myth and ritual (it being a question in both of exploring the limits of civilization), myth can enrich ritual action at the level of the imaginary; it can rethink the categories constructed by the ritual as it unfolds. This combination of identity and specificity can be clearly seen on the spatial plane. In myth as in ritual, the protagonist, because he enunciates space, is his own enunciator; he makes the narrative space into a mirror, one that then redefines him. But ritual creates space using predetermined sites, while myth can break away from that limitation. Myth thus confers on the action of a cult an ideological dimension which conforms to the social and political context in which that ritual action is performed.

[21] Cf. Calame 1990, 47ff.

Appendix

(*Translations by* DEREK COLLINS)

Texts A

1. Homeric Hymn to Demeter 1–5

> Δήμητρ' ἠΰκομον, σεμνὴν θεόν, ἄρχομ' ἀείδειν,
> αὐτὴν ἠδὲ θύγατρα τανύσφυρον, ἣν Ἀϊδωνεὺς
> ἥρπαξεν, δῶκεν δὲ βαρύκτυπος εὐρύοπα Ζεύς,
> νόσφιν Δήμητρος χρυσαόρου ἀγλαοκάρπου
> παίζουσαν κούρῃσι σὺν Ὠκεανοῦ βαθυκόλποις.

Of lovely-haired Demeter, revered goddess, I begin to sing,
of her and her slender-ankled daughter, whom Aïdōneus
seized—and loud-thundering, far-seeing Zeus consented—
while, far from Demeter of the golden sword and splendid fruit,
she was playing with the daughters of Okeanos, whose dresses fall
  in deep folds.

2. Homeric Hymn to Apollo 1–4

> Μνήσομαι οὐδὲ λάθωμαι Ἀπόλλωνος ἑκάτοιο
> ὅν τε θεοὶ κατὰ δῶμα Διὸς τρομέουσιν ἰόντα·
> καί ῥά τ' ἀναΐσσουσιν ἐπὶ σχεδὸν ἐρχομένοιο
> πάντες ἀφ' ἑδράων, ὅτε φαίδιμα τόξα τιταίνει.

I shall keep in mind and not leave out far-shooting Apollo
at whose coming the gods in the house of Zeus tremble;
and all spring up from their seats at his approach,
when he bends his shining bow.

3. Homer, Iliad *2.493*

᾽Αρχοὺς αὖ νηῶν ἐρέω νῆάς τε προπάσας.

The commanders of the ships in turn I shall tell, and all
the ships together.

Texts B

1. Homeric Hymn 9 (to Artemis), 1–9

῎Αρτεμιν ὕμνει, Μοῦσα, κασιγνήτην ῾Εκάτοιο,
παρθένον ἰοχέαιραν, ὁμότροφον ᾽Απόλλωνος,
ἥ θ᾽ ἵππους ἄρσασα βαθυσχοίνοιο Μέλητος
ῥίμφα διὰ Σμύρνης παγχρύσεον ἅρμα διώκει
ἐς Κλάρον ἀμπελόεσσαν, ὅθ᾽ ἀργυρότοξος ᾽Απόλλων
ἧσται μιμνάζων ἑκατηβόλον ἰοχέαιραν.
   Καὶ σὺ μὲν οὕτω χαῖρε θεαί θ᾽ ἅμα πᾶσαι ἀοιδῇ·
αὐτὰρ ἐγώ σε πρῶτα καὶ ἐκ σέθεν ἄρχομ᾽ ἀείδειν,
σεῦ δ᾽ ἐγὼ ἀρξάμενος μεταβήσομαι ἄλλον ἐς ὕμνον.

   Sing Muse, of Artemis, sister of the Far-Shooter,
arrow-shooting maiden, reared with Apollo.
she, watering her horses near Meles with its deep rushes,
swiftly courses her solid gold chariot through Smyrna
to richly vined Klaros, where Apollo of the silver bow
sits awaiting her, the far-darting archer.
   May you and all the goddesses take pleasure in my song, as it is;
but first I begin to sing of you, starting with you,
then, having started with you, I shall pass to another song.

2. Homer, Iliad *1.1–7*

Μῆνιν ἄειδε, θεά, Πηληϊάδεω ᾽Αχιλῆος
οὐλομένην, ἣ μυρί᾽ ᾽Αχαιοῖς ἄλγε᾽ ἔθηκε,

πολλὰς δ' ἰφθίμους ψυχὰς Ἄϊδι προΐαψεν
ἡρώων, αὐτοὺς δὲ ἐλώρια τεῦχε κύνεσσιν
οἰωνοῖσί τε πᾶσι· Διὸς δ' ἐτελείετο βουλή,
ἐξ οὗ δὴ τὰ πρῶτα διαστήτην ἐρίσαντε
'Ατρεΐδης τε ἄναξ ἀνδρῶν καὶ δῖος 'Αχιλλεύς.

Wrath, make it your song, goddess, the wrath of Peleus's son Akhilleus.
Ruinous, it caused countless pains for the Akhaians
and sent to Hades many brave souls
of heroes, making their bodies prey for dogs
and birds of all kinds; and the will of Zeus was accomplished,
since that time when the two first stood divided in quarrel,
the son of Atreus lord of men and godlike Akhilleus.

Texts C

1. Homeric Hymn to Aphrodite 1–6

Μοῦσά μοι ἔννεπε ἔργα πολυχρύσου 'Αφροδίτης,
Κύπριδος, ἥ τε θεοῖσιν ἐπὶ γλυκὺν ἵμερον ὦρσε,
καί τ' ἐδαμάσσατο φῦλα καταθνητῶν ἀνθρώπων,
οἰωνούς τε διϊπετέας καὶ θηρία πάντα
ἠμὲν ὅσ' ἤπειρος πολλὰ τρέφει ἠδ' ὅσα πόντος·
πᾶσιν δ' ἔργα μέμηλεν ἐϋστεφάνου Κυθερείης.

Muse, tell me the deeds of richly golden Aphrodite
of Cyprus, who stirred sweet longing in gods
and subdued the races of mortal men
as well as the hovering birds and beasts of all kinds,
which both earth and sea nourish in their multitude;
all indeed have a care for the deeds of the fair-crowned Cytherian.

2. Homeric Hymn 19 (to Pan), 1–7

'Αμφί μοι 'Ερμείαο φίλον γόνον ἔννεπε, Μοῦσα,
αἰγοπόδην, δικέρωτα, φιλόκροτον, ὅς τ' ἀνὰ πίση
δενδρήεντ' ἄμυδις φοιτᾷ χορογήθεσι νύμφαις,
αἵ τε κατ' αἰγίλιπος πέτρης στείβουσι κάρηνα
Πᾶν' ἀνακεκλόμεναι, νόμιον θεόν, ἀγλαέθειρον,

μὶχμήενθ', ὃς πάντα λόφον νιφόεντα λέλογχε
καὶ κορυφὰς ὀρέων καὶ πετρήεντα κέλευθα.

Of Hermes' dear son tell me, Muse,
the goat-hooved, two-horned, noise-loving one who over
wooded meadows roams together with chorus-wont nymphs
who tread the heights of ledges too sheer for goats
invoking Pan, the god of herds, the splendid-haired,
unkempt one, who has as his domain all snowy crests
and mountain peaks and rocky paths.

3. Homer, Odyssey 1.1–9

Ἄνδρά μοι ἔννεπε, Μοῦσα, πολύτροπον, ὃς μάλα πολλὰ
πλάγχθη, ἐπεὶ Τροίης ἱερὸν πτολίεθρον ἔπερσε,
πολλῶν δ' ἀνθρώπων ἴδεν ἄστεα καὶ νόον ἔγνω·
πολλὰδ' ὅ γ' ἐν πόντῳ πάθεν ἄλγεα ὃν κατὰ θυμόν,
ἀρνύμενος ἥν τε ψυχὴν καὶ νόστον ἑταίρων,
ἀλλ' οὐδ' ὣς ἑτάρους ἐρρύσατο ἱέμενός περ·
αὐτῶν γὰρ σφετέρῃσιν ἀτασθαλίῃσιν ὄλοντο,
νήπιοι, οἳ κατὰ βοῦς Ὑπερίονος Ἠελίοιο
ἤσθιον· αὐτὰρ ὁ τοῖσιν ἀφείλετο νόστιμον ἦμαρ.

Tell me, Muse, about that man, the one of many turns who
     in many ways
wandered after he destroyed the holy citadel of Troy
and saw the cities of many men and learned their mind;
many were the pains he suffered at sea in his spirit,
vying for his life and for the homecoming of his companions,
but even so he could not rescue his companions, despite his eagerness;
for they perished of their own recklessness,
fools who consumed the oxen of Hyperion Helios;
and that one took away their homecoming day.

4. Homer, Iliad 2.484–93

Ἔσπετε νῦν μοι, Μοῦσαι Ὀλύμπια δώματ' ἔχουσαι—
ὑμεῖς γὰρ θεαί ἐστε, πάρεστέ τε, ἴστέ τε πάντα,
ἡμεῖς δὲ κλέος οἶον ἀκούομεν οὐδέ τι ἴδμεν—

οἵ τινες ἡγεμόνες Δαναῶν καὶ κοίρανοι ἦσαν·
πληθὺν δ' οὐκ ἂν ἐγὼ μυθήσομαι οὐδ' ὀνομήνω,
οὐδ' εἴ μοι δέκα μὲν γλῶσσαι, δέκα δὲ στόματ' εἶεν,
φωνὴ δ' ἄρρηκτος, χάλκεον δέ μοι ἦτορ ἐνείη,
εἰ μὴ Ὀλυμπιάδες Μοῦσαι, Διὸς αἰγιόχοιο
θυγατέρες, μνησαίαθ' ὅσοι ὑπὸ Ἴλιον ἦλθον·
ἀρχοὺς αὖ νηῶν ἐρέω νῆάς τε προπάσας.

Tell me now, Muses dwelling in Olympian homes—
for you are goddesses, you are there, and you know everything,
while we hear only report, but we know nothing—
who were the leaders and rulers of the Danaans.
I could not recount or name their full number,
not if I had ten tongues or ten mouths,
a voice unbroken or a bronze heart within,
not unless the Olympian Muses, daughters of aegis-bearing Zeus,
recall the many who came up to the walls of Ilion.
The commanders of the ships in turn I shall tell, and all
            the ships together.

Texts D

1. *Hesiod,* Theogony 1–52

    Μουσάων Ἑλικωνιάδων ἀρχώμεθ' ἀείδειν,
αἵ θ' Ἑλικῶνος ἔχουσιν ὄρος μέγα τε ζάθεόν τε·
καί τε περὶ κρήνην ἰοειδέα πόσσ' ἁπαλοῖσιν
ὀρχεῦνται καὶ βωμὸν ἐρισθενέος Κρονίωνος·
καί τε λοεσσάμεναι τέρενα χρόα Περμησσοῖο
ἢ Ἵππου κρήνης ἢ Ὀλμειοῦ ζαθέοιο
ἀκροτάτῳ Ἑλικῶνι χοροὺς ἐνεποιήσαντο
καλοὺς ἱμερόεντας, ἐπερρώσαντο δὲ ποσσίν·
ἔνθεν ἀπορνύμεναι, κεκαλυμμέναι ἠέρι πολλῇ,
ἐννύχιαι στεῖχον περικαλλέα ὄσσαν ἱεῖσαι,
ὑμνεῦσαι Δία τ' αἰγίοχον καὶ πότνιαν Ἥρην
Ἀργείην, χρυσέοισι πεδίλοις ἐμβεβαυῖαν,
κούρην τ' αἰγιόχοιο Διὸς γλαυκῶπιν Ἀθήνην
Φοῖβόν τ' Ἀπόλλωνα καὶ Ἄρτεμιν ἰοχέαιραν
ἠδὲ Ποσειδάωνα γαιήοχον ἐννοσίγαιον

καὶ Θέμιν αἰδοίην ἑλικοβλέφαρόν τ' Ἀφροδίτην
Ἥβην τε χρυσοστέφανον καλήν τε Διώνην
Λητώ τ' Ἰαπετόν τε ἰδὲ Κρόνον ἀγκυλομήτην
Ἠῶ τ' Ἠέλιόν τε μέγαν λαμπράν τε Σελήνην
Γαῖάν τ' Ὠκεανόν τε μέγαν καὶ Νύκτα μέλαιναν
ἄλλων τ' ἀθανάτων ἱερὸν γένος αἰὲν ἐόντων.

Let us begin to sing of the Helikonian Muses, who dwell on great and sacred Mount Helikon; around the dark-blue spring, with delicate feet, they dance, and around the altar of the very mighty son of Kronos; after washing their soft skin in the spring of Permessos or of the Horse or of sacred Olmeios, at the topmost point of Helikon they created beautiful, lovely choral dances, and they nimbly moved their feet; starting from there, covered in much mist, they moved along at night sending forth a very beautiful voice, hymning aegis-bearing Zeus and Lady Hera of Argos, who walks in golden sandals, and the daughter of aegis-bearing Zeus, bright-eyed Athene, and Phoibos Apollo and Artemis the arrow-shooter and Poseidon, master of the earth and earth-shaker, and venerable Themis and quick-glancing Aphrodite and golden-crowned Hebe and beautiful Dione and Leto and Iapetos and Kronos of the devious counsel and Eos and great Helios and radiant Selene and Earth and great Okeanos and black Night and the holy race of the other immortals who exist forever.

Αἵ νύ ποθ' Ἡσίοδον καλὴν ἐδίδαξαν ἀοιδήν,
ἄρνας ποιμαίνονθ' Ἑλικῶνος ὑπὸ ζαθέοιο·
τόνδε δέ με πρώτιστα θεαὶ πρὸς μῦθον ἔειπον,
Μοῦσαι Ὀλυμπιάδες, κοῦραι Διὸς αἰγιόχοιο·
«Ποιμένες ἄγραυλοι, κάκ' ἐλέγχεα, γαστέρες οἶον,
ἴδμεν ψεύδεα πολλὰ λέγειν ἐτύμοισιν ὁμοῖα·
ἴδμεν δ', εὖτ' ἐθέλωμεν, ἀληθέα γηρύσασθαι.»
Ὣς ἔφασαν κοῦραι μεγάλου Διὸς ἀρτιέπειαι,
καί μοι σκῆπτρον ἔδον δάφνης ἐριθηλέος ὄζον
δρέψασαι θηητόν· ἐνέπνευσαν δέ μοι ἀοιδὴν
θέσπιν, ἵνα κλείοιμι τά τ' ἐσσόμενα πρό τ' ἐόντα,
καί μ' ἐκέλονθ' ὑμνεῖν μακάρων γένος αἰὲν ἐόντων,
σφᾶς δ' αὐτὰς πρῶτόν τε καὶ ὕστατον αἰὲν ἀείδειν.

These are the ones who one day taught Hesiod beautiful song while he was tending his sheep at the foot of sacred Helikon; these are the very first words the goddesses, the Olympian Muses, daughters of aegis-bearing Zeus, said to me: "Shepherds dwelling in the fields, base cowards, mere bellies; we know how to say many false things that resemble real things; and we know also, whenever we are willing, how to say true things." Thus spoke the daughters of great Zeus, they whose words are exactly fitted, and they gave me a scepter, a wondrous branch of luxuriant laurel, having plucked it; then they breathed into me divine song so that I may celebrate the things that will be and the things that have been, and they commanded me to hymn the race of the blessed ones who exist forever but to sing always of them at the beginning and at the end of my song.

> Ἀλλὰ τίη μοι ταῦτα περὶ δρῦν ἢ περὶ πέτρην;
> τύνη, Μουσάων ἀρχώμεθα, ταὶ Διὶ πατρὶ
> ὑμνεῦσαι τέρπουσι μέγαν νόον ἐντὸς Ὀλύμπου,
> εἰρεῦσαι τά τ' ἐόντα τά τ' ἐσσόμενα πρό τ' ἐόντα,
> φωνῇ ὁμηρεῦσαι· τῶν δ' ἀκάματος ῥέει αὐδὴ
> ἐκ στομάτων ἡδεῖα· γελᾷ δέ τε δώματα πατρὸς
> Ζηνὸς ἐριγδούποιο θεᾶν ὀπὶ λειριοέσσῃ
> σκιδναμένῃ· ἠχεῖ δὲ κάρη νιφόεντος Ὀλύμπου
> δώματά τ' ἀθανάτων· αἳ δ' ἄμβροτον ὄσσαν ἰεῖσαι
> θεῶν γένος αἰδοῖον πρῶτον κλείουσιν ἀοιδῇ
> ἐξ ἀρχῆς, οὓς Γαῖα καὶ Οὐρανὸς εὐρὺς ἔτικτεν,
> οἵ τ' ἐκ τῶν ἐγένοντο θεοὶ δωτῆρες ἐάων·
> δεύτερον αὖτε Ζῆνα, θεῶν πατέρ' ἠδὲ καὶ ἀνδρῶν,
> ἀρχόμεναί θ' ὑμνεῦσι θεαὶ λήγουσί τ' ἀοιδῆς,
> ὅσσον φέρτατός ἐστι θεῶν κράτεΐ τε μέγιστος·
> αὖτις δ' ἀνθρώπων τε γένος κρατερῶν τε Γιγάντων
> ὑμνεῦσαι τέρπουσι Διὸς νόον ἐντὸς Ὀλύμπου
> Μοῦσαι Ὀλυμπιάδες, κοῦραι Διὸς αἰγιόχοιο.

But what are these words to me about an oak or a rock? Listen, let us begin with the Muses, who in hymning please the great mind of Zeus the father in Olympos, telling the things that are, the things that will be, and the things that have been, agreeing in tone; and their sweet voice flows unwearying from their mouths; and the palace of father Zeus the loud-thunderer smiles at the delicate, dispersing voice of the goddesses; it resounds in the peaks of snowy Olympos and the abodes of the immortals; and they, sending forth an immortal voice, celebrate in song, first, the venerable race of gods, from the beginning, those whom

Gaia and vast Ouranos bore and those gods, givers of good things, who were generated from them; next they sing of Zeus, father of gods and men, both when the goddesses begin to hymn and end their song, of how he is the most important of gods and the greatest in power; then, again, hymning the race of men and of powerful Giants, they please the mind of Zeus in Olympos, the Olympian Muses, daughters of aegis-bearing Zeus.

2. Hesiod, Theogony 104–18

Χαίρετε, τέκνα Διός, δότε δ' ἱμερόεσσαν ἀοιδήν·
κλείετε δ' ἀθανάτων ἱερὸν γένος αἰὲν ἐόντων,
οἳ Γῆς τ' ἐξεγένοντο καὶ Οὐρανοῦ ἀστερόεντος,
Νυκτός τε δνοφερῆς, οὕς θ' ἁλμυρὸς ἔτρεφε Πόντος·
εἴπατε δ' ὡς τὰ πρῶτα θεοὶ καὶ γαῖα γένοντο
καὶ ποταμοὶ καὶ πόντος ἀπείριτος, οἴδματι θυίων,
ἄστρα τε λαμπετόωντα καὶ οὐρανὸς εὐρὺς ὕπερθεν·
οἵ τ' ἐκ τῶν ἐγένοντο θεοὶ δωτῆρες ἐάων,
ὥς τ' ἄφενος δάσσαντο καὶ ὡς τιμὰς διέλοντο
ἠδὲ καὶ ὡς τὰ πρῶτα πολύπτυχον ἔσχον Ὄλυμπον.
Ταῦτά μοι ἔσπετε Μοῦσαι, Ὀλύμπια δώματ' ἔχουσαι,
ἐξ ἀρχῆς, καὶ εἴπαθ' ὅ τι πρῶτον γένετ' αὐτῶν.
    Ἦ τοι μὲν πρώτιστα Χάος γένετ', αὐτὰρ ἔπειτα
Γαῖ' εὐρύστερνος, πάντων ἕδος ἀσφαλὲς αἰεὶ
ἀθανάτων οἳ ἔχουσι κάρη νιφόεντος Ὀλύμπου

Take pleasure, children of Zeus, and give me a lovely song; celebrate the holy race of the immortals who exist forever, who were born of Ge and starry Ouranos and of dark Night, those whom salty Pontos nurtured; tell how the gods and earth were generated along with the rivers and boundless sea, raging with waves, and the shining stars and the vast heaven above; and the gods, givers of good things, who were generated from them and how they divided their wealth and how they parceled out their honors and how in the beginning they came to possess Olympos with its many ridges. Tell me these things, Muses, who have Olympian dwellings, from the beginning, and say what was first generated from them.

    In truth, first Chaos was generated, and then wide-bosomed Gaia, ever steadfast seat of all the gods who live on the peaks of snowy Olympus.

Text E

Hesiod, Works and Days *650–62*

Οὐ γάρ πώ ποτε νηί γ᾽ ἐπέπλων εὐρέα πόντον,
εἰ μὴ ἐς Εὔβοιαν ἐξ Αὐλίδος, ᾗ ποτ᾽ Ἀχαιοὶ
μείναντες χειμῶνα πολὺν σὺν λαὸν ἄγειραν
Ἑλλάδος ἐξ ἱερῆς Τροίην ἐς καλλιγύναικα·
ἔνθα δ᾽ ἐγὼν ἐπ᾽ ἄεθλα δαΐφρονος Ἀμφιδάμαντος
Χαλκίδα τ᾽ εἶσε ἐπέρησα· τὰ δὲ προπεφραδμένα πολλὰ
ἄεθλ᾽ ἔθεσαν παῖδες μεγαλήτορος· ἔνθα μέ φημι
ὕμνῳ νικήσαντα φέρειν τρίποδ᾽ ὠτώεντα·
τὸν μὲν ἐγὼ Μούσῃς Ἑλικωνιάδεσσ᾽ ἀνέθηκα
ἔνθα με τὸ πρῶτον λιγυρῆς ἐπέβησαν ἀοιδῆς·
τόσσον τοι νηῶν γε πεπείρημαι πολυγόμφων·
ἀλλὰ καὶ ὧς ἐρέω Ζηνὸς νόον αἰγιόχοιο·
Μοῦσαι γάρ μ᾽ ἐδίδαξαν ἀθέσφατον ὕμνον ἀείδειν.

For never yet have I sailed the wide sea in a ship, unless you count the time I went to Euboea from Aulis, the place where once the Akhaians, having waited out a storm, gathered together a vast host of fighting men from sacred Hellas to head for Troy with its beautiful women; there, heading for the games of warlike Amphidamas, I crossed over to Khalkis; and the children of the greathearted one arranged many prizes proposed in advance; I affirm that it was there that I won a contest in song and that I carried off a tripod with handles on it; this I dedicated to the Helikonian Muses in the place where they first set me upon the path of clear-voiced song; this much I have experienced of well-bolted ships; even so I shall tell the mind of aegis-bearing Zeus; for the Muses have taught me to sing a marvelous hymn.

Text F

Theognis 19–26

Κύρνε, σοφιζομένῳ μὲν ἐμοὶ σφρηγὶς ἐπικείσθω
τοῖσδ᾽ ἔπεσιν, λήσει δ᾽ οὔποτε κλεπτόμενα,
οὐδέ τις ἀλλάξει κάκιον τοὐσθλοῦ παρεόντος,
ὧδε δὲ πᾶς τις ἐρεῖ· «Θεύγνιδός ἐστιν ἔπη

τοῦ Μεγαρέως· πάντας δὲ κατ' ἀνθρώπους ὀνομαστός,»
  Ἀστοῖσιν δ' οὔπω πᾶσιν ἀδεῖν δύναμαι·
οὐδὲν θαυμαστόν, Πολυπαΐδη· οὐδὲ γὰρ ὁ Ζεὺς
  οὔθ' ὕων πάντεσσ' ἀνδάνει οὔτ' ἀνέχων.

Kyrnos, let a seal be placed by my skillful speaking
upon these words, and they will never be stolen without notice,
and no one shall exchange a bad thing for the good that is there,
and thus everyone will say: "These are the words of Theognis
of Megara; renowned among all men."
But I am not yet able to please all citizens;
not at all surprising, son of Polypaos; for not even Zeus
is pleasing to everyone, either in making rain or in holding it back.

Text G

Theognis 1055–58

Ἀλλὰ λόγον μὲν τοῦτον ἐάσομεν. αὐτὰρ ἐμοὶ σὺ
  αὔλει, καὶ Μουσῶν μνησόμεθ' ἀμφότεροι·
αὗται γὰρ τάδ' ἔδωκαν ἔχειν κεχαρισμένα δῶρα
  σοὶ καὶ ἐμοί, <μελέ>μεν δ' ἀμφιπερικτίοσιν.

But we shall have done with this talk; next you
play me the pipe, and we shall keep in mind, each of us, the Muses;
for they themselves gave these pleasurable gifts
to you and me, to be on the minds of the neighboring peoples.

Text H

Herodotus 1.1

Ἡροδότου Θουρίου ἱστορίης ἀπόδεξις ἥδε, ὡς μήτε τὰ γενόμενα ἐξ
ἀνθρώπων τῷ χρόνῳ ἐξίτηλα γένηται, μήτε ἔργα μεγάλα τε καὶ θωμασ-
τά, τὰ μὲν Ἕλλησι, τὰ δὲ βαρβάροισι ἀποδεχθέντα, ἀκλέα γένηται, τά
τε ἄλλα καὶ δι' ἣν αἰτίην ἐπολέμησαν ἀλλήλοισι.
  Περσέων μέν νυν οἱ λόγιοι Φοίνικας αἰτίους φασὶ γενέσθαι τῆς δια-
φορῆς.

This is the public disclosure of the inquiry of Herodotus of Thurii, so that the events of men will not become faded in time and that great and marvelous deeds, some performed by the Hellenes, and some by barbarians, will not lose their fame, especially what caused them to wage war with each other.

The learned men of the Persians say that the Phoenicians were the cause of the disagreement.

Selected Bibliography

Adam, J. M. *Le récit*. Paris: P.U.F., [3]1991.

——. *Le texte narratif: Traité d'analyse textuelle des récits*. Paris: Nathan, 1985.

Adam, J. M., and J. P. Goldenstein. *Linguistique et discours littéraire*. Paris: Larousse, 1976.

Adrados, F. R. *Origines de la lirica griega*. Madrid: Revista de Occidente, 1976.

Barthes, R. "Le discours de l'histoire." *Social Science Information* 6, no. 4 (1967): 65–75.

Benveniste, E. *Problèmes de linguistique générale*. Paris: Gallimard, 1966.

——. *Problèmes de linguistique générale*, vol. 2. Paris: Gallimard, 1974.

Borel, M. J., J. B. Grize, and D. Miéville. *Essai de logique naturelle*. Berne: Lang, 1983.

Bowra, C. M. *Greek Lyric Poetry: From Alcman to Simonides*. Oxford: Oxford University Press, [2]1961.

Calame, C. *Les choeurs de jeunes filles en Grèce archaïque*, 2 vols. Rome: Ateneo, 1977.

——. *Thésée et l'imaginaire athénien: Légende et culte en Grèce antique*. Lausanne: Payot, 1990.

Caron, J. *Les régulations du discours: Psycholinguistique et pragmatique du langage*. Paris: P.U.F., 1983.

Certeau, M. de. *L'écriture de l'histoire*. Paris: Gallimard, 1975.

Coquet, J.-C. *Le discours et son sujet*. Vol. 1, *Essai de grammaire modale*. Paris: Klincksieck, [2]1989.

Darbo-Peschanski, C. *Le discours du particulier: Essai sur l'enquête hérodotéenne*. Paris: Seuil, 1987.

Detienne, M. *L'invention de la mythologie*. Paris: Gallimard, 1981.

——. *Les maîtres de vérité dans la Grèce archaïque*. Paris: Maspero, 1967.

Deubner, L. *Attische Feste*. Berlin: Weidmann, 1932.

Dubois, J. *L'institution de la littérature: Introduction à une sociologie.* Brussels: Nathan-Labor, 1978.

Ducrot, O. *Le dire et le dit.* Paris: Minuit, 1984.

Dupont-Roc, R., and J. Lallot. *Aristote: La Poétique.* Paris: Seuil, 1980.

Finnegan, R. *Oral Poetry: Its Nature, Significance, and Social Context.* Cambridge: Cambridge University Press, 1977.

Frontisi-Ducroux, F. "Au miroir du masque." In *La cité des images: Religion et société en Grèce antique.* (Paris: Nathan-LEP, 1984), 147–62.

Genette, G. *Figures III.* Paris: Seuil, 1972.

Gentili, B. *Poesia e pubblico nella Grecia antica da Omero al V secolo.* Rome: Laterza, ²1988.

Gianotti, G. F. *Per una poetica pindarica.* Turin: Paravia, 1975.

Goldhill, S. *The Poet's Voice: Essays on Poetics and Greek Literature.* Cambridge: Cambridge University Press, 1991.

Greimas, A. J. *Du sens: Essais sémiotiques.* Paris: Seuil, 1970.

——. *Du sens: Essais sémiotiques,* vol. 2. Paris: Seuil, 1983.

Greimas, A. J., and J. Courtés. *Sémiotique: Dictionnaire raisonné de la théorie du langage.* Paris: Hachette, 1979.

——. *Sémiotique: Dictionnaire raisonné de la théorie du langage,* vol. 2. Paris: Hachette, 1986.

Hartog, F. *Le miroir d'Hérodote: Essai sur la représentation de l'autre.* Paris: Gallimard, ²1992.

Havelock, E. A. *The Greek Concept of Justice: From Its Shadow in Homer to Its Substance in Plato.* Cambridge: Harvard University Press, 1978.

Heubeck, A. *Schrift (Archaeologica Homerica* fasc. II, X). Göttingen: Vandenhoeck and Ruprecht, 1979.

Jakobson, R. *Essais de linguistique générale.* Paris: Minuit, 1963.

Jong, I. J. F. de. *Narrators and Focalizers: The Presentation of the Story in the* Iliad. Amsterdam: Grüner, 1987.

Kerbrat-Orecchioni, C. *L'énonciation de la subjectivité dans le langage.* Paris: Colin, 1980.

Kirk, G. S. *The Songs of Homer.* Cambridge: Cambridge University Press, 1962.

Landowski, E. *La société réfléchie: Essais de socio-sémiotique.* Paris: Seuil, 1989.

Leclerc, M.-C. *La parole d'Hésiode: A la recherche de l'harmonie perdue.* Paris: Belles Lettres, 1993.

Lenz, A. *Das Proöm des frühen griechischen Epos: Ein Beitrag zum poetischen Selbstverständnis.* Bonn: Habelt, 1980.

Lesky, A. "Homeros." *Realencyclopädie der classischen Altertumswissenschaft, Suppl.-Band* XI. Stuttgart: Druckenmüller, 1968, columns 687–846.

Lévi-Strauss, C. *Anthropologie structurale.* Paris: Plon, 1958.

Lord, A. B. *The Singer of Tales.* Cambridge: Harvard University Press, 1960.

Maehler, H. *Die Auffassung des Dichterberufs im frühen Griechentum bis zur Zeit des Pindars.* Göttingen: Vandenhoeck and Ruprecht, 1963.

Momigliano, A. *La storiografia greca.* Turin: Einaudi, 1982.

Musti, D. *L'economia in Grecia.* Rome: Laterza, 1981.

Nagy, G. *The Best of the Achaeans: Concepts of the Hero in Archaic Greek Poetry.* Baltimore: Johns Hopkins University Press, 1979.

———. *Pindar's Homer: The Lyric Possession of an Epic Past.* Baltimore: Johns Hopkins University Press, 1990.

Notopoulos, J. A. "Studies in Early Greek Oral Poetry." *Harvard Studies in Classical Philology* 68 (1964): 1–77.

Ong, W. J. *Orality and Literacy: The Technologizing of the Word.* London: Methuen, 1982.

Parke, H. W. *Festivals of the Athenians.* London: Thames and Hudson, 1977.

Pavese, C. O. *Tradizioni e generi poetici della Grecia arcaica.* Rome: Ateneo, 1972.

Pickard-Cambridge, A. *The Dramatic Festivals of Athens.* Oxford: Clarendon Press, ²1968.

Pucci, P. *Hesiod and the Language of Poetry.* Baltimore: Johns Hopkins University Press, 1977.

Race, W. H. "How Greek Poems Begin." *Yale Classical Studies* 29 (1992): 13–38.

Ricoeur, P. *Temps et récit,* vol. 1. Paris: Seuil, 1983.

———. *Temps et récit.* Vol. 2. *La configuration dans le récit de fiction.* Paris: Seuil, 1984.

Rösler, W. *Dichter und Gruppe: Eine Untersuchung zu den Bedingungen und zur historischen Funktion früher griechischer Lyrik am Beispiel Alkaios.* Munich: Fink, 1980.

Russo, J., and B. Simon. "Homeric Psychology and the Oral Epic Tradition." *Journal of the History of Ideas* 29 (1968): 483–98.

Simondon, M. *La mémoire et l'oubli dans la pensée grecque jusqu'à la fin du Ve siècle avant J.-C.* Paris: Belles Lettres, 1982.

Svenbro, J. *La parole et le marbre: Aux origines de la poétique grecque.* Lund: Studentlitteratur, 1976.

Travlos, J. *Pictorial Dictionary of Ancient Athens.* New York: Hacker Art Books, 1971.

Ubersfeld, A. *Lire le théâtre.* Paris: Editions sociales, 1977.

Vernant, J.-P. *La mort dans les yeux: Figures de l'autre en Grèce ancienne.* Paris: Hachette, 1985.

Vernant, J.-P., and P. Vidal-Naquet. *Mythe et tragédie en Grèce ancienne,* vol. 2. Paris: La Découverte, 1986.

Waters, K. H. *Herodotos the Historian: His Problems, Methods, and Originality.* London: Croom Helm, 1985.

West, M. L. *Hesiod: Theogony.* Oxford: Oxford University Press, 1966.

———. *Hesiod: Works and Days.* Oxford: Oxford University Press, 1978.

Winkler, J. J., and F. I. Zeitlin. *Nothing to Do with Dionysos: Athenian Drama in Its Social Context.* Princeton: Princeton University Press, 1990.

Index

MYTH AND POETICS

A series edited by

GREGORY NAGY

Singers, Heroes, and Gods in the Odyssey
by Charles Segal
The Mute Immortals Speak: Pre-Islamic Poetry and the Poetics of Ritual
by Suzanne Pinckney Stetkevych
Phrasikleia: An Anthropology of Reading in Ancient Greece
by Jesper Svenbro
translated by Janet Lloyd
The Jewish Novel in the Ancient World
by Lawrence M. Wills